Seventh Sense

A Collection of True, Unsolved Mysteries from the World of Animals

To Carol ~

Thanks for being my next door neighbor while I wrote this book!

The best to you always,

Seventh Sense

*A Collection of True,
Unsolved Mysteries
from the World of Animals*

by

Diane Arrington

All of the stories in this book are documented and true. They have been dramatized for literary value. Some of the names have been changed to protect the privacy of pet owners.

Copyright © 1993, 1996, 2000, 2001 Diane Arrington
All rights reserved. No part of this book may be reproduced, stored in a retrieval system, or transmitted by any means, electronic, mechanical, photocopying, recording, or otherwise, without written permission from the author.

ISBN: 0-75961-037-1

This book is printed on acid free paper.

1stBooks – rev. 4/24/01

*For my father, who taught by example a reverence for all life.
He fostered the wisdom of knowing the creatures of the earth,
and unknowingly engendered a timeless devotion
to honor and enrich their existence.*

TABLE OF CONTENTS

Chapter 1 Lady & Burr
Incredible tale of canine-for-canine rescue. Thisdog shows a presence of mind, a conceptual grasp of a situation and an ability to communicate
that approximates human behavior in crisis. Exhibits uncanny and enviable canine perseverance.

Chapter 2 Mickey
Curious and thought provoking story of a cat with a playful spirit, even to the point of putting one over on his human owner. Typifies the secretive behavior for which cats are notorious.

Chapter 3 Cookie
Spooky tale of a dog who suffered early trauma in her life and then, once she was safe, recognized the same danger to others and took action on their behalf. This story shows strong evidence that canines possess long-term memory and have an understanding of cause and effect.

Chapter 4 Magic
Deeply thought-provoking incident occurring between dolphin and human. Shows dolphin ability to reason, comprehend and imagine. Inconceivable dolphin understanding of physics and its abstract concepts. Gives the tingles.

Chapter 5 Polar Bear
This story proves fact is stranger than fiction. The canine inventiveness in this tale manifests in an unbelievable behavior for which the dog's motivation is unknown, but far too easy to anthropomorphize.

Docktale 1 Ramsey
> *This short accounting of the antics of an African Gray parrot offers comical insight into the parrot mind. Ramsey's rantings make one wonder where the parrot mind is really coming from.*

Chapter 6 Charles
> This story will change the mind of any cat-hater. Shows remarkable inter-species communication among cats. Who says cats are asocial?

Chapter 7 Hannah
> This tale makes one wonder if dogs can be reincarnated from humans. A four-month-old puppy shows, through spontaneous and voluntary behavior, a convenient sense of order.

Docktale 2 Agnes
> *A story short on words but long on dog shows a Great Dane's remarkable intelligence, insight, divisiveness...and just plain scheming.*

Chapter 8 Frammis
> One of those stories of animal behavior (in this case a cat) that triggers in all of us a primordial fascination for the mysterious and the wonder that accompanies it.

Docktale 3 Tara
> *A description of truly laughable behavior from a small dog. How seriously she takes her dog job!*

Chapter 9 Teddy
> A fun, comical look at canine obsessive compulsive behavior. Although this is becoming increasingly common among dogs, this particular dog exhibits notable originality.

Chapter 10 Lari
> A grin-inspiring tale of a cat able to follow a long-term pattern of behavior until a specific

goal is achieved. It's too easy to think one can accurately determine her motivation.

Chapter 11 Beatrice & Chewy
Remarkable account of what vigorous and determined efforts a dog will make to entertain herself and her playmate. This dog outsmarts her human owners time after time.

Docktale 4 Three
This short tale describes an eery, silent, three-way communication among three cats. It is about three cats simultaneously living one life.

Chapter 12 Bubba
Amazing account of a dog whose behavior exhibits an understanding of if-then conceptual thinking. It is difficult to believe this true story.

Chapter 13 Honey
A rewarding tale not surprising to those who know dogs well. Shows strong and alluring evidence that dogs may fully comprehend what humans say to them, even regarding future events.

Chapter 14 Joseph
A cute story about an unusual puppy who regularly carries out a human behavior. This report shows strong evidence that dogs actually possess a sense of Self. Adoring account of cross-species bonding. Confirms evidence that dogs share human emotions.

Chapter 15 Sid
Stockpiling is fairly common in cats, but this tale tells of a cat's singular and strange habits in this regard. Shows cat behavior that is unusually mysterious, not in its actions, but in its choices.

Docktale 5 Zoe
This story of a keen dog's remarkable ability to manipulate others gives stunning evidence that

canines are capable of surprisingly convoluted thinking and reasoning.

Chapter 16 Scruffy

This is the tale of the incredible journey of a dog. Puts to mind the age old migration ritual of water fowl.

Chapter 17 Abbe

A short story that shows uncanny conceptual thinking in a canine. This dog's ability to adapt her behavior to both solve a problem and achieve a goal is awesome.

Chapter 18 Q Tip

Ponderous story of a cat's radar, not for catching prey but for communication with humans. Truly a mystery.

Chapter 19 Max

Tearful tale describing the extreme of allelomimetic behavior in dogs. Describes an endearing family closeness and provides proof that dogs perceive their families as their packs.

Chapter 20 Katie

A gifted Golden Retriever evidently possesses some mysterious high-tech radar system. A story which offers evidence that, to a dog, out of sight does not necessarily mean out of mind.

Chapter 21 Buddy

This curious and fascinating tale of a dog's secrecy supplies insight into how a dog's ideas differ from humans.

Chapter 22 Amos

Heartwarming tale of cross-species and cross-gender love and acceptance. This story shows that the male canine can be as happy about motherhood as a real mother, even to the remarkable nurturing behavior shown here.

Docktale 6 Louie
A short take on a fascinating peek at the young feline mind and its infant struggle with decision-making. Life isn't easy for a kitten.

Chapter 23 Star
Delightful tale of a Neapolitan Mastiff using her brawn and brains to get her way. Shows human-like reasoning in dogs, willful behavior at its utmost.

Chapter 24 Houdini
This story makes one wonder about the mind of a dog as it relates to human technology.

Chapter 25 Gus
Gus the dog shows remarkable talents regarding barriers. He is utterly unfazed by humans.

Chapter 26 T Bone
This is the tale of a cat's unusual method of self-entertainment, a cat who might have been reincarnated from a fish. It is a story to end to all myths about cats hating water.

Docktale 7 Sugar
Short account of a well trained dog with a mysterious global hang up. Sugar's behavior defies explanation on any level.

Chapter 27 Lolly & Cubby
Impassioned action tale of canine rescue. Two-year-old puppy shows innate understanding of implication, and offers proof that some dogs are born heroes.

Chapter 28 Manor
Awe-inspiring tale of a dog who demonstrates unusual adaptive intelligence. Shows evidence of clear understanding of physics and physiology in dogs. An unbelievable mystery. This dog will win your heart.

Chapter 29 Chuckie
>This cat shows exceptional ability where barriers are concerned, and extreme conceptual ability where his desires are concerned. Chuckie knows what he wants and he gets it.

Docktale 8 Murphy
>*Amusing short story of a six-month-old puppy's skills for problem-solving. Shows droll reasoning in the canine mind.*

Chapter 30 Ralph & Steve
>This accounting leaves plenty to the imagination...and leaves one thinking it can't possibly be true. Reveals the canine sense of order in an unsuspected way.

Chapter 31 Sampson
>A tale of inexplicable feline obsession with an object everyone remembers: the Troll doll. Is Sampson's behavior insult, or is it something else?

Chapter 32 Amy & Arnold
>Touching story of how true and strong the bond between felines can be. Offers compelling evidence that the feline species shares emotions in common with humans.

Chapter 33 Piffles
>Dogs are opportunists, but this one takes the cake...and keeps it for herself! Surprising story of what a bored dog with an eating disorder is capable of.

Docktale 9 Obie
>*Remarkable account of a cat who overheard and plainly understood human language. Demonstrates strong evidence that cats understand the implications of, at least in this case, certain human words.*

Chapter 34 Rosie
    Truly incredible tale showing parrot intelligence. Confirms recent findings about parrot ability to accurately interpret surroundings...and comment on them!

Chapter 35 Gretchen
    This story about a Chesapeake Bay Retriever with no sense of humor tugs at the human heart. Demonstrates instinctive canine ability to comprehend audio only direction from humans.

Chapter 36 Kate
    A warm and funny tale of a dog behavior so overdone it could be labeled hysterical. Shows strong evidence that dogs feel a sense of accomplishment.

Chapter 37 Noel
    This story makes one wonder if dogs don't just know everything about humans, even to sharing our interest in sports. Shows extreme canine talent for originality.

Chapter 38 Fergie
    Hard-to-believe anecdote of human-to-feline communication. The humor lies in its absurd simplicity.

Docktale 10 Holly
    Short and jovial account of childlike behavior in a Collie and her comical attempts to go unnoticed in a roomful of humans.

Chapter 39 Prince
    Frisky account of a dog, aptly named, who shows admirable inventiveness and originality in his mysterious behavior. This dog does not learn his lessons.

Chapter 40 Chris
A truly inspiring story of canine comprehension made possible by an understanding human. Shows how remarkably non-complex cross-species communication can be.

Docktale 11 French Fry
Ticklish anecdote of a feline fetish, fully without explanation.

Chapter 41 Sissie
This heart-wrenching story offers an unforgettable look at how the canine mind works. We can seldom give dogs too much credit.

Chapter 42 Clique
Jolly tale of an incorrigible dog with an intractable habit. Her humans are comically forced to adapt their behavior to the dog's chosen lifestyle.

Chapter 43 Sasha
Sasha's behavior makes one wonder if dogs don't aspire to be human. Shows the canine mind's admirable attention to detail.

Docktale 12 Abbey
A profound short story of a dog's sense of future peril. Confirms the reputation canines have for protecting children.

Chapter 44 Meisha
Some may wish this cat's act of passion would occur regularly within the animal kingdom.

Chapter 45 Silkie
Chilling story of a singular dog's deliberate act. The obvious forethought of this shaggy canine leaves one tearful and speechless.

Chapter 46 Sandy & Waldo
Narrative of a clever and dignified dog learning to cope with an obnoxious duck. Teeming with fascinating canine ingenuity.

A very special thanks to the pet owners who so selflessly offered your stories for inclusion in this book. Thanks for understanding the necessity of probing personal lives to ensure accuracy.

FROM THE AUTHOR

Behavioral scientists know the origins of the social behavior of animals and the way in which it is directed by ancestry. Biologists can explain how animal behavior is governed by physiology. Research can tell us how animals learn and, of late, scientific studies have been conducted regarding whether or not animals think, experience emotion and possess self-awareness. But what of the deeper mysteries, activities our animal companions undertake independently which are not governed by genetics, behavioral conditioning or by ancestry -- activities without scientific explanation?

News reports amaze us with unbelievable animal stories: a pet pig who reasons to stop a car in the road outside to save her disabled owner from a gas leak inside, a Rottweiler who escaped through a heavy wooden door to go dig up her puppies her owner had buried alive, dogs who can detect cancer in the human body, dogs who can predict the onset of human epileptic seizure, and cats, dogs, birds and other animals who can detect and signal humans of an impending earthquake disaster. From what source, by what sense, comes the inventiveness, creativity, and ingenuity that is exhibited daily by those animals with whom we have chosen to share our lives, homes and hearts?

Many pet owners have experienced animal mysteries. As a practitioner of pet behavior modification and training, I am frequently privy to accounts of animal intrigue. Initially I was simply entertained by these tales. But as one who has forever possessed an endless fascination for the animal mind, the stories stayed with me. By the late 1980s, after more than a decade in practice, I had mentally collected a wide array of interesting tales, tales which ordinary people could not read about in the news. I re-interviewed the pet owners for verification of details, veracity and adjunct behaviors so the stories could then be dramatized.

Selectivity was crucial. There were many stories -- cats who fetched like dogs, dogs who seemed capable of distinguishing between your fishing shirt and your office skirt, animals who hid things, played tricks on their owners and invented their own games. There were dogs who could climb trees, play basketball, pick up five tennis balls at once, and snatch a frisbee from the sky fifteen feet over their heads. There were cats who covered in the box for their housemates and even cats who reprimanded their housemates for not covering.

All of these tales flirt with the human mind and its traditional concept of the animal mind. Most of them had a scientific or environmentally-induced explanation. What captivated me were the mysteries. For this volume I have compiled those descriptions of enigmatic animal behaviors which have no justification in the scientific community, for it is the unexplained which fascinates, titillates, and stimulates the human imagination.

There are two stories which deserve to be included in this book but could not be. I was privileged to hear them first-hand, but when I set about my research, the owners had moved out of state and could not be reached to verify names, dates and other details.

One story told of a fat cat whose roommate had passed away. The cat who passed had been cremated. The grieving cat was excessively overweight, so much so that he could neither jump nor climb up onto any piece of furniture. It was all he could do to make it over the edge of his litter box. He and the cat who had passed were virtually joined at the hip. For three days and three nights the poor lonesome cat paced and cried and cried some more, looking for his brother. On the fourth day, a Sunday I believe, the owners had gone out for an early dinner. When they returned, the house was quiet. As they entered the house they did not hear their cat calling for his lost roommate. As they entered the den they discovered why: there, up on top of the television set five feet off the floor was their overweight cat. He was sniffing at the jar of ashes. He had found his lost brother. What drove this cat to execute the impossibly high leap? Does a cat's scent remain after cremation, or did the cat somehow 'sense' his brother's remains?

The other story told of a stray cat who appeared in a woman's yard just about the time her marriage was beginning to collapse. The woman took in the little female cat. Over the ensuing few months the soon-to-be ex-husband grew increasingly abusive to the woman. The violence was mounting. Finally one horrible day the husband had the wife bent backwards over the kitchen sink, vowing he would kill her this time. In his hand was a knife. The woman was helpless in the grasp of his insane, homicidal hands. He placed the knife at the woman's throat. Suddenly, explosively, out of nowhere, came the little female cat. With a primal, angry howl she leapt onto the evil man's back, biting and clawing in her frenzied attack. The surprised attacker shrieked in pain and dropped the knife, giving the woman enough time to run from the house to safety with a neighbor. The agile cat also escaped the bad man's hands, and was able to hide successfully from his rabid, angry pursuit. Two months later the cat passed away from natural causes. The woman was devastated, in agony over the short life of the cat who had so heroically saved her life. But the cat had stayed only as long as the woman needed her. Was she an angel, sent to stay just long enough to save the woman's life and then depart this world?

The behavioral endeavors undertaken by the animals in this book cannot be explained. They are displays for which there is no accounting in the behavioral, sociological or biological sciences. They are animal antics so curious and fascinating as to warrant our closer scrutiny. The activities these animals exhibit are not behavior problems in need of modification, but rather harmless activities. Some stories are comical, some are sad. There are tales of big heroes and small heroes. Others stories are bizarre or endearing, and some are just plain spooky. All describe activities invented by animals alone. All are mysteries. When taken together, a startling trend emerges.

Animals have evolved in lockstep with mankind. Who can say with absolute certainty that animals today do not think, feel and interpret exactly as we do? Down through the ages, the human mind has overflowed with new ideas. Could it be that animals are equally as inventive and creative as human men and women, as full of thoughts and ideas which are not biologically motivated? Who can assure us unequivocally that animals do not understand our exact words and their meaning? Until such proof arrives, we can continue to enjoy looking at the fascinating and incontrovertible evidence the animals themselves provide us.

I believe each single animal to be an individual work, designed and crafted with care by our Creator. It is my belief that those who acknowledge and respect this possibility, those who feel it deeply and behave with kindness to all beasts of the earth, will receive the maximum abundance and joy they desire in their lives on earth. Those who do not, will not.

Perhaps this volume will awaken those who are asleep to the fact that animals maintain thoughts, decision-making and imaginations all their own. To those who already know, may you enjoy the journey.

Seventh Sense

Diane Arrington

Chapter 1
Lady and Burr

This true story exemplifies the intelligence of the Labrador Retriever. The mystery lies not in what Burr did, but in how he knew what to do. His actions dissolve the myth that a dog is just a dog, incapable of thinking for himself. They are empirical proof that problem-solving as a means to an end does take place in at least one canine mind.

It was a suede grey Monday in late October, 1993 in north central Texas. Driving through the late-day chill, Joe Marsh was returning home from work when he noticed a large yellow dog on the gravel shoulder of the road. The dog was agitated, pacing and barking at passing cars.

Several other residents of the small farm community reported having seen the dog at the same spot on the isolated country road several days in succession. All had sighted him at the same location. The dog seemed to be staying near a narrow path that cut through the thick woods behind him. Passersby simply assumed he had lost his way and would soon find his own way home. No one stopped.

Joe saw the dog again on Tuesday. By Wednesday the dog was still there, still in the same spot. Joe wondered what kept the dog from leaving that particular place on the road. The dog looked strong and healthy and did not possess the slinking posture of free-roaming dogs. This dog stood straight and tall. Joe had always been a dog lover. Unable to override his compassion or his curiosity, Joe slowed and pulled his truck to the shoulder, stopping just a few yards short of the worried dog.

The dog was a yellow Labrador Retriever, obviously purebred and unusually handsome. It was a young male, perhaps two years of age. Beneath a shiny coat his ribs were beginning to show from hunger, but his muscles were clearly defined. His bark sounded hoarse from his constant, vigilant barking. As Joe pulled over and stopped, the dog grew silent.

Joe climbed from the truck and eased around the front fender. He could see immediately the dog was not dangerous, but friendly. With his ears held low, the dog trotted right up to Joe, his huge paws crunching the gravel. His jaws opened in a happy grin. He waved his big tail respectfully, hopefully. Joe decided to take the dog home and at least feed him before looking for his rightful owner.

"Come on, boy, let's go," Joe said as he opened the passenger door of the truck. He patted his own leg, encouraging the dog to hop in. The dog started toward the open cab but stopped short. He hesitated, and their eyes met. Then the dog turned and loped to the mouth of the path, his tail swinging.

Though Joe was stunned by the way the dog had looked at him — so directly, so meaningfully — he convinced himself he had imagined it and again called to the dog.

"Come on, let's go, fella! Aren't you hungry, boy?"

The dog again started toward the truck as if to indicate a desire to go, but he turned away a second time. He jogged purposefully a few yards up the path and stopped. He looked at Joe over his shoulder, swung his plumed, gold-white tail and whined softly. It was clear the dog wanted Joe to follow. Joe did.

With the dog anxiously leading the way, they made their way together up the narrow path and deep into the woods. Past brambles and briars, pin oak, poison oak and mesquite trees the dog led the man. Disturbed birds exploded from the underbrush, fluttering and squawking protest. Noisy crickets and toads grew silent as they passed.

After half a mile of struggling along a not so well-worn path covered with undergrowth, Joe's patience was slipping. *This is silly*, he thought to himself. *This big, sloppy, happy dog is just taking me on a little jaunt, and I'm not falling for it.*

He reversed his direction and began the trek back to his truck.

The dog turned with him. Initially he panted worriedly at Joe's heels. Then he tried to get Joe to stop. He moved out in front of Joe, yelping and nipping at the man's feet. He tried standing still across the path to completely block the way. But Joe, assuming the dog only wanted play, managed to continue on to the roadway.

Once back at the truck, Joe again opened the door and offered the big dog one last chance to get in. The dog lifted his ears and tipped his big square head. His golden eyes cleared, and he suddenly seemed to understand Joe did not intend to follow him into the woods.

Suddenly the dog became desperate. He barked and whined and yelped and raced repeatedly the few yards to the trees and then back to Joe. There was something in his behavior, something more than just play — something dreadful and urgent.

Joe removed his cap and scratched his head, watching the dog's odd, compulsive behavior. With one quick, decisive motion he snugged his cap back onto his head.

They ventured back into the thicket for a second time. The smell of burning leaves flirted faintly in the air. A chilly wind whisked through the trees overhead. The sound of four paws and two feet snapping twigs and crunching dead leaves echoed through the silent woods.

The athletic dog seemed to know precisely where he was heading. He leapt boulders and fallen trees effortlessly in his rush. His gait was purposeful, determined.

A dog's vision differs from human vision only in spectrum, not in detail. The dog knew the way by identifying landmarks, just as humans do on a trail hike.

The surprise was where the trail led.

This time the pair had gone almost a mile along the tortuous trail when Joe suddenly heard the faint, musical sound of running water. He sensed a mounting urgency in the dog's demeanor. A few paces more and the dog began to tremble. He ran faster, stretching his neck forward and barking short, loud bursts, his tail wagging high over his back. Suddenly he dashed forward and disappeared over a small rise.

At that precise moment, the sun broke through the clouds. Instantly the mood of the day shifted from dreary to sparkling autumn yellow.

Joe climbed over the rise. The dog had stopped about ten yards ahead. He was standing in a shallow, icy creek, up to his elbows in water, near a fallen log. There was relief on his face and triumph in his barks. He wriggled and smiled his dog smile, prancing high and proudly on the tips of his toes in the mud, his tail fiercely wagging his body. The source of his joy lay at his feet. It was another dog.

A second creamy Labrador, a large female, was helplessly submerged in the chilly water up to her neck. Through the water, its clarity now aided by the brilliance of the sunlight, Joe could see the female dog's body. She had evidently tried to swim beneath the fallen log but the water had been too shallow. Her hips and hind legs had become trapped beneath the obstruction, ensnaring her, pinning her to the mud-and-clay creek bottom. For three days she had lain helpless in the water, unable to do anything to help herself. All she could do was struggle to keep her head above water. When she saw Joe approaching, she whined softly and made a tired attempt to wag her tail underwater.

***

In DeSoto, Texas, fifty miles to the northwest, Chad Haginsaw went about his Monday routine absent-mindedly. His heart was heavy. He had lost his two yellow Labrador Retrievers, Lady and Burr. Burr was Lady's offspring, and Lady just loved showing the youngster the ropes on their weekend hunting trips.

Deep in the Texas country, Chad permitted the high-energy pair to run free. When it came time to leave on Sunday afternoons, the two keen dogs always seemed to know. They were promptly front-and-center, just in time to vault into the truck for the hour-long ride back home.

But Sunday had been different for Chad and his dogs.

The dogs had been more or less with him most of the day. If he looked quickly, he could catch glimpses of their light, gleaming coats through the trees. They romped and frisked. They pored over the many rich and vivid scents of the country in fall and splashed joyously through the creek, by now numbing cold with the change in weather. But when it had come time to leave that day, the dogs were mysteriously absent. The country air was silent.

Chad hiked mile after mile of woods and field, searching frantically for his dogs, a gnawing pain of fear and loss spreading like hot grease through his gut. For hours he whistled and bellowed into ominous silence. It grew late, and with darkness came a bitter chill in the air. By eleven p.m. he could search no longer. He would have to return home for work in the morning.

He left word in town that his dogs were missing, and his phone number. Dejected, Chad climbed alone into the truck. He drove slowly, away from his beloved dogs. He was heartsick, knowing his dogs were in trouble and finding himself unable to help them.

***

Burr had led Joe to Lady.

Quickly, carefully, Joe lifted the log and released Lady. She was stiff from lying so long in one position and exhausted from struggling not to. Joe did not hesitate to plunge knee-deep into the cramp-cold water boots and all, to help Lady to her feet and out of the creek. She did not appear to be seriously injured, just

Seventh Sense

purely exhausted. While she limped around him on her twisted leg, she could not stop licking Joe's hands in gratitude.

Every sinew of Burr's muscular body radiated jubilance as he wriggled and whined and bounced a tight circle around his mother. She shook herself dry, and creek water streamed in all directions. While Joe fell back a pace or two, Burr never flinched. He sniffed his mother anxiously. He tried to lick her entire coat dry all at once. He nuzzled her and kissed her face and mouth. She nudged him weakly in return, and they entwined their necks, the heartwarming equivalent of a canine hug.

Through sheer canine courage Lady had stayed alive. And by way of intelligence, determined perseverance and love, true and absolute, Burr had saved his mother's life.

Joe looked at Burr differently now. He knew the big dog had accomplished something almost too heroic to believe. Not only had Burr found his way to civilization, he had stayed there for three days and three nights trying to get someone to stop and help. He somehow knew that barking until someone stopped would be his mother's only hope for survival. He had denied his own need for food and water in the interest of saving the life of another dog.

With the two dogs' vanilla coats gleaming in the sun, the man and two dogs headed back down the trail to the truck. This time Burr did not hesitate to jump in. Joe leaned down and gently lifted Lady into the truck. He found a blanket to put around her, and headed straight for the vet.

***

It had been three desperately lonely days for Chad. He plodded through his duties and chores half-heartedly. He could not seem to concentrate. After three bleak, miserable, meaningless days, he drove away from work. He barely noticed when the sun found a portal in the slate cover of clouds. He had surrendered nearly all hope of finding his dogs.

Diane Arrington

Word travels fast in a small town. On Wednesday night following that dreadful Sunday, Chad Haginsaw received the answer to a prayer: a phone call.

"We have your dogs and they're fine," an unknown but jubilant voice declared.

A warm thrill filled Chad's spirit as he listened to Joe's tale of Burr's heroism, the rescue, the medical treatment. Lady was treated for hypothermia and a sprained hip, Burr was treated for dehydration. The following day, both dogs were treated to a big, juicy, mesquite-smoked steak in the dry warmth and comfort of their own safe home.

Seventh Sense

Diane Arrington

Chapter 2
Mickey

In this tale of feline trickery at it's finest, Mickey's behavior appears to be evidence of a protracted thought process to goal achievement in the feline brain. The significance of the goal in Mickey's mind will always remain a mystery.

Cats who fetch like dogs are becoming increasingly more common. Such cats are special but not rare. Mickey was rare. Mickey fetched and much, much more. There was nothing visibly exceptional about him as a pet, but who can say what lurks in the mysterious mind of a cat?

***

The scrawny black furball was just six weeks old when his founder, a co-worker, showed him to Steve and Laura of Richardson, Texas. The moment they had him in their sight they had him in their hearts. They named him Mickey for his comical, mule-eared resemblance to Mickey Mouse, and took the 16-ounce thing home.

When found, Mickey was skinny and weak and covered with fleas. But over the ensuing months the couple's lavish form of love and care nurtured Mickey to a healthy, beautiful feline. It wasn't long before his coat was flowing ebony and his emerald eyes, too big for his face, glistened with good health and mischief.

As a youngster Mickey was not particularly enraptured by common kitten games. He enjoyed Boo-Cat and Sheet Monsters like any well-balanced cat, but retrieving was his game of choice. His love for the pastime bordered on obsession.

Seventh Sense

Some cats will fetch balls, some prefer cat toys, some have even been known to retrieve coins. Mickey's passion was cigarette wrappers, rolled into a ball. Mickey took the game a few giant steps further than expected, which is where his mystery begins.

Each evening without fail, Mickey meowed and purred and snaked around Steve's legs, begging him to toss the "ball." If Steve refused, Mickey hopped onto his lap and waved his tail in Steve's face until he broke down. A certain wildness crept into Mickey's eyes as he sprang after the little ball, pinned it with his paws, picked it up and carried it in his mouth back to Steve. At times, in his frenzy, he uttered strange, muttering noises in his throat.

Steve would toss the toy for Mickey several times in succession until Mickey appeared to tire of the game and casually wandered away, the cellophane-wrapped ball left alone on the rug. It wasn't until later Laura realized she never saw the toys again, and that each evening Steve would wad up a new one for Mickey's nightly ritual.

One day while housecleaning Laura pulled back the couch cushions and, to her surprise, discovered an unbelievable stash: about two dozen balled-up cigarette packs.

This explained why the toys had disappeared after the fetch games were over. Laura realized that all these months she and Steve had been watching TV while sitting on Mickey's stash. Mickey had been hiding his toys at the very spot his humans relaxed. They literally leaned against them nightly, and hadn't a clue as to the huge cache just six inches behind their backs.

Laura's discovery might have ended the matter, but in a moment of creative clarity, just to see what would happen, Laura decided to re-hide the treasures. Making sure Mickey didn't see her, Laura moved his collection across the room and hid the balls behind the cushion on the chair. With company arriving in just a few days, she promptly forgot that she had done so, and carried on with life.

Diane Arrington

It wasn't until a month later that Laura remembered her experiment. She went to check her hiding place behind the cushion on the chair. It was empty!

Her first thought was Steve had discovered the toys and thrown them out. In view of Steve's less-than-ideal housecleaning habits, it took Laura only a few moments to discard this idea.

Trying to think where so many toys could have gone, she looked underneath the furniture. Perhaps they had all fallen out on the floor and been kicked under. They had not. She searched deep in the bottom of the umbrella stand where she had found cat toys before. Nothing was there. Finally, certain they couldn't be there but as a last guess, she pulled back the cushion on the couch and peeked down behind. Lo and behold, there sat twenty-three rolled up cigarette wrappers!

Laura never saw Mickey hide the objects. With the exception of a game-in-progress, she never even saw him with one in his mouth. Neither she or Steve ever had a clue as to what Mickey was up to, not a hint, not an inkling. The secretive cat had managed to move every last one of his 23 coveted playmates back to its original location without detection. It was not retrieving Mickey loved, but concealment.

When you consider the feline — domesticated a mere 5,000 years and limited by a human presumption of insufficient language, and consider the feline mind — restricted by what the scientific community believes to be "nearsighted" and deficient of cognitive reasoning abilities — Mickey's little caper is astonishing.

It is irresistible to form a mental picture of Mickey in the night, creeping down the hallway and into the living room on silent cat paws. Here is the lone black cat, stealthy, lustrous eyes shining in the dark, glancing furtively this way and that — with a paper and cellophane ball clenched in his jaws.

What were these objects to Mickey? A surrogate litter? Why these and not cat toys — fake mice or sponge balls? Did he enjoy the scent of fresh tobacco? Were they items of food to be stored for later? Perhaps they were a reserve stock to be presented for play in the unfortunate event Steve's supply ran out.

Consider the manner in which Mickey ended each game so casually, even off-handedly. Was he consciously manipulating his own behavior so Laura and Steve would not suspect his scheming? Was this a serious issue for Mickey or simply an elaborate, recreational form of cat self-entertainment?

Perhaps Mickey stayed up nights to hide his treasures. Or possibly he hid each one in some secret holding cell to await human absence and an opportunity to hide it more deeply. Why did Mickey hide all the toys in the same place? Even a cat should know never to put all your eggs in one basket.

How did Mickey discover his stash missing? He would have been forced to either conduct nightly security checks or baby-sit it through the night. When he did detect the absence, by means of what sense did he find his toys behind the cushion on the chair in order to move them back to the couch? And why did Mickey insist on hiding them in the couch and not any other available hiding spot?

Consider, too, the logistics of the matter. When Mickey moved the items back to the couch, did he pull an all-nighter to transfer them at once, or did he relocate two or three each night, his nocturnal work spanning weeks?

To Laura, the one who lived with this cat on a daily basis, the most curious fact was that on no occasion did she see Mickey move or carry the objects other than during actual fetch games.

Whatever lurked in the mind of Mickey, the pitiful little stray, of one thing Laura was certain: she would never be able to spoof Mickey more than Mickey could spoof her.

Diane Arrington

Chapter 3
Cookie

This is a story that wasn't a story until after Cookie's adoption. It was then that her mystery came to light. It happens daily, around the world; wherever people and dogs share the same space, dogs silently endure the terrible neglect Cookie did — and worse. This little dog's actions reveal a chilling awareness and a heroic heart.

The simple act of growing bigger was the puppy's only mistake, and it nearly killed her.

The springtime sun was bright that morning, but she barely noticed. Her days were dark and her nights, lonely. Yet, because she's a dog, she awoke each morning with renewed hope. She crawled from beneath the broken-down Chevy, her only shelter from the cold and rain. She was unaware of the grease and oil smeared along her back.

The puppy yawned and stretched, but waking brought back the pain. She knew the ache of hunger, the suffering of thirst. But most of all the searing, throbbing pain around her neck was what the puppy knew. She shook her head and started to scratch, but could not bring herself to do it. Breathing was difficult, at moments impossible. It hurt to swallow.

The hide on her neck was wide open, almost to her trachea. The injury was teeming with infection, and she had lost so much blood she felt weak and dizzy. Her chest, normally the color of coffee with cream, was crusted with dark, matted blood. There was too much of it for her to clean with her feeble tongue. The puppy was dying a slow, agonizing death by strangulation. Still, her will to live was fierce.

At the tender age of nine months, the dog named Cookie already knew plenty about pain and suffering. It is not known exactly when — four or five months previously, perhaps — someone knotted the length of twine firmly around her neck. Whoever did never bothered to remove it — and then Cookie grew up. As she grew, the twine etched slowly into her neck, through the skin and the tissue beneath, to a depth of almost a full inch.

Each morning Cookie roamed the neighborhood, wanting desperately to find someone to care about her. She would lift her floppy brown ears and wag a hopeful tail at passing humans, but they would take one look at the bloody little dog and hurry on in disgust. Cookie did not understand, and her almond eyes would cloud with sadness as she quietly watched them turn away.

But Cookie had the luck of the Irish. On March 17, 1994 — St. Patrick's Day — the Good Samaritan the puppy had been searching for stopped to help at last. Cookie was rushed to a nearby veterinarian for treatment.

The puppy could feel the probing of her swollen, inflamed injury, the smart sting of penicillin. There was a scary soak in the tub to remove the clotted blood. There was clipping and shaving to endure and, worst of all, painful removal of the embedded twine. But cookies are sweet, and this one deserves an award for bravery.

Through it all, Cookie never once whimpered, growled or even winced. Intense pain had been a part of her life for a very long time. Cookie was a survivor. Sweet as sugar, she was twenty-two puppy pounds of innocent love.

Cookie loved everyone and trusted those who helped her, but she had no one to belong to. She needed a home and someone to love her forever. Not just any home would do, though. Her new owners would need to follow medical instructions and treat her wounds until they healed. Cookie would need a family willing to use a harness and not a collar to walk her and to teach her fun things. Most of all, Cookie needed a safe, nurturing place, a sanctuary where she could heal her spirit and restore her faith in humankind.

Cookie's golden-haired Irish luck held true. Her story was spread across the region via newspapers, radio and television. Donations for her medical care poured in, and dog lovers from all over the city lined up to adopt her.

Cookie selected a middle-aged couple, Bonnie and Ben, whose old dog had passed away not long before. The couple had recently moved to the country; Cookie would have five rolling acres in which to run and play and heal.

No one but Cookie might have guessed what would happen next.

Cookie and her new home turned out to be a perfect match. She fit into the family like the last piece in a puzzle. She loved her new digs, and particularly enjoyed chewing on Ivan, the family cat. Ivan loved it.

Bonnie and Ben had expected some soiling, but Cookie was impeccable. The couple also planned on some destructive chewing from a nine-month-old puppy. It wouldn't have mattered, because they loved her just the way she was. They understood the healing process. They anticipated a few ruined table legs or cabinets or baseboards. That Cookie might be interested in Bonnie's stuffed animals, of which she had quite a collection, never occurred to Bonnie.

The couple was fully prepared to let nature take its course, even in their absence. They knew that, with the exception of Ivan, Cookie would find herself home alone in her new and strange surroundings. There were many temptations for a puppy. Still, they chose not to confine Cookie. The first evening Bonnie returned home from work not knowing what she would find.

But when Bonnie returned, almost everything was in order. There was only one exception. On a baby chair in a bedroom, Cookie had discovered a stuffed teddy bear with a ribbon round its neck. She had pulled the bear to the floor and chewed the ribbon off, leaving both the untouched bear and the severed ribbon on the floor.

On the second day of Bonnie's absence, Cookie found a stuffed koala bear, about the same color she was, fitted with a

Diane Arrington

ribbon around its neck. She chewed the ribbon off, but she left the koala unmolested to nap on the carpet. On the third day Cookie found a stuffed alligator with a ribbon for a collar, which she removed without harming the alligator. On the fourth day she discovered a stuffed dinosaur. Cookie cut the ribbon from around its neck.

Within the first week in her new home Cookie had removed all neck gear from every stuffed animal in the house. Why?

Cookie's demeanor on discovery was innocent and matter-of-fact. She never looked guilty or slunk away when Bonnie found evidence of Cookie's daytime activities. Except for tasting a couple of irresistible wooden figurines, the only destructive chewing Cookie undertook were the "collars" from around necks.

Cookie never chewed the stuffed animals. Never did she attack the eyes or noses or ears or tails, which is customary when puppies get hold of stuffed toys, just the neck ribbons. Just the danger. Heroically, Cookie cleared away the danger for her new-found friends.

Cookie's motivation will always remain a mystery. One wonders if, with Cookie around, Ivan could ever wear a collar.

Seventh Sense

Diane Arrington

Chapter 4
Magic

Some theorize that dolphin intelligence is beyond the capacity or even the imagination of the human mind. The behavior displayed by this three-day-old infant offers strong support for this theory. Magic's inventive behavior will make one a believer.

Magic was not her real name. But magical she was, and mysterious is what she did in this piece of film aired in 1993 on public broadcasting television stations across the country. Magic's behavior was not the focus of the story. It was a matter of good fortune to have captured it on film, because it is almost impossible to believe.

Magic was an infant bottle-nosed dolphin, born in captivity just a few days before the documentary was filmed. As the film progressed, the narrator spoke of dolphins, their habits, Magic's birth. The narrator noted the species' renowned love for human imitation. A few moments later, Magic revealed startling evidence of a wondrous thought process. The narrator made note of her behavior in passing, but it seems the full import of her behavior was overlooked.

There was a man in the film, watching Magic swim with her mother. The man was observing through an underwater window. He was smoking a cigarette. Out of the corner of her eye, Magic noticed the man. In the way of a curious infant, she strayed from her mother and swam to the window to get a closer look.

Fearlessly, Magic maneuvered right up to the six-foot-square window pane and stopped. Magic peered at the man. The man looked at Magic. There occurred a moment in time as the human and the dolphin were bottle nose-to-face with only the glass between them.

The baby dolphin hovered there, scrutinizing the man. What the man did next seemed to delight little Magic. He drew on his cigarette, then released a stream of smoke. The smoke hit the glass and puffed gracefully upwards, forming a pillowy cloud of white.

Magic's small face and high brow suddenly took on a look of inquisitive surprise. She watched curiously, intently, as the smoke billowed. Her tail waved slowly in the clear water. Had she been born a dog, she might have perked up her ears and tipped her head. Magic hesitated, appearing to think for a moment.

Then, all at once, tiny Magic dashed away in a great, big, infant hurry. Her small tail pumped furiously as she churned a beeline to her mother. Through the crystal blue water of her tank she went, leaving a trail of bubbles in her wake. She located mom's milk spigot and nursed hastily. Then Magic turned on a dime and charged back through the water to the window where the man still stood. She raced up to the window and screeched to a stop. She positioned herself precisely opposite the human, facing him squarely, preparing herself.

Then, unbelievably, Magic pushed a mouthful of milk at the glass. The milk hit the glass and puffed gracefully upwards, forming a pillowy cloud of white in the water — just like the smoke. Magic's behavior was flawless mimicry.

To consider the thought process of this three-day-old infant stuns the human mind.

First, Magic had to imagine. *Imagine*. She had to search her memory banks for a substance that would resemble smoke. Perhaps she tried pushing pure water at the man and found it an unsuitable duplication. This cannot be known. But how could she possibly have known that milk, when mixed with water, would resemble smoke? Do dolphins have knowledge of chemistry?

In addition, it was necessary for Magic to decide quickly where to obtain the substance she needed. Once procured, she had to know to hold the milk in her mouth without dribbling or swallowing. This would involve a conscious decision. And, holding the milk in her mouth could possibly take an extraordinary amount of physical maneuvering of mouth, tongue, air and esophagus.

Finally, to complete her imitation, Magic had to know to carry the "smoke" from her Mom clear across the tank and back to the window without releasing it a moment too soon. These last two behaviors, the act of holding the milk in her mouth and the act of pushing the milk from her mouth would not only be difficult mechanically, but are two behaviors profoundly opposite her instinct for survival. It was an act of conscious self-restraint not to ingest the precious, life-giving fluid. Did Magic override her instinct for survival for the exclusive purpose of playing a joke on a human?

Habits, activities, societal rituals and general intelligence are passed from mother to infant in all animal species, but these teachings customarily involve mother-to-infant consultation. Magic did not consult with her mother on this. Independently, inside a brain only 72 hours outside the womb, Magic perceived, originated and executed an idea.

It is not known where Magic is now, but perhaps she will be the one, in her lifetime, to offer humans a measure of promise. Perhaps Magic will give humans the key to unlock the mystery of dolphin intelligence.

Seventh Sense

Diane Arrington

Chapter 5
Polar Bear

Bear displays a behavior which politically correct humans would applaud. Curiously, his bizarre fetish was the product of spontaneous generation. No explanation can be culled from the behavioral repertoires of either the wolf or the domestic dog. The motivation of this American Eskimo dog can only be presumed. Perhaps another canine would know. To humans, it is a mystery.

He looked like a baby seal. A perfectly round ball of pure white fluff. His whiteness was broken only by three black dots — two shiny eyes and a wet, black nose. He was six weeks old.

Linda kneeled to the box on the floor, lifted the puppy out, gave him a big squeeze and placed him on the carpet to show her friend Sherry. Panting happily and wagging his small, skewed tail, the puppy promptly left a puddle. Then, without the briefest moment of guilt, he paddled away to play.

It was that warm spring day in May of 1987 that Sherry and her husband Doug accepted their friend's gift. How could they resist? They named him Polar Bear for his appearance, and took him home.

When Sherry and Doug first plopped puppy Polar Bear down in his own yard, now replete with fresh spring grass, his paws barely touched the ground. He bolted away, thrilled to have a whole yard all to himself. He ran huge circles, growling his happy puppy growl. Round and round he went, ninety miles an hour, the Doggie Bunny Run. He ran continuously for five minutes, dissipating energy and pouring out joy. Doug, Sherry and their son Billy laughed like hyenas as the white puppy zoomed past them again and again.

Seventh Sense

On one pass-by, without stopping, Bear snatched a stuffed white bear Sherry had given him. Ironically because it looked so much like him, that bear would later become Polar Bear's favorite toy. He circled once with it, then executed a noisy attempt on its life. By all appearances, the cat-sized American Eskimo puppy loved his new home.

As a rule, extremely intelligent dogs need more than other dogs in terms of education, supervision, attention, and physical exercise. Bear was not dumb. He was an alert and decidedly active dog. But because he was not annoyingly brilliant, his needs in terms of training and direction were minimal. This made his upbringing easier than it otherwise might have been. During Bear's first year of life there was no indication of the peculiar habit he would acquire and keep for years to come.

The raising of Bear went as smoothly as raising any puppy can. He grew into an exceptionally happy dog who spent most of his time with his little black eyes smiling and a huge grin plastered across his snowy white face. His thick white tail was perpetual motion. It stopped wiggling on only two occasions: when he fell asleep, and when everyone left him in the morning. Indeed, most appealing about Bear was his ever-present glee. He loved everything, and his harmless, Pickwickian nature made him easy to love. Whatever activity the family was to undertake, Bear insisted on being included. The sole exception was rides in the car. As far as Bear was concerned, car rides too often led to the man in the white coat with the big needle.

Cookouts were a family favorite. Bear considered the yard his, and enjoyed sharing it with his family on summer evenings. It was just such an evening when Bear first displayed his strange behavior.

In early June of 1988, Bear was a year old. The sun slanted low through the trees as crickets began evening overtures. A gentle breeze carried the heady scent of springtime honeysuckle. The air was moist and balmy. It was the kind of summer evening made for carnivals, softball and barbecues.

Diane Arrington

The couple finished dinner and Sherry had gone inside with the dishes. Doug relaxed outside, smoking his usual after-dinner cigarette. After thirty minutes of luckless campaigning for a hamburger of his own, Bear had finally conceded. Busy as always, he scooted around his yard, sniffing here and there, lost in his canine world of scents and insect prey.

Doug finished his cigarette. He flipped the glowing remains into the grass. Whether Bear heard it land or smelled it, no one can be certain. Suddenly, the dog spun around. His ears shot forward. He spotted the neon glow and raced for it.

Sniffing frantically, Bear located the butt. To Doug's amazement, the puppy actually picked up the lit cigarette in his teeth. He did this gingerly, the coal protruding from the side of his mouth like a Groucho Marx cigar.

Suddenly Bear tossed his head hard and released the cigarette, dashing the butt to the ground. He sniffed it, picked it up again, and slammed it down a second time. He pitched it to the ground three times. In this way Bear broke up the coal.

Next Bear punched at the smaller coals with his wet nose, deft, quick little punches to avoid being burned. The coals spread through the grass. Punch and sniff, punch and sniff. Most of the coals went out.

Bear then bowed to his chest, rump in the air, front paws curled under. He began to rub his face on the coals, first one cheek, then the other. Doug was fascinated, watching the snow-white dog smudge sooty, burnt coals all over himself.

Next, Bear tossed his entire body on the ground and smeared the snuffed cigarette with his neck. This led to rolling on it as if he were rolling in something of the smelly things with which dogs too often like to coat themselves. Paws flailing above him, the white dog twisted and writhed on his back and shoulders for a full sixty seconds until he was certain the cigarette was completely extinguished.

Finally, Bear stood up. He sniffed at the dead butt on the ground. He circled it once. Then, to make sure the offending thing had truly perished, Bear raised his hind leg and sprayed its remains. Satisfied, he turned away and trotted off.

Bear did not run to Doug for approval or praise. He did not expect a reaction from anyone present. It seemed this was something he did strictly for his own benefit. The compulsion existed only in Bear's own mind.

Doug had flipped cigarettes into the grass many times. Bear had never been interested. Why now, so suddenly? He wondered if Bear would do it again. He lit another cigarette, smoked it and flipped the hot coal into the grass.

Again Bear went to work on the cigarette butt. He performed precisely the same behaviors in exactly the same order. He finished the job thoroughly in the same way as before: the leg lift.

Bear seemed surprised when humans reacted to his cigarette-snuffing activities. Whether his motivation became, over time, the human reaction or whether it was purely a matter of self-interest, Bear continued. The attitude with which he carried out the behavior was not bravado or braggadocio. Rather, it was addictive and nervous. Bear was obsessive about putting the cigarette out as quickly as possible.

Whatever his instigation, Bear's activities became a source of unequaled entertainment at parties. He knew just how to extinguish the cigarette without burning his nose, singeing his face or sparking holes in his thick white fur. Because Bear was so intense about snuffing them out, it seemed almost unkind to flip more than a few cigarettes. The dog seemed incapable of permitting even one cigarette to escape his immediate attention. And, in each and every case, he ended his performance with the same coup de grace, the elevated hind leg.

Snuffing cigarettes out with his face is a peculiarity Polar Bear will apparently never lose. As events turned the following year, Doug left the family and did not return for eleven months. Sherry does not smoke. Eleven months later Doug tossed a cigarette. Bear went for it. Although Bear had not performed it

Diane Arrington

for nearly a year, the behavior did not extinguish. The cigarette did.

Always, without exception, Bear picked up the cigarette and threw it down three or four times, tamped it with his nose, rubbed first his cheeks on it, then his neck followed by his shoulders and back, then the raised leg. Always the same behaviors, always in the same order.

Bear was raised as a seemingly normal dog with an uneventful puppyhood. No traumatic events involving cigarettes occurred. Bear's life was full and happy. The random behavior he so suddenly developed cannot be explained.

Five years passed. Sherry, Billy and Bear moved to a different house. By then Bear was six years old. Though he had a different yard, he still had the same reaction to a lit cigarette flipped into the grass.

Perhaps someone should notify Smokey Bear he has a new recruit.

Seventh Sense

Diane Arrington

Docktale 1
Ramsey

Ramsey may be the parrot from hell. This five-year-old African Gray makes life interesting for his owner Jim Schuler of Dallas and a six-month-old white Boxer named Missy.

When Ramsey is out of his cage, he waddles on the floor and permits Missy to kiss him on the back. When he's trapped inside his cage he gazes down on Missy and says, *"You're a bad girl."* Missy folds her ears back and her tail under and slinks into her kennel.

When Ramsey is in a better mood, he sits on his perch and pitches food to Missy with his beak. First the bird tells the dog to sit. Missy does it. Then Ramsey tosses peanuts, apples, peaches and grapes out through his cage door to Missy who is sitting obediently below. As she consumes his gifts Ramsey says, *"You're a good girl."* Missy wags her tail.

If he isn't thinking like a human, then how does Ramsey suit his comments to the situation? He speaks in his own voice and is not imitating Jim.

In the morning, Ramsey wakes Jim with a style all his own. In the quiet house his parrot voice rips through the silence: *"NO! LEAVE ME ALONE!"* This occurs suddenly, without warning or provocation, and the wayward bird screams with maximum use of his parrot lungs.

Occasionally, presumably for variation, Ramsey uses a down-home country accent to awaken Jim. In the voice of a radio DJ, Ramsey quite loudly announces, *"And the next song will be—"* But Ramsey never quite manages to name the song. As one can well imagine, this leaves Jim pretty much on edge without much hope of returning to sleep.

When Ramsey wants something to eat, such as a grape, he asks Jim the question.

"You want a grape?"

Jim answers, *"No, do you want a grape?"*

"You want a grape?" counters Ramsey.

"No, do you want a grape?"

"Wanna grape?" Ramsey tips his head at Jim.

"You want a grape?"

"Okay, yes, grape," Ramsey decides at last, as though Ramsey getting a grape was originally Jim's idea.

It appears as though, in Ramsey's mind, others were created for Ramsey's use. He annoys the dog, pesters Jim and terrorizes Jim's visitors. When an unsuspecting guest puts his finger in Ramsey's cage, Ramsey sinks his black beak hard into the finger and then complains loudly, *"Ow! That hurts!"*

Jim has a friend named Rick whom Ramsey for some reason adores. When Rick comes over, Ramsey calls to the man from his cage in the dining room.

"Rick!"

If Rick ignores him, Ramsey yells.

"RICK!"

If Rick still ignores him, Ramsey screams, *"R-I-I-I-CK!"* If Rick still pays no attention, Ramsey mutters, *"You're a brat,"* and turns his feathered back.

Jim has no idea how Ramsey picked up what he seems to "know." He has not spent any time teaching or coaching the bird. Still, Ramsey seems to know everything and be a very smart bird. Just ask him; he'll tell you.

"I'm a smart boy."

Diane Arrington

Chapter 6
Charles

Whether human or animal, evidence suggests the learning process to be identical in all mammals. This story of feline cognizance will make all humans think twice about euthanasia, animal medical experimentation or even de-clawing the dignified feline. The behavior Charles undertakes occurs continually in the animal world. It is the opportunity of witnessing it that is a rare honor.

Charles was an oversized grey and white short-haired domestic cat, very dignified as his name implies. Charles was extremely well aware that he was a cat. Exquisitely blended in four-year-old Charles were the dignity of an adult and the spirit and mischief of a kitten. He lived with three other cats. Charles was the oldest and clearly the wisest. Charles must have had higher education all through his astrological chart, because he was a teacher of the finest quality.

Charles had another quality of dubious pleasure, an apparently inherent ability to make life intriguing for owners Jay and Sonya of Buckingham, Texas. For example, if Jay took a break from his computer work and forgot to close the keyboard, he returned to a screen full of alien tongue.

Although Charles was invisible when Jay left the room, he materialized long enough to walk onto the keyboard, stand for a second on his large feet, then walk off. He was careful to disappear before Jay returned. No frisky *see what I did want to play some more* for Charles. That one simple act of walking, standing and leaving, not more than three seconds in duration, caused Jay nightmares untangling the mess on a confused computer. Ever the educator, Charles taught Jay to close the keyboard, if even for a simple bathroom break.

Diane Arrington

At all times, Charles knew precisely what he was doing.

On more than one occasion Charles quietly pushed the phone off the hook. Important callers heard a busy signal hour after hour. Or, Charles walked his big self across the clock radio in the night, turning off the alarm. Both Jay and Sonya were repeatedly late for work until they ingeniously thought to tuck the radio inside the desk drawer. Once Charles was caught red-handed playing one of his devilish tricks, he stopped that one and invented another.

By far the most annoying habit Charles developed took place in the kitchen. He learned to open the kitchen cupboards. There are other cats in the world who have learned to do this, but Charles always took things beyond reason, and beyond the realm of human tolerance.

The cupboards Charles chose to frequent were located on the floor below the counters. One Saturday in May as Sonya put away some dishes, she noticed Charles sitting quietly in one corner of the kitchen, watching her intently. Evidently that day was the day Charles learned by observation how to manipulate the cabinet doors.

Later the same day Charles walked his holier-than-thou walk to the same cupboard and sat thinking for a moment. He lifted his right paw, extended his claws into the crack of the cabinet door where it met the frame. He spared not a glance at the side with the hinges; Charles already knew which side of the panel would open.

With a chunky white paw as smooth as milk Charles pulled the cupboard open. Magnets pulled it closed. Again he pulled it open, but this time Charles slid his paw inside, then his arm, head, body — and he was in. Two attempts was all it took. A third attempt was unnecessary for Charles to be successful at meeting his objective. The door closed on his tail, but this was not a problem for Charles. He simply reeled it in, like a woman pulling her skirt free of an elevator door.

Seventh Sense

Once inside the cupboard, Charles discovered a marvelous, magically dark place to sleep. It was perfect for a cat. There were large, cool glass casserole dishes just like boxes to sleep in. There were big round metal pots wonderfully similar to large holes to cram himself into. He fell asleep inside Sonya's crock pot.

Early evening the same Saturday Sonya was preparing to fix supper. She opened the cabinet and nearly fainted with fright. A large hairy *thing* bounded out from the darkness of the cupboard. Charles was through with his nap.

After Charles acquired his peevish habit of making pots, pans and platters his beds, all cookware had to be washed before use. In a busy, two-income family this was intolerable. Jay thought to install baby-proof latches, but he unfortuitously chose the wrong kind. Charles soon learned a firm push on the panels would spring the doors open. Charles thought this new development made things much easier.

Charles' ultimate came soon after the new latches, before Jay had a chance to replace them. Charles was four. Jay was standing in the kitchen at the sink when the most uncommon sight approached.

Charles strode purposefully into the kitchen. Behind him, all three other cats followed him in single file, tails straight out behind them. It was a cat convoy. Jay had never before seen all four of his cats gathered together at once. Charles had not seen Jay, so intent was he on his mission. Jay stayed quiet, waiting to see what would happen next.

Charles marched straight to his favorite cupboard and stopped. He paused for a moment in front of the cabinet and looked back over his shoulder at the others. The three sat down, as if on cue, in a horizontal row like pupils in a classroom.

Charles turned his attention back to the cupboard. He took a step forward. He raised his right front paw to the cupboard door. He pushed in firmly, putting his weight behind the action. The door sprang open, then eased shut. Charles again turned his head and looked over his shoulder at his class. He seemed to say, *See there?* He faced back and repeated the paw lesson. All three cats continued to watch intently. Again, Charles looked around at his roommates. *See how?* Jay half-expected three student cats to nod in unison like a Disney animation.

Then Charles stood back a few paces and sat down, just off to the side but still at the head of the class. Jay could not believe what happened next.

Mandy, a small orange tabby, stood and approached the cabinet. She raised her right front paw and softly stroked the cabinet door. It did not open. Mandy looked at Charles. Pedantic Charles gazed back. A moment occurred. Mandy's classmates watched. Then Mandy turned back, reached up and pushed on the door, this time putting her weight into it. The door clicked and popped open, then whispered shut.

The small cat raised her paw and pushed again. The panel paged open, then quietly closed. Mandy then turned away from the cupboard and, with her tail high in the air, walked back and sat down, taking her place beside the two others.

In the silent kitchen Jay was awestruck, but the class bell had not yet sounded. There was more.

Next Timothy stepped forward. While Charles looked on, Timothy proceeded through the same ritual Mandy had. Then it was Elliot's turn, but Elliot used his left paw while the others had used the right. Each cat in turn learned the lesson. How To Open Mom's Cupboards. Throughout the entire process, about a ten-minute event, Charles attended as the stately professor.

When the lesson had concluded, all cats stood and filed out of the room, tails high, Charles in the lead. They dispersed for a snack, a bath and a nap.

Jay stood in shock and disbelief, wishing he'd had his camcorder handy to prove to himself — and others — what he had just witnessed: a cat class. For obvious reasons, he was at once amused and terrified.

The degree of silent communication that occurred among these cats is inconceivable to humans who blabber endlessly with their mouths all of their lives. Most are strangers, at least consciously, to the idea of thought transference.

It is irresistible to wonder how the telepathy occurred in this case. Did Charles wake each cat individually, or was he able to stand in one place and mutely holler, calling them from all parts of the house for class?

How was Charles able to influence all three cats simultaneously? Perhaps the feline social structure is more ordered than humans have ever before realized. Does their conversation occur in some form of feline verbiage or does it take place in mental pictures and images?

Charles' motivation in teaching the other cats his trick is an enigma. A human would likely choose to keep his private hiding place a secret, selfishly preserve it for himself. It is possible cats have huge egos and Charles was showing off? Or was there some particular survival-linked purpose for Charles to teach other cats how to sleep inside the cabinets?

It would have been interesting to see if Mandy, Timothy and Elliot would have taken up residence inside the cupboards with Charles. But we will never know.

That very day in May Jay installed the proper latches on the kitchen cupboards.

Diane Arrington

Chapter 7
Hannah

Hannah's story shows a surprisingly fixed purpose for a young canine mind. Her behavior cannot be classified, categorized or explained, but it exemplifies firm decision-making. It is evidence that dogs are capable of making choices and can have clear preferences. Hannah exhibits a voluntary recipe for puppy play that is systematic and classic.

Hannah was an unusual puppy in both breed and in temperament. The Welsh Springer Spaniel has not been made common by the Hollywood, Disney or advertising communities, so its genes remain reasonably pure. Generally speaking, the more undiluted the genes, the more true to bred purpose, and the more intelligent the dog.

In the behavioral arena, the more intelligent the dog, the more difficult to appease, particularly in an environment which, to a dog, is non-working, non-stimulating and boring. Such is the average household, and such was Hannah's household.

Adopted from a breeder at the age of twelve weeks, Hannah had saffron eyes, a pink nose and a smooth vanilla coat interrupted here and there by random rusty splotches. Her coat may have been a reflection of her brain waves. Nevertheless, Hannah was a housetraining dream. Her sagacity and ability to comprehend were a blessing on that issue. But her high IQ caused other problems. She was a serious puppy-biter, wouldn't come when called and, in fact, ignored her owners most of the time.

But there was a kernel of brilliance in Hannah, and she showed it at the tender age of four months. Her unusual choice of behavior, though a mystery, is a pet-owner's fantasy. Hannah's

Diane Arrington

family, Helen, Paul and two young children, were surprised to learn Hannah was a neatnik.

All of Hannah's toys, almost a footlocker full, were kept in a bright yellow plastic laundry basket. Hannah also had a bed of her own, a large, round, stuffed and washable one. Hannah's was red and black plaid.

Helen had called in a behaviorist for her Princess of Willfulness. As the two women discussed the problems and their solutions regarding her behavior, Hannah was lost in her own world.

To watch a dog when she thinks she is alone is most illuminating. Without the detraction of human interaction, one gets a secret look into the canine world. It was such a moment.

Restless, hyperactive Hannah was actually resting for a change. She was on her bed, heedless of anyone around her. Nearby, just a few feet away, was her yellow toy basket. After a short nap Hannah stirred, yawned and stretched her trim, youngster's body. She was awake. She appeared to think for a moment about what to do next, appeared to be considering her options.

Hannah spotted her toy basket brimming with toys. She climbed off her huge bed and toddled over. Through the waffled sides of the basket, Hannah surveyed the toys inside, sniffed and eyed them thoughtfully.

Then, appearing to have made a decision, Hannah stretched her short neck up and over the side of the basket and, with her pink nose, rooted around like a pig in the mud. She surfaced with a brown stuffed bear. She carried the bear the few feet back to her bed, circled once and settled down to chew him up.

Four minutes later Hannah grew bored with Mr. Bear. She rose with Mr. Bear clutched in her mouth. She carried him back to her basket. She lifted him over the edge and dropped him in.

Still unaware she was under observation, Hannah again put her head in the basket and grubbed around, burying her nose deep in the jumbled, colorful pile of toys. Evidently she had a specific toy in mind, and Hannah persisted until she obtained it. She emerged with a fat stuffed sock. She carried the sock back to her bed, circled once, sank down and began to chew.

Another five minutes and Hannah was tired of the sock. She got to her feet. She carried the sock to her basket. She lifted it over the side and dropped it in.

This time Hannah tunneled even more deeply into her basket of treasures. She wagged her tail slightly as her head all but disappeared beneath the contained pile of playthings. As before, Hannah targeted a specific item. This time she selected a red rubber Kong toy. She carried it back to her bed, circled once, lay down and began to chew, holding the brightly-colored toy vertically between white satiny paws.

After a few minutes Hannah tired of the Kong. She stood and carried it in her mouth back to the basket. Again she stretched up her neck and dropped the toy back inside the basket.

Fifteen minutes had passed. The women pretended to carry on despite Hannah's amusing activities over in the corner all by herself.

A fourth time Hannah searched the basket. Again she seemed to have pre-chosen a special toy. The one she wanted this time was on the bottom of the pile, way at the bottom of the basket. Because she was only a puppy, she was too short to reach over the edge and to the bottom, though she gave it the college try.

Hannah first thought to seek the toy through the side of the basket, and tried to pull it through the slots. She could not. She could scent it through the side, though, and may have wondered why she couldn't pull it through. She circled the basket and attempted retrieval through the other side. Despite punching several times at the basket with her puppy muzzle, she was still unable to acquire what she wanted. But hard-headed Hannah did not, would not, settle for a different toy.

Instead, Hannah stood on her hind legs, put her front paws on the lip of the basket and gave a mighty shove, tipping the basket over and spilling its contents in a tangled layer across the hardwood floor.

Hannah sniffed eagerly over the array of toys, tail wagging happily. She was nearing her goal. In a flash Hannah located the toy she sought and, with a happy face, pounced victorious on her old smelly tennis shoe, just the toy she wanted. She carried the shoe proudly by the laces, neck arched, chest out and tail high. The old gray sneaker swung between her front legs and kicked her white feathered chest. Back on her red and green bed, Hannah circled once, plopped down and chewed for a long twenty minutes this time. With this toy the puppy was happy.

When Hannah was through with the tennis shoe, she climbed off her bed and carried it to the pile of toys on the family room floor. She stood directly over the pile, very deliberately lifted the shoe by the laces into the air and, with a flourish, dropped it on top. Then she trucked off to her water bowl, brown toenails clicking on the hardwood floor. She was still mindless of anyone else around her, still unaware that she had been observed.

Helen and Paul had not instructed Hannah in any manner to put her toys away when finished playing with them. She was not taught this behavior at the breeder's facility. At home she was kept confined in an area away from the children and their toys, so the likelihood of her actions being mimic behavior are too remote to consider. According to her owners, Hannah had undertaken this practice since her adoption. Her behavior was fully spontaneous.

Aside from the wonderfully reassuring idea of a puppy putting away her own toys when finished playing with them, how did Hannah decide exactly which toy she preferred? Did she choose by color, scent or texture? What cerebral mechanism told her she was through with one toy, that she should choose another? And what of her peculiar habit of circling once without fail before lying down?

Seventh Sense

Most unexpected, how could a dog possibly, at four months of age, understand the concept *there's a place for everything and everything in its place*?

Hannah's bumpy upbringing eventually smoothed out. She continued her mysterious, systematic behavior throughout her entire puppyhood and for many years thereafter.

To humans, it will remain a mystery for many more years than that.

Diane Arrington

Docktale 2
Agnes

Agnes was a mammoth, hard-headed, strong-willed, smart, intelligent, beautiful, slobbery, happy eight-month-old Harlequin Great Dane as lovable as Marmaduke. She was all legs, paws and mouth. To hear it from her family, Agnes learned too early in life to use her smarts to get the better of them.

Agnes had a pecan tree in her back yard. She loved to crack the shells with her huge jaws and, though it's a wonder how she did it with her oversized mouth, separate the nutmeat for eating. She spent happy hours at this avocation.

Sometimes, though, when the weather was cold or damp, Agnes dreamed of how nice it would be to stretch out on a warm, soft, comfortable sofa to eat her nuts. But Agnes knew she was not permitted inside the house with the nuts—so Agnes tried to sneak them in. Like a way overgrown chipmunk, she packed her jowls full, then scratched the door to be let in, thinking no one would notice.

Most often Agnes got caught on her way through the door, but she seemed to think it was worth a try anyway. Occasionally the big dog with the mammoth jowls was victorious, and was able to secret one or two pecans inside. This, however, presented a dilemma: where to hide the nuts to avoid discovery.

There was an end table by the couch. Its pedestal foot would have a rectangular bottom but for small alcoves or cutouts on all four sides of the square. This seemed to Agnes like the perfect hiding place.

Ever so delicately the huge dog placed the nuts inside the cutout that was least visible from the room, the one at the back. Like a squirrel stockpiling for a lean winter ahead, Agnes used her fat nose to cover her nuts over with imaginary dirt to preserve them for a future, more idle time.

Diane Arrington

What Agnes didn't seem to know is that her "hidden" nuts were in plain view. She galloped off to play, secure in the knowledge that her edibles were safely hidden away.

Seventh Sense

Diane Arrington

Chapter 8
Frammis

There are several interesting theories to explain feline homing technique. Most often these involve cats who do the job once. Only occasionally do they include cats like Frammis. He puts an erratic new shine on feline homing. Was it by instinct or scent or the angle of the sun that Frammis found his way? Or was it strictly by means of a sixth or seventh sense outside the realm of human conception?

Across the world, stories abound of cats and dogs returning to old homes. Some of these are documented, others undocumented. All are captivating.

One well-documented story involved a cat who was re-homed in New York only to leave and follow a commercial airplane 3,000 miles to cling to his relocating owner. It took the determined cat six months to arrive battered and bruised on the original owner's California doorstep. Not only had he found the correct town, he'd found the proper porch step.

***

A 1986 spring day, a trip to the store and love at first sight threw the two together. At seven weeks of age he was a one-potato cat, a stunning buff against spring grass the same lustrous green as his eyes. He precisely equaled in size one Russet potato.

Feral cats and kittens rarely stay in the open when a towering, fifty-story human happens along. They take cover. Not this one. Fate had him not crouching but sitting like a dog on the lawn at the apartment community where Ellen and her husband

Seventh Sense

Tom lived. Oddly enough, the kitten stayed put as Ellen approached.

Not only did the kitten permit Ellen to pick him up, he melted into her arms. His immature coat, which would ultimately grow long and flowing, looked as if he had stuck his tail into a light socket. Tufted and stiff, his hair stood out from his body. He resembled a small, toasty cactus. Ellen named the kitten Frammis.

As he grew, the jocular cat endeared the couple. Frammis' favorite game was Toothpicks. He may be the first cat in history to play this game, and he never tired of it. His willow eyes twinkled and his pink nose reddened with excitement as he tried to catch the sticks, either with mouth or paws. He dived and flipped for them with the enthusiasm of a minor-leaguer in training.

Frammie spent most of his time flat on his back like a turtle on its shell, four legs waving. He was famous for this. Friends called and asked to come over so they could watch Frammie roll on his back, belly flattening out like a pancake. Whether for sleeping, during which he snored like a rhinoceros, playing, brushing or tummy rubs, it was his favorite position.

For three happy years Frammie brought to the couple's home the love, joy and entertainment only a cat can contribute. The couple was aware that cats who are permitted outside unsupervised have an approximate average life span of only two years as compared to ten years for indoor cats. But the smart cat so plainly enjoyed the outdoors, Ellen and Tom could not deny him his natural joy. Frammie played out most days, but slept indoors at night.

Frammis learned to come when called, which may have kept him a particle safer than he otherwise might have been. Ellen called with her human meow. Frammie answered with his own, more skillful call, and bounded up the stairs to his second-floor habitat. Without fail, Frammie was eager to come inside when called.

Diane Arrington

Frammie had a strange time schedule of his own. He awoke each morning at four a.m. to go out. Invariably, he returned precisely at seven for breakfast.

In February 1989 Tom, Ellen and Frammie moved from the apartment into a quiet residential neighborhood. Frammie's new home was big and beautiful and comfortable. It was 1.5 miles away from the old apartment.

Upon the advice of their veterinarian, Ellen kept Frammie inside the new location for the first three weeks. Allowing him time to acclimate before being permitted free run of a strange new neighborhood would decrease the likelihood of Frammie trying to return "home." The eleven-pound cat seemed to enjoy his new surroundings. He explored endlessly each interesting new space, no matter how small.

It is interesting that in the mornings during his three weeks of confinement indoors, Frammie still awoke at four a.m. to ask out. He had retained his original timetable.

But the first time Ellen did let him out, Frammie was gone. He simply disappeared, like a raindrop in grass or a speck of sand in water. Ellen and Tom were heartbroken. For ten days they searched frantically, checked the newspapers and shelters. Frammie did not turn up.

On the tenth day they received a phone call. Frammie had been found, alive and well. Where he was found is where his mystery begins.

The new tenants in Frammie's old apartment opened the door one morning to a strange but handsome toasted marshmallow, cat-napping on their welcome mat. Frammie had found his way through yards and over fences, across a creek, through scores of high-speed automobiles on two major traffic arteries, around corners, into the complex, past building after building each identical to the next. Up the stairs of the correct unit he had gone, to wait at the door which had been his for three years. It had taken Frammie ten days to find his way a mile and-a-half distant.

Seventh Sense

Frammis may have wondered at the fact of finding someone other than Ellen inside "his" apartment. When Ellen arrived to retrieve him, Frammie meowed big and quivered his tail, overwhelmed with joy at seeing her again. He wrapped his wheaty paws around her neck, rubbed his cheeks on hers, and purred mightily in her ear.

During Frammie's ten-day absence, a stray cat living in the back yard of the new house had given birth to a litter of kittens. Frammie came home to a yard full of unfamiliar cat smells. He had his cat nose a bit out of joint over this new development. He recognized home, seemed glad to be back, but stayed only two weeks.

On his second disappearance Frammie was quicker. It took him only three days to find his way. Once more the new tenants discovered him on their mat, once again Ellen fetched him, again he was thrilled to see her.

Back home, the kittens opened their eyes, then their ears, then began to wobble on spindly legs. As spring turned to summer, they romped and played in the fresh grass. And finally there was Frammie, smack in the middle of all the fun. He had changed his mind about the kittens and now seemed to enjoy the fun and play they provided him.

Frammis now adored the kittens and their mother. For six heavenly months they kept him happy. He helped raise the kittens and invented new games for them with their mother Puff. Frammie taught Puff how to cross the street without getting hurt and how to hide under the neighbor's eves in case it should rain. Frammie liked his new home even better than before the cat family. He seemed finally to have settled in.

The time came to home the playful Russian Blue mutts, and they were taken to a no-kill shelter for adoption. For two weeks Frammie and Puff together searched the bushes, the yard, under the deck. But the kittens had disappeared and could not be found.

Just a few weeks after the kittens departed, so did Frammie, for the third time. Ellen leaned out the door one evening to call him in, only to receive sound silence in return.

Diane Arrington

Not again, Ellen and Tom thought. Now they wrestled with their emotions. They were torn between their responsibility to keep Frammis safe and his clear and evident love for his freedom. Indeed, he had been free and wild when Ellen found him three years earlier. He was unhappy when kept indoors at all times, moping and declining play. But still, should they keep him inside?

A few days passed before Ellen got the call. Certain as sunrise, Frammie was back at his old apartment.

This time Ellen had an idea. Perhaps if, instead of driving him back, she were to walk him home on his own four paws he would be able to find his way if he should run away again. She wished desperately to discover a way to make him understand the house was his new home, that they had actually moved, and she hoped this might be the way to get that message across to him. She would show him the terrain from his own perspective.

Ellen used food treats to encourage Frammis along with her. She coaxed him and he followed through the heat and dryness of a Texas summer. But Frammie had a limit.

Ellen managed to lure the cat only about a half mile away from the complex. Then dear, sweet Frammie, the gentle, loving boy who slept on his back, loved brushing and came when called, bit and scratched Ellen when she tried to make him go any further. One-half mile was as far from his original home he planned to go, voluntarily at least. Tom had to leave work and pick them up in the car.

Ellen felt she may have imposed her will too strongly on Frammie; he stayed only two days before leaving again for the fourth time. This time Ellen followed him.

Thinking he was alone and unobserved, Frammie assumed the slinking posture of a feral cat as he crept along the alley and across yards. As he approached McCree Road, a four-lane street with heavy traffic spinning along at 45 miles an hour, he began looking for the cars even before reaching the curb. Amazingly, Frammis waited at the curb for an opening in the traffic.

Looking both ways, the cat watched for a break in traffic. When it came, he dashed across the hot pavement as fast as his legs would carry him. Frammis seemed as terrified of the cars as Ellen was that he would get hit, but not afraid enough to stay behind. By some unknown force, Frammis was driven.

Ellen did her best to follow, but eventually she lost him. A few hours later she retrieved him back from the apartment. Now like a yo-yo, Frammie left home for the fifth time less than a week later.

Ellen reports that after his tantrum in the woods he no longer seemed happy at the new house. In the space of three years, Frammie returned to his old apartment, his original home, six times. He did so even though his owners no longer lived there.

Ellen lived and loved with Frammie for most of his six years. His most outstanding quality was his keen, almost neon intelligence. Because of this, Ellen thinks he may have associated his collar and tags with being found and fetched back home again. He may ultimately have found a way to remove his own collar, freeing him to go where he pleased when he pleased.

While we think of cats as asocial animals, time and evolution do not stand still. Are felines evolving into social animals? Did Frammie have standing relationships with other cats in the area? Like a human, did he miss them emotionally and go back for visits?

Some unknown biological need drove Frammie, but was it a need for the company of other cats or simply the place of his birth? Was his mother still there? And what of his half-mile limit? Studies show feral cats in high-density areas range approximately two to four blocks, while cats in low-density areas range up to two miles. Frammie's limit conforms to neither of these.

It cannot be known why Frammie could not or would not adapt permanently to his new home. In human terms it would seem to be a desirable home. It contained others of his own species whom he obviously loved, a big, green yard to play in, food when he wanted.

Diane Arrington

But the biggest mystery of all is what in Frammie's mind or brain or hormones or instincts made him decide to leave when he did? He did not go back at every opportunity. He stayed six months, three days, two weeks, each time mysteriously choosing to leave for no known reason.

It is possible, in mind of literary history on the subject, that cats have psychic abilities that would enable them to signal telepathically to each other. Was Frammie, for reasons unknown to humans, needed at "home" on certain occasions?

Frammie was six when he left the final time and could not be found, not at his old apartment, and not alive or dead. Ultimately all resources were exhausted. There is no way of knowing what became of the smart, toast-colored feline.

There is also no way of knowing that Frammie won't mysteriously appear again at some time in the future. For Ellen and Tom, hope roams eternal.

Docktale 3
Tara

This short, stocky mixed breed took her job as Guard Dog Supreme way too seriously.

Tara, who lived near Flower Mound, Texas and weighed only twenty pounds, could scale an eight-foot privacy fence. Once at the top, the small stick of dynamite hung by the ankles of her forepaws. She chinned up to peek over the top of the fence and bark ferociously at anyone passing by her house and her property on her sidewalk.

The inside onlooker would see seven feet of cedar fence between the grass and a little dog rear. The outside observer would see eight feet of fence between the ground and two light brown paws, two glistening eyes and many white teeth as the mighty tyke guarded her premises.

Most dogs are satisfied with peeking through the cracks and barking from behind the fence. Not Tara. Can a dog have a Napoleon complex?

From what is known, Tara thankfully never went over the fence. Momentum took her to the top, upper-body strength kept her there, and, when satisfied she had achieved her goal of terrorizing even the most passive intruder, gravity brought her safely back to earth.

Tara would land back in the grass unharmed, unhurt and all puffed up about herself. The intruders were gone. As far as Tara was concerned, she got the job done, big-time.

Diane Arrington

Chapter 9
Teddy

There are many thousands of ball-obsessive dogs in the world. Teddy was one. But Teddy showed an ability to anticipate human behavior outside the realm of what humans consider normal for a dog. How he did it is beyond the human capacity for understanding, and Teddy wouldn't tell.

Teddy was only six months old when the doctor discovered the handsome German Shepherd had developed hip dysplasia. It may have been this fact and Teddy's resulting inability to run and fetch that he learned instead how to catch. A ball was the most convenient item to use for his daily games. This explains why Teddy formed an early attachment to the ball, but it does not explain how Teddy was able to visualize future events in order to quench his appetite for the game.

During his upbringing, Teddy was never hurt, scolded, struck by a human or made afraid in any way. The absence of fear for his own safety and welfare kept his natural spirit and identity intact. It left him free to think and scheme.

Teddy had a system. He was the creator of a plan so delectable in its subtlety it would intrigue even the most avid dog-dismisser. The plan required of Teddy foresight, intuition and telepathic anticipation. Teddy's power to foresee the short-term future even Wall Street would covet — if it could only determine how he did it.

Teddy was a ball connoisseur. Ultimately he "owned" at once an average of a dozen balls. He knew where all of them were at all times by means of his mysterious yet conscientious accounting system. He had all kinds, from tennis balls to squeaky rubber to the brightly-colored kind with the porcupine nubs. Having proclaimed himself the Ballmeister, Teddy made sure no vermin (the other dogs in the house) had custody of one of the balls for too long a time.

The balls were not necessarily Teddy's security blanket. He did unquestionably want one nearby at any given moment, in the delightful event some benevolent human soul might choose to throw it to him. Teddy took good care of the orbs, cleaning them occasionally by means of a dunk in the pool; he would sit on the ledge at one end of the pool and toss a ball out into the water for himself to leap in and swim after. Upon retrieval he would swim back and climb out of the pool with the ball still in his huge Shepherd jaws, only to throw it in again so he could fetch it again. This he would do for hours on end, amusing himself as the day sidled by.

Teddy's angled obsession did not occur suddenly. True, he loved to catch, but that was the easy part. To Teddy the challenge seemed to be devising ways to connive a throw of the ball. He tricked people. He made use of natural human behavior to serve his own desires. He developed his skill gradually into a ritual which ultimately worked perfectly for him.

During his puppyhood a ball acted as pacifier for the plump black-and-tan infant. As he settled down to sleep, Teddy held a squeaky ball in his mouth. Still wakeful, the puppy chomped the ball absently, the way a human might grind his teeth, squeaking it loudly in the darkened room. The repetition of sound appeared to make him sleepy. To a dog obsessed, having a ball right there in his mouth might be a comfort.

Momentarily the sound of squeaking was replaced with the sound of steady breathing. Then he'd stir, squeak and chomp some more, then drift off again into quiet breathing. Squeak-squeak-squeak-snore—squeak-squeak-squeak-snore. This repeated several times. As Mr. Sandman overtook his puppy brain, Teddy relaxed his grip on the ball. The squeaking stopped and the ball rolled from his spongy jaws to the carpet, there to rest nearby for ready access in the morning. The puppy was asleep.

Before long Teddy began to take the ball with him to meals. He set it nearby while he ate, just to keep it in view. Then one night over the dishes owner Jane turned to the dishwasher to find Teddy's ball in the silverware basket. Another night as Jane was finishing dinner she rose to soak her plate and found Teddy's ball in the sink. Teddy and his ball got there before she did. He knew her ritual. He knew she would go to the kitchen sink after dinner.

Soon the ball was appearing everywhere. In the mornings, if Jane turned a moment from the mirror, she turned back to find Teddy's ball stuffed inside her makeup case. She found the ball on the bottom shelf inside the refrigerator. While transferring wet clothes from washer to dryer, she would find Teddy's ball lying innocently inside the dryer, not there one minute, there the next. Teddy's ball always seemed to materialize just before Jane's next move.

Of course Teddy's scheming worked for him because on each occasion Jane was required to move the ball out of the way. It consequently got tossed away, giving Teddy just one more opportunity to catch, on the fly, first bounce, or second bounce. Then Teddy could dream up a new strategy for providing himself another golden opportunity.

Teddy's ball pursuits were not geographically limited. He and it were omnipresent.

While cleaning the skimmer in the pool, Jane turned away for a moment only to turn back and find the ball in the skimmer. While gardening and filling a wheelbarrow full of dirt, a moment's distraction only produced Teddy's ball, placed strategically on top of the mountain of dirt. Jane never seemed to be able to catch Teddy placing the ball, so sneaky was he. Planting flowers or trees, she dug out the hole, reached to fetch the tree or plant, turned back to find the clever dog's ball in the hole.

Teddy never bothered Jane with the ball, pushing it at her like so many ball-obsessive dogs do. He was simply there, unobtrusive, silent, stealthy, to place the ball in her way, in the way of her life.

Diane Arrington

Countless balls were lost, buried, drowned, chopped up. Countless balls went through the dishwasher, laundry, or spent the night in the refrigerator.

With each passing day, Teddy's scheming grew increasingly more sophisticated.

While watching television at night, Jane got up for a snack and returned to find the ball in her chair. In the mornings she rose to find her way to the bathroom, only to discover Teddy and his ball had beaten her to the commode. The ball floated in the clean water. While Jane mowed the lawn, Teddy annoyingly anticipated and placed the ball in the next row to be mowed.

Initially Jane tried hiding the balls from Teddy. But brainy Teddy, whether by scent or sight or telepathy, was always able to find it. If she put it on top of the refrigerator, Teddy would dig and scrape and claw at the refrigerator door to get to it. If she tried hiding it at the top of the bookshelves, Teddy would pull books down with his mighty paws until he obtained the ball. If she put it in a drawer or cupboard, Teddy simply tracked it down, opened the drawer or cupboard and got it back out again, an elementary task for a dog as big as Teddy.

By far Teddy's most intriguing demonstration of anticipating Jane's activities happened one day in summer. Jane was preparing to leave in the car. While she gathered her things inside the house, the front door stood open. The screen door was closed but not latched. Teddy, of course, knew Jane would be leaving through that very door. This time Jane had a rare opportunity to witness Teddy in action.

Thinking himself unobserved, Teddy clamped a tennis ball in his gold and black muzzle. He nosed open the screen door and slid his head and shoulders through. While birds chatted in the quiet yard out front, Teddy let the screen door rest easily against his ribs while he crouched with his forward half outside the door and his rear inside the house. Sneakily, Teddy quietly placed the ball just outside the door. Always thinking, the dog pressed the ball firmly with his nose, making sure it stayed in place and did not roll away. He withdrew then, retracting himself soundlessly like a turtle into its shell. He let the screen close silently in front of him. Then Teddy, ever so proud of himself, stood back and waited, perpetually ready, always in proximity of an airborne ball. Surely enough, when Jane innocently exited the house she picked up the ball and tossed it back inside, providing Teddy with just one more coveted opportunity to snatch it wildly.

How was Teddy able to so accurately foresee where his owner would be next? We think of intelligent dogs as possessing an if-then genesis of behavior. *If I hear keys, then a car ride is imminent. If I see a leash, then a walk is coming.*

But *if my owner gets up then she will be returning and if I place my ball in her chair then she will be forced to throw it for me to get it out of her way* is a bit of a stretch, at least on as many different occasions in as many different contexts for as many years as Teddy entertained himself in this manner.

For what canine purpose did Teddy appoint himself Ball Steward? Teddy directed his behavior to a specific purpose. The thinking and reasoning of most dogs is reversed. If a human sits down, *then* you bring the ball and ask that it be thrown. The fault and flaw in that process, however, which Teddy apparently recognized, is that the human could then decline to throw the ball. Teddy's plan ensured that the human could not refuse and would be forced to put or toss the ball somewhere in order to continue the activity at hand. Teddy interrupted the very flow of human life to serve his own purpose.

What Jane learned after all her years with Teddy was to be prepared to be surprised. She also learned that there was only one place on earth in which it was possible to hide a ball from Teddy, a place where he could neither see it nor smell it: inside the freezer.

Diane Arrington

Chapter 10
Lari

Cats are strange and secretive creatures. Tireless, high-energy Lari proves this fact. While the feline fondness for hiding things is omnipresent, Lari's mysterious behavior shows an intensity of imagination and resourcefulness unequaled by even the most prescient Easter Bunny.

Some mysterious things happened at the house on Dwyer Street, all of them perpetrated by a winsome mixed-breed kitten named Lari.

Lari was a Calico kitten with a white chest, huge orange ears and big, round, buttercup eyes. Her tail was longer than average, and the black patches in her markings were splattered in strange patterns across her short fur coat. At six months of age Lari was willowy, spry and athletic. More packed with mischief than the average kitten, her mysterious behavior apparently began when she was adopted, though it was not discovered until months later.

In her youth, Lari's owner Dorothy had been a dancer, a member of the bawdry era of bars and burlesque. But the years and two children had taken their toll, and little evidence of her youthful, attractive figure remained. There was no going back. Now in her sixties, Dorothy's figure was not sloppy but had matured to round and voluptuous.

Dorothy's husband had passed away, the end result of a devastating stroke. A full-time housekeeper, Mattie, was now Dorothy's only companion. Dorothy loved animals and wanted company in the evenings after Mattie had gone home. She thought a nice, low-maintenance cat would be perfect, something warm to lie in her lap and cuddle. With Lari, this was not to be.

Dorothy went to the SPCA in Dallas, Texas and adopted what she was told was a male kitten eight weeks of age. She

Diane Arrington

named him Larry. A few months hence, Larry morphed into a girl. Already too attached to return the kitten, Dorothy adapted by simply changing the spelling of her name.

Lari loved her new home. She was sagacious, and took full advantage of the two women. She was fond of throwing herself to the carpet directly into Dorothy's path. The kitten particularly enjoyed a game called Boo Cat, which involved sneaking up on Mattie and scaring the life out of her. One of Lari's most annoying joys was dancing on the piano keys at three o'clock in the morning.

Dorothy's house was filled with cellophane-wrapped hard candies. The sweets were everywhere. There was every kind of candy one can imagine, in every color in every conceivable container.

And it was elegance. The candies were the finest available. They were not tossed into old cigar boxes and dime-store dishes. Candy was placed with care in Baccarat crystal and Wedgewood china, sterling bowls, and hand-blown, long-stemmed goblets. There were butterscotch and lemon and raspberry-filled candies. There were red-and-white striped peppermints, and green-and-white striped winter mints. There were orange candies, cinnamon candies, lime, cherry and licorice, and there were root beer balls too. All were wrapped in cellophane—it was a cat's version of heaven.

The cat as a hunter is attracted to cellophane. It is theorized that the cellophane on its own generates sounds of cat quarry. Even better, when wadded into a tight ball, cellophane re-opens itself, moving of its own volition—just like prey.

It wasn't until Lari had been in the house about four months that both Dorothy and Mattie began to notice the candy disappearing at a faster rate than usual. It occurred to Dorothy she really ought to cut back, and she thought no more of it.

One day Mattie discovered a golden butterscotch behind the cookie jar in the kitchen. She supposed Dorothy had dropped it there. She came across a cinnamon ball on the kitchen windowsill, hidden among the plants. She dismissed it as Dorothy's absent-mindedness, having had it in her hand while pinching back the plants. A few days later Mattie found a sunny lemon drop on the dining room windowsill, tucked behind the curtain. This discovery was more difficult to explain away. When she found two pieces tucked beneath the cat's dinner mat on the floor, she had an idea someone in the house needed therapy.

Soon nearly all the candy had disappeared. Literally hundreds of candies were gone. It was not difficult to determine that Lari had been stealing and hiding the candy. Indeed, it might be expected that she chose to hide the treasures. That she might be attracted to cellophane is not unusual. The intriguing thing was where Lari did the hiding. The mystery was why.

Fascinating were the hiding places Lari selected. Not one piece was in plain view. Most were so well hidden it would take years to find them all.

Lari dropped two mints in front of the couch, then presumably used her paw to push them far underneath a sofa so close to the ground even Lari's tiny paw would have barely fit beneath. Under the coffee table, of which the bottom shelf was no more than two inches above the floor, also seemed like a good hiding place to Lari. She hid an orange ball there. She stashed two flat pieces, a green-and-white spiral and a cinnamon disk, beneath the mat at her feed station.

As the weeks went by Lari either ran out of floor space or became more creative in the selection of her hiding places. She pushed candies beneath the seat cushions on both the couch and loveseat. Lari thought behind the cushions on the sofa would be a good place for a Raspberry Zinger. Carrying a creamy coconut wafer in her mouth, ivory whiskers protruding from behind it, she leaped to the dining room table. On top of that expansive Broyhill table, the little kitten dropped the prize into a two-inch hole: the mouth of an eighteen-inch-high Wedgewood vase. She did this without disturbing the vase.

Diane Arrington

The books in the built-in bookshelves fit closely, with perhaps an inch to spare at the top. Possibly aided by her extra-long tail, Lari was somehow able to balance her lithe body on a two-inch ledge five feet above the ground, a holiday sweet in her mouth. She tucked the candy into the tiny space on top of the books. Then she stretched a Dreamsicle paw over the books and pushed, sliding the sweet back until it fell down behind. An antique lamp with feet at the base made a small space above the surface of its table. Lari must have thought this a superb hiding spot: three pieces of candy were found there.

Ultimately, candy was discovered concealed in every room of the house, under, behind or inside nearly every object available.

Lari never played with the candy in the presence of Dorothy or Mattie. Not once did they see Lari with the candy. Never in their presence did she investigate it or show any interest in it whatsoever. Her favorite toy as far as they knew was an old tennis ball she had unearthed from the secret place in which it had remained hidden months since the dog left.

It is impossible to avoid wondering what was taking place in Lari's mind as she performed her secret work. Could a cat have consciously reasoned to hide the candy from Dorothy to help her with her diet? If in fact Lari thought the candies were prey, why would she hide them and not try to gut and eat them? And why did she never play with the cellophane? Instead, Lari played with a slobber-soaked dog toy.

Lari's true feline motivation will always remain a mystery. So will how she managed to hide hundreds of pieces of candy in her short, four-month residence. One wonders if she ever slept a wink.

There may be little left of Dorothy's youth but a good mind, but there will always be something left of Lari's youth and weird mind, hidden somewhere in the house on Dwyer Street.

Seventh Sense

Diane Arrington

Chapter 11
Beatrice & Chewy

Beatrice was a sharp, clear-minded dog. A handsome German Shepherd, her behaviors and activities appeared to be premeditated and deliberate, showing evidence of goal-seeking in the canine mind. The fact that her goal was a common human goal makes her story all the more appealing.

Beatrice had a pal. Her name was Chewy. Chewy was also a German Shepherd. Beatrice adored Chewy. She mothered her. She cleaned her ears. She nibbled her fleas for her. Chewy loved Bea just as much as Bea loved Chewy, and sprawled out dreamily when big sister Bea took care of her. They were two dogs engaged in a joyous, almost celestial relationship together. If ever two dogs were humanesque in their love for each other, these two were. They were inseparable except when human intervention prevented their togetherness.

There was a problem, though. Bea and Chewy had too much fun together. Inside their small frame house the two 65-pound Shepherds would race wildly, chasing back and forth between the kitchen and the living room, up and down the hallway and around and around the couch. It was as though they had no concept of their size and thought they might be Chihuahuas. They skidded on the hardwood floors, leaving long, white toenail gouges. When one finally caught the other, they wrestled like two rowdy teenage boys, only they were two very large dogs. They bit and tumbled gleefully, and in their zeal knocked over furniture and broke things. While owner Lacy was away, the dogs got into the trash and the closets and treated the drapes as a tugging towel and the TV remote control as a rawhide chew toy.

Seventh Sense

Lacy was at a loss as to how to control her two crazy dogs when she wasn't there. Though they had always been permitted free run of the house in her absence, she decided the dogs were too happy and their horseplay too rambunctious. She determined they must be left in the back yard. It was this very decision which led Bea to her ingenious behavior. After all, dogs adapt to the current situation, regardless.

***

Bea and Chewy lay together in the dappled shade of a silver maple, idly snapping flies. They panted rhythmically in the Texas heat, healthy pink tongues dripping. A jetliner flying high above the earth crept across the pale blue sky of summer. Muzzle to the clouds and brown eyes keen, Bea watched it pass. She yawned, her formidable jaws stretching wide. Ho-hum. What to do, what to do. Closed out of the house, don't know why. She and Chewy had already played five games of Tug-of-War with a lawn chair, Keep-Away with the patio umbrella, re-landscaped the yard, pruned the new azaleas and snacked on what remained of the marigolds. It was only 9:30 in the morning.

Bea, whose middle name should be Mischief, rose and wandered to the back door. Still locked. Her morning nap always took place on the living room couch, but she couldn't get to it. She stood by the door, not knowing what to do with herself. As she turned away she tripped over something sticking up from the ground. It was the water faucet. The attached garden hose lay coiled like a green snake nearby. Exploring this new find, Bea opened her teeth and, with characteristic German Shepherd over-exuberance, she tasted the faucet handle.

Suddenly she heard water running. There it was, wet and fresh and cool. Chewy heard it too, and wandered over to see. Together they licked the clear water from the mouth of the hose. Bea's ancestors whispered; she picked up the green coiled hose and shook it. Suddenly Chewy was all wet and cool. The dogs exchanged a look. They couldn't believe their luck.

Diane Arrington

***

Lacy arrived home tired from a long day at work. It was hot. In the back yard she found Bea and Chewy together as usual. They were fast asleep. They were also rib-deep in a monolithic puddle of mud. The water hose was running nearby, keeping the mud nice and cool. The Shepherds were in hot dog heaven, flat on their sides and snoring, cool as cucumbers in the early June heat. From whiskers to paws they were covered with mud half wet and sloppy, half dried and caked.

When the infuriation wore off, Lacy made a mental note to remind her husband Robert to turn off the faucet after watering the yard.

But the next day when Lacy returned home, the dogs were in the same condition — wet, sloppy and ecstatic, very much like two barnyard pigs. The water flooded freely from the garden hose onto the ground nearby. In their joy to see her home again, Bea and Chewy shared the mud with Lacy's work clothes.

Hours later, after the laundry was done, Lacy again reminded Robert about the water. He was certain he had remembered to turn it off.

Robert and Lacy put the evidence together. By the fourth day, although they had not seen her in action, they deduced the truth: Bea was turning the water on during the day when everyone was gone. To solve the problem, Lacy removed the handle from the faucet. That would be the end of it, she was certain of it.

The next day Lacy and Robert returned home to two messy, mud-coated shepherds. The water ran independently from the hose into the earth. Though the handle had been removed, Beatrice had discovered a way to twist the stump with her teeth. To solve the problem, Robert secured the faucet with wire. This would solve the problem, he just knew it; a dog has no fingers to bend the wire away.

Seventh Sense

But the next day when he came home Bea had proved to him that a dog doesn't need fingers. She had turned on the hose despite the wire.

Next, Lacy thought to cover the faucet with an empty plastic container. It was a simple matter to sink the hard plastic several inches into the soft mud. The mud would dry overnight, cementing the cover in place.

The next day Bea removed the cover and played in the water anyway.

Human exasperation reigned. Doggie challenge sustained. Day after day, upon Lacy and Robert's arrival home, Beatrice looked innocent. Had she shown the tiniest bit of remorse they might have felt better. Instead, she gazed at them with a look of delighted victory. She appeared to be enjoying this new game.

Still, the problem was at hand and Bea rose to the challenge of untangling the puzzle each new day brought. Each night Lacy and Robert would shake their heads in wonder. How could they keep Bea from transforming their water bill into the national debt?

This time Robert turned a large galvanized bucket upside down over the faucet and sank its edges nearly ten inches into the mud. Surely a dog would not be clever enough to get it off. But they underestimated Bea. She was a dog driven. The couple returned home to water pouring unrestrained into the yard. The galvanized bucket lay dead at the back of the property, mangled, bent and full of tiny tooth holes, the unfortunate victim of a sincere game of Chase-and-Tug.

Bea's resolve went undaunted, and Robert and Lacy were at their wit's end. As a final attempt to foil the spunky dog, Robert fashioned a faucet cover using heavy concrete. Bea found a way to remove it. She thwarted every human effort. She used adaptive intelligence, her wiles, her teeth, her paws — whatever would achieve her goal of playing in the water. Bea may have thought if she and Chewy were going to be locked outside in the heat, then it would be her responsibility to keep herself and pal

Diane Arrington

Chewy cool. It is common knowledge that dogs take their responsibilities very, very seriously.

Once, on a mutual vacation day, Robert and Lacy had one rare opportunity to see Bea and Chewy in action. As they observed through the window, Bea used her jaws to turn on the faucet. She grabbed the hose in her teeth about a foot back from the end. She shook it once, then actually turned her head in order to aim the hose directly at Chewy. Bea hosed Chewy down.

Chewy snapped at the water and turned her body this way and that, allowing herself to be squirted and deriving full benefit from the fresh, cold water. Then the two played tug with the hose while both dogs got soaking wet. After a few minutes it was Bea's turn to get squirted. Chewy took the hose in her mouth and squirted it at Bea, the same way she had seen Bea do. Bea appeared equally pleased with being squirted. They took turns squirting each other for perhaps 20 minutes. When they'd worn themselves out and nap time came, they deliberately lay down in the path of the running water the way humans relax in a cool pool.

There was also something odd about Chewy. When Lacy would arrive home and verbally accuse Bea of malbehavior, whether for the hose or some other malfeasance, Chewy spun. She spun frantically, round and round, chasing her tail in a frenzied circle. Faster and faster she went. The madder Lacy got, the faster Chewy spun, until she was nothing but a blur of black and tan with tongue streaks. Chewy would spin until Lacy was laughing hysterically and no longer angry. Without fail, Chewy in her silliness spun on every occasion of Lacy's anger.

Regardless of what Robert and Lacy invented to prevent Beatrice from turning on the faucet, their efforts went unrewarded. When the hose was detached from the faucet, Bea turned on the water anyway. Like two kids in discovering an open hydrant in the street, they dipped their heads and splashed in the puddles. Whatever the situation, Bea always managed to adapt. She was determined to use the hose to suit her own needs.

Human endeavors progressed until all thoughts had been exhausted. The couple stopped short of having the city water department completely remove the spigot from the ground. Ultimately the water had to be turned off at the source, spoiling all Bea's fun.

Step inside Bea's mind. Consider the focus, the determination. She handled the situation with uncanny clearness of mind and purpose. She seemed stimulated by the challenge of outwitting the humans. Having been once reinforced, she knew what she wanted and she figured a way to get it, day after day after day. This was canine goal achievement at its finest.

Think of the canine, a wolf descendant, a hunter, driven by the need for food and survival. How does playing squirt games relate to her wolf ancestry? Was her motivation the water, or was it outsmarting her owners? Most amusing, how were Bea and Chewy able to aim the hose so expertly in order to achieve their purpose?

Consider also the way in which Chewy manipulated Lacy's emotions when the human was angry at her friend. Was her manipulation conscious? Was it an intentional, determined effort to distract her owner and keep Bea out of trouble? The Omega or bottom-ranked wolf in the pack has two functions. One of them is to dissipate tension among the pack. Could Chewy's spinning have been ancestrally driven? Whatever drove Chewy, her efforts succeeded, far better than human efforts succeeded with Bea.

Bea and Chewy's behavior may not be the last great mystery, but it certainly paints a picture of pure doggie fun.

Diane Arrington

Docktale 4
Three

And then there were Rudy, Gracie and Bob. Three cats. Three stooges. Three strikes. Three hearts. Together they participated in life as it came to them.

There was Bob, a male gray tabby eighteen months of age, the back-scratch addict. There was Rudy, a long-haired silver domestic, nine months of age, the dog milk bone eater. And there was Gracie, a smudgy, six-month-old Snowshoe mix of some silly sort, the feather-lover. A motley crew, it was.

The trio conducted life by virtue of some mysterious, silent telepathy known only to them. Perhaps it was the same species-inherent code that causes dolphins to swim in perfect unison or a flock of geese to turn at once across the sky in fall.

On some eery, unheard cue a unanimous decision was made. All three would glide together to the feed station and enjoy a meal in tandem, crunching the dry kibble in each other's ears. Then some unknown mental courier took them to the next concordance. On ghostly signal, all traveled to the powder room. There they minded their business, immodestly in the company of one another. A cloud of dust arose like halos as they performed a scratching ensemble.

Next agreement: they bathe together. They bathed themselves, they bathed each other. Gracie, not a pro yet, often found herself unwillingly pinned to carpet or couch as both her brothers groomed her at once, lovingly but efficiently.

After bathing, the three determined collectively to nap. They slept touching. Even while asleep some three-way extrasensory message awakened them simultaneously. *It is time for play*, agreed their mute conversation, and they would play three-way Hide and Seek.

Once play was over, the secret watchword was "observe," an essential element in the life of a healthy cat. On cue, the three walked single file with sister Gracie taking up the rear or, all

Diane Arrington

three abreast, Gracie in the middle. Side-by-side on spongy cat feet they strutted through the house, each knowing perfectly well the destination.

Once there, they hopped to the desk by the big window, one after the other. Bob first, Rudy second, Gracie third. They lined up and crouched, three parallel meatloaves in a row, looking like a shell game.

Together, in perfect harmony, the three cats observed life as it passed by the rear glass of the house they shared together. By all appearances, they would not have had it any other way.

Seventh Sense

Chapter 12
Bubba

It is inconceivable to the prosaic human mind that the canine mind may be capable of anticipating, even pre-conceiving, an abstract event. Bubba offers proof that a keen mind can be disguised behind a toothy dog smile.

Audrey, in her mid-twenties and single, had recently suffered the breakup of a relationship. She needed a new friend. She could accomplish two goals at once, she thought: give a homeless dog a home, and give herself someone to love and cherish. She set out for the animal shelter.

Audrey walked slowly past the rows and rows of cages. Her heart broke at each cage. It is overwhelming, the numbers of unwanted dogs sitting in cold concrete cages, homeless through no fault of their own. It may never be known for certain whether it is a dog's silent plea or a human heart aching that brings one of each together. Perhaps it is a bit of both. Audrey succumbed to the sad brown eyes, lowered black ears and soft, pleading whimpers of a leggy, mixed Labrador puppy. She brought him home and named him Bubba.

Little Bubba grew in spurts. At seven months of age he weighed nearly seventy pounds. Audrey raised Bubba the best she could, seeking advice of trainers, co-workers, friends, relatives, and many different books. Each gave different advice. Audrey would try one method for a few days and then change things on him. The effect of so much inconsistency on Bubba was devastating. By the time he was seven months old he was hopelessly confused.

As a result of his confusion, Bubba was wild and frenzied for most of his hours in a day. He seemed to think everything was funny, and he passed much of the time with his mouth

Seventh Sense

gaping widely. This made him thirsty. As a consequence of his infinite water intake and his perpetual state of bewilderment, Bubba was still having problems housebreaking.

Bubba was a very large dog living in a very small apartment. Not much could be done about his size or his level of enthusiasm. He bludgeoned anyone at the front door with club-like feet and full body weight. His juvenile body was all legs. Those spindly black sticks carried him nicely onto bed and furniture. This might not have been a problem were it not for his resemblance to a goat in a pickle barrel in the tiny apartment.

Bubba's brand new teeth were huge and gleaming white, which served him well for chewing just about anything he could wrap his jaws around. He seemed to have a fetish for lipstick. On more than one occasion, Audrey came home to red lipstick smeared down Bubba's white throat, chest and front paws. At Audrey's anger, Bubba simply grinned hugely and went for a drink.

When Bubba was a mere nine months of age, he spooked Audrey and incurred a new respect with his awesome, almost telepathic grasp of a situation.

The configuration of Audrey's particular apartment complex was standard. Two-story buildings were set in parallel rows facing one another. Auto drives ran between. Covered parking was perpendicular to the curbs, and residents parked facing the fronts of their buildings.

Audrey's apartment was located at street level. It had floor-to-ceiling windows in the living room and bedroom. These windows overlooked a 30-foot patch of grass that stretched from the windows to the curb. Walkways led from the parking up to windowless alcoves harboring the doors to four units, two downstairs and two upstairs. Apartment doors faced each other with the stairs in between.

It was a crispy fall morning just a few weeks before Audrey began caging Bubba full days because of his destructive chewing. Audrey said goodbye to Bubba, leaving useless instructions to be a good boy while she was at work. She left the

Diane Arrington

drapes open in both living room and bedroom. The apartment was in managed order — the dishes were washed, the bed was made, and her nightgown was folded neatly at the foot of Audrey's bed. She gathered her things, locked the door behind her and walked to her car. She could see clearly inside her own apartment. Bubba apparently did not know he could see out or didn't care, because he never watched Audrey leave.

Video research studies have shown that destructive dogs undertake their errant behavior an average of 45 minutes after or before owners leave or return. Bubba was no exception.

As she climbed into her car, Audrey looked into her own apartment. What happened next took place in a matter of seconds.

Through the bedroom window she could see Bubba already hunting up something to chew. She happened to see Bubba swipe her nylon sleeper off the bed. As she scrambled to jump out of the car, she saw him carrying the nightgown in his mouth. He disappeared from the bedroom, then reappeared in the living room. She could see him settle to the floor in the center of the living room, Sphinx position, with the gown between his paws. It was clear he was preparing to make spaghetti.

Audrey leaped from the car. She had left the television on for Bubba, so she knew it would be futile to call his name as she raced back to her apartment. She must stop him physically before he shredded her gown. She watched him with the gown through the window until she passed the corner of the alcove. Wonderfully focused on his new discovery which smelled like Audrey, Bubba did not see her returning. Audrey reached the door, jammed the key in the lock and burst inside.

Surprisingly, Bubba was still lying in the same position in the same spot in the very center of the living room carpet. The nightgown was nowhere in sight. Whether feigned or not, Bubba looked surprised when Audrey entered. The big dog was literally glowing with innocence. If she looked hard enough, she could barely make out the faint outline of a halo hovering above his big, goofy face and flying-nun ears.

Did he eat it? Wondering if Bubba could possibly have swallowed the entire garment so rapidly, she frantically searched the apartment. She found the pale blue chemise lying in a heap, not in the kitchen, not in the hallway, not in the bathroom. She found it in the bedroom. Unbelievably, the gown was not on the floor but *on the bed, precisely where she had left it.*

Audrey is certain Bubba did not see her coming up the sidewalk. If Bubba reacted the second he heard Audrey's key in the front door, how quickly he must have moved! Like a video on fast forward, he would have had to streak from the living room all the way down the hallway carrying the full-length nightie in his mouth without tripping over it, reach up and place it back on the bed where he had found it, race back to the living room and lie down and compose himself, all in the few seconds it took for Audrey to get the key in the lock and open the door.

The incident happened so fast, Audrey thought she must have been dreaming. Just one tiny thing made her certain she wasn't, just one canine limitation that caused Bubba to inadvertently divulge his guilt. Audrey had left the nightgown folded. Now it was not.

If Bubba did not see or hear Audrey, how did he know she was coming back? It is difficult to imagine that all his activity would be possible had he sprung to action only when he heard the key in the lock. It is presumed he intuited her return as she passed behind the wall of the entryway. Furthermore, how did Bubba know what he was *about* to do was wrong? Indeed, Bubba's behavior was much like the human child caught with a hand in the cookie jar. With truly linear thinking, it appears Bubba somehow knew there would be some consequence to his activities, so he got rid of the evidence. Most intriguing, how did Bubba know that to put the nightgown back where he found it would be the best insurance against a scolding? Finally, what made Bubba return to the exact same spot and assume the exact

Diane Arrington

same position after he had rid himself of the incriminating evidence?

With a pragmatic dog like Bubba, it's impossible to say what went on in his mind. That's why his mystery will live on in canine history. His actions revealed an inexplicable pre-comprehension of human action and reaction that leaves one wondering if dogs could be superior to mankind, knowing everything man knows and more.

Bubba. Out of a pandemonial mind comes brilliance.

Seventh Sense

Diane Arrington

Chapter 13
Honey

Honey provides stunning evidence that dogs can and do understand our spoken words, even outside the realm of conditioned responses to everyday experiences. Honey can't tell us how she understands, but she shows us that dogs have "stuff" too.

The ditch had been quiet, but there was no food there. Here there was food to eat and clean water to drink, but it was awfully noisy. The small, golden-vanilla puppy trembled in the corner of the cold steel cage. Her baby-brown eyes watched the people filing past.

Suddenly two of the people stopped at the front of her cage. They said something to the prison guard and then the gate was opened. The lady held out a piece of crunchy biscuit. The puppy could smell it, even four feet away. Slowly, step by step, the shy puppy moved away from the corner and accepted the cracker. As she ate, she heard soothing voices and felt gentle hands on her back. The hands touched her softly, stroking her, comforting her. It felt good and she wanted more, but first she finished her biscuit.

The puppy turned and put her feet on the lady's knee. She reached to sniff the lady's face and wound up giving out a kiss. The lady picked her up and hugged her. It may have been the first human hug the lost puppy had ever had.

The puppy had found a home.

Honey grew up to be small, blond and all dog. Named for her color, Honey may have been a cross of Golden Retriever and Shetland Sheepdog. The size of the Sheltie, she looked like a miniature Golden Retriever with fly-away ears. She was mild-mannered and sweet, with not as rich a sense of humor as one might expect from a dog with Golden Retriever genes. But Honey had a golden spirit.

Honey liked her new house and yard. She was permitted to do anything she liked in her yard, which made it hers alone. All through her puppyhood she dug and rolled and snoozed and played ball with owners Jo and Jon. Honey liked the house, too, except that she had to behave in the house.

Honey had a habit of burying any rawhide chews or bones her owners might chance to give her, anything she might want to savor. The biscuits she ate right away, but the chews, large or small, she buried.

First, Honey would carry the chew all around her yard until she found just the right spot, usually beneath a bush or near a tree. She would hold the chew in her mouth as she dug a hole just as big around as her chew and about four inches deep. With one quick, furtive look about to be sure no one was watching, she then dropped her chewie into the hole. She quickly covered it over by pushing at the soft earth repeatedly with her small black nose until the chew was fully concealed.

Honey's back yard was large enough to accommodate all the chews she could want to sink. The disturbing thing was, Honey never seemed to be able to remember where she buried what, and always begged more. Perhaps this was divisive on her part, but day or night, upon receipt of a new chew, she turned on her toes and dashed through her doggie door to inter her new treasure somewhere safe.

Burying is behavior often occurring in dogs with highly-competitive backgrounds. Burying is fairly common among dogs, and it is not uncommon for Honey to forget exactly where she buried things. These activities alone were not unusual. But when Honey was one year old, she did an amazing and eery thing.

In the fall of 1991 Jon and Jo were preparing to relocate to a new home a few miles away. Honey had been "helping" with the packing. Jo would just fill a box, turn away for a moment, and turn back only to find Honey had emptied the box of the top layer of items. In her dog mind she may have thought it was Christmas, a day she dearly loved.

The night before the actual move, the three were in the family room. The last of the boxes had been packed up and bedtime on the last night in this house was near.

"Honey, we're leaving in the morning. You'd better go dig up your things," Jon joked.

"That's right," Jo concurred. "We're out of here in the morning, Honey. We're never coming back. Better go pack your suitcase."

They laughed as Honey wiggled and wagged and panted, not cocking an ear. She seemed to think it was another game as they petted her and ruffled her fur. The words seemed to sail right over her smooth, coppery head, and, as expected, had no immediate effect on her behavior.

"What a silly dog you are," Jon chuckled as he stroked her affectionately.

"Not a very smart one, are you, sweetie?" Jo agreed, "but we love you." She gave Honey a big hug and they went to bed. Honey followed them in, and as the lights went out she settled on the foot of the bed where she always slept.

Morning dawned cool and sunny. A crisp, red-apple feel of fall was in the air. A perfect moving day. Not too hot, and not raining. Jon made coffee, Jo was dressing and packing up last-minute items. Honey yawned, stretched both ends, and hopped off the bed.

In the kitchen, Jon poured a cup of coffee, steadying himself for a long and strenuous day. He wandered to the back door to let in the fresh air. He stepped outside. He happened to look down, and was stunned at what he saw at his feet.

There, placed with care at the back door, were three old, moldy, half-eaten, dirt-covered chews.

In the full year the couple had owned her, Honey had never before dug up one of her chews. She did not seem to be a particularly smart dog. She was not human-like in her behavior.

How did Honey interpret and understand what had been said to her about moving? How would a dog even know what "leaving" means? Honey had only known one house and home and yard.

If she had understood, why did she not go and dig up her toys immediately, when the words were spoken? Why did she wait until the middle of the night? Perhaps she feared detection and was unwilling to reveal her hiding places. Could it be that, as the human mind is startled awake by something urgent temporarily forgotten, the realization of their words startled her from sleep, causing her to race out her dog door and take care of business? And why did she not bring her precious possessions inside through her dog door? Why did she instead leave them at the back door? Even more curious, there must have been dozens of chews buried in her yard. Why did she dig up only three?

Further, had Honey known all along where her chewies were buried and only pretended to forget? To a dog, this trick could possibly lead to the garnering of another chew. But does a dog know how to pretend, to feign innocence to achieve some higher goal?

The answers to these questions will never be revealed. But the first thing Honey did at her new house in her new yard was — yes — bury her three precious chewies.

Diane Arrington

Chapter 14
Joseph

Joseph shows stunningly humanesque deportment in many of the activities which engage him. His actions and intentions are not subject simply to whimsical human interpretation, but are clear and indisputable in the emotionality of the body language he displays. The ties he forms are not only strange for a dog, Joseph also develops a cross-species bond that runs counter to all historical canine tradition.

Named after a human saint, Joseph could have been human, but he would not qualify as a saint. He did not easily form ties. He was wary of newcomers. He was a gadfly with strange dogs, grumbled about his obedience and liked to bite his trainer. But he was in large part a good and happy dog, particularly when things went his way. Once Joey approved, though, the bonds he did form were deep, permanent and mysterious.

Joseph was also the mother-lode of canine idiosyncracy.

From the beginning owner Beth might have known Joey, an ewok-like Lhasa Apso, would be a different duck. He was not marked like the common pet-quality Lhasa. Joseph was a mixture of coppery brown, golden, black, white and gray — like Joseph's Coat, a second reason for his name.

The smarter the dog, the harder to raise successfully. As a puppy, Joey was serious about puppy-biting being the most popular puppy sport. He was feisty, hard-headed and smart. With the exception of Heel, Joey had learned all of his obedience commands by the time he was twelve weeks old.

Joseph didn't walk anywhere, nor did he run; he skipped. He loved a good back scratch. He spent interminable hours at this pursuit, most commonly when company came to visit. He would

Diane Arrington

heave himself to the floor and, writhing like a fish out of water, hairy paws punching the air, rabidly scratch his back on the carpet until someone took pity on him and knelt down to do it for him.

Some dogs notice television, some don't. Joey didn't notice it, he bonded with it. Joey was a TV maven. Like a human being, watching television was, above all others, Joseph's favorite pastime.

At Joey's house in Dallas, Texas, a built-in floor-to-ceiling bookshelf held a 28-inch television. Three feet in front of this, running parallel and facing out from the bookshelf, was a beige cloth couch with plush, thick seat-back cushions. It was a perfect nesting place for Joey to plant his behind for TV viewing. He liked animal shows and the Muppet Babies the best.

Dogs and cats who notice television are either attracted to the motion of the images on the screen or they are curious about the unusual sounds. Most appear to have no concept of context or story line, and quickly become bored and disinterested. Joey was an exception. Strangely, he seemed to have some cognizance of both action and story line.

Joey actually concentrated on the screen. His ears were up and forward as he listened closely. His bearded, little-old-man face was focused and intent. His generous black eyes watched and followed the images. He tipped his head. He snorted, wagged or changed position as a direct reaction to what he saw on the screen. Once Joey had decided he liked a program, only the doorbell could distract him away. Some nights he was so like a human Beth was tempted to fetch him a bag of popcorn and a beer.

On a blustery day in late autumn when Joey was a year old, he snuggled deep in his cushions as he watched PBS with Beth. Flowing across the screen was a colorful documentary investigating the Everglades, Florida. A wide assortment of mystifying new animals held Joey vividly enthralled. He was glued to the screen, and he reacted appropriately as the program progressed.

Raucous parrots made Joey visibly jiggle, just as if he were giggling. Swinging monkeys seemed to make him dizzy as he swayed on his cushion with their motions on the screen. Nesting egrets he watched passively.

The narrator's voice was pleasant — low-toned and hypnotic. Joey was getting sleepy as he moved with the camera through rivers and jungles. As the camera floated peacefully down a gently flowing creek, Joey looked as though he were going into trance. *Your eyes are getting heavy. You are getting very, very sleepy.*

Suddenly a crocodile exploded from silent black water. Huge, powerful, tooth-studded jaws snapped savagely at the camera. Joey was so startled his body lurched involuntarily. The shock launched him straight into the air like a missile with ears. He hovered momentarily three feet above the couch, then fell back with a thud, all askew on his cushion.

That wasn't funny enough. When he landed, Joey was incensed. He stood stiffly on all fours and barked angrily at the screen. Could he truly have been enraged at having been so rudely jerked from his state of bliss, like a human yanked from sleep by a nerve-jangling telephone? Or was Joey embarrassed that he had been so startled he jumped?

Joey's couch potato favorite was a home video of himself and Lila. Lila was Joseph's girlfriend.

Also a Lhasa Apso, Lila was younger than Joey. The two dogs' owners frequently visited socially. That Joey selected Lila as acceptable is an understatement. He had a big, fat, sweetheart crush on her.

When the two dogs were together, there was no doubt to any who witnessed Joey's behavior that he was absolutely love-struck. Heartily bitten by the love bug. Star-struck. Shot through the heart by cupid. With her, Joey lost every last shred of decorum and dignity. In Lila's presence, Joseph was transformed into a wimp, a pansy. He utterly adored Lila. He took her out to

Diane Arrington

potty, and he took her away from other dogs' rough play. He permitted her to lead him around by the nose and have her way with him.

It was not a matter of dog hormones. Both were altered. It was, however, a thing of beauty and comedy at once to see Joey acting like a teenager in love with the prettiest, perkiest, flirtiest, most lovely girl in school. When a man loves a woman he can't keep his mind on anything else. When a man loves a woman she can do no wrong.

Lila bit his ears and feet as hard as she could; Joseph loved it. She knocked him to the ground; he rolled on his back and stayed there, grinning up at her while she bit his windpipe. Lila would steal his favorite toys from him; he let her, something he absolutely would not permit with the other dogs at home. One could say Lila had Joseph wrapped around her paw—and he was captivated by their video.

Joseph's power of concentration was immense when he watched their video. Again and again, he watched every move she made, followed every game they played together on the screen. He even vocalized during his viewing, offering small guttural sounds from high in his throat. At certain parts, always the same parts, he wagged his sorrel tail. Occasionally he would stand on his cushion and lean forward to get a closer look, his push-button face ecstatic. When Joey was watching Lila, nothing could distract him, not even the doorbell.

For Joey's owners the video was a dog babysitter, keeping him entertained for long hours. Like a kid with his favorite Barney tape, he watched it over and over again. It was a good way for Joey to get in more time with Lila, since he could not seem to get his fill of her in real life. Joey was a starry-eyed dog over Lila the Lhasa.

When Lila was not visiting or cavorting for him on television, Joey played by himself in his yard. Well, almost by himself. In place of the traditional Get Out Of My Yard You

Scrawny Obnoxious Intruder canine demeanor, Joey instead seemed to enjoy the company of squirrels.

Joey played with squirrels as if they were dogs he loved. In turn, the squirrels seemed to participate voluntarily and respond to his puppy-like invitations to play. This was fully uncharacteristic of both species.

After his strange behavior unfolded, Beth realized in hindsight Joey had actually developed a bond with one squirrel in particular.

Each morning, eleven-pound Joey skipped out to his small yard and, after taking care of first things first, plopped down in the green grass to wait. Soon he snapped to attention as he heard the squirrels coming from neighboring treetops. Was it some mysterious collective consciousness that brought them to him?

Three or four squirrels participated in the fun, but only one squirrel had the chutzpa to venture as far as he did down the trunk of a large pecan tree. In the scurrying manner of all squirrels, he sneaked up on the dog gradually, hiding behind a leaf here, a twig there.

Joey waited excitedly, his whole body quivering, but he smartly stayed quiet and did not vocalize. He bowed and wagged his tail in anticipation, rump high, inviting the squirrel to play the way puppies invite play from one another.

Eventually the squirrel made himself visible and ventured down the trunk, almost within Joey's reach. Joey put his paws against the trunk and sniffed impetuously, stretching his neck toward the squirrel. His tail could not wag any faster. He continued to remain silent lest he frighten his friend away. The squirrel sneaked down the tree until the dog and the squirrel almost touched noses. Then the playful squirrel dashed away and up the tree while Joey lurched and vaulted and did his best to follow.

Round and round the tree the squirrel ran with Joey in hot pursuit until the dog was dizzy. During their games Joey remained quiet, but he barked victoriously when by chance he managed to catch the squirrel off guard and come within inches of tasting the squirrel's busy tail.

Joey and his squirrel played for hours at a time, most times the entire morning. Joey quietly sprang and ran and wagged his feathered tail, playing Hide-and-Seek with the squirrel until both were bushed. The daily morning ritual between Joey and the squirrel continued for several months.

One beautiful August morning when all dogs should be playing outside, Beth discovered Joey inside the house. This was unlike Joey. To see his normally bright, sunflower face so wilted was an unfamiliar sight. He lay dejectedly in the living room on his red plaid bed, chin between his paws, eyes open and downcast. He was not sleeping. Beth thought he was ill. Through the morning she kept an eye on him. If he did not perk up by that evening she planned to take him to the vet.

Later Beth went out to water plants in the yard. She discovered a squirrel dead on the ground at the base of the tree around which Joey's wild games took place. It was then that Beth realized Joey had been the first to discover the squirrel's lifeless body. Saddened, he had gone inside.

It is not certain precisely how the squirrel met its death. Beth is reasonably certain that Joey did not catch and kill him accidentally. The mystery lies in the fact that Joey literally mourned the death of that squirrel. For more than three days he lay miserably on his bed, not interested in food or activity of any sort.

To make certain he was not ill, Beth took Joey to the vet. He was in perfect health. Possible medical causes for his sudden turn in behavior were ruled out. Joey was, in fact, grieving the loss of the squirrel with whom he had made such good and fast friends.

Joey grieved for almost three weeks. He never again played the games so constantly and so regularly with any other squirrel in his yard.

Seventh Sense

All species form relationships. As time progresses, a growing number of these bonds are cross-species. In many households today, dogs are friends and playmates with cats, rabbits, ferrets, pigs and even birds. It is not unusual to enter a house where a dog and cat or puppy and kitten roll and tumble and wrestle like two puppies. There have even been stories of farm animals — ducks and horses, ponies and swine — showing clear evidence of bonding. These incidents of cross-species bonding defy long-held traditional human beliefs.

But dogs and squirrels? Rarely. Joey may be the first in history to have crossed that line in the sand.

Research indicates that domestic dogs share approximately eleven different emotions with humans. What made Joey, above other dogs, so expressly capable of displaying his emotions with the body language of a human?

Humans assume that emotions, if and when they are experienced by a dog, must be different in some way—not as poignant or not as painful, because they are "only" the canine equivalent. Could it be that the emotional wellspring of animals is identical to that of humans?

If Joey's behavior is any indication, the two are mirror images.

Diane Arrington

Chapter 15
Sid

Sid's behavior defies explanation. Today's cats are domesticated and consequently well-fed, having no practical cause to do what Sid does. Sid's gathering behavior was not unusual in itself, but mysterious in the what and where of it.

A cat's world is one of discovery. Sid's world took discovery a step further than normal. He did not display his mysterious behavior suddenly, but undertook his weird thing most of his life.

Sid's entry into the lives of Karen and Keith was as mysterious as he was. He simply appeared one day from nowhere. There he was on their doorstep, as if dropped from the sky. He was the size of a single black glove. They took him in, and raised him with their two other cats.

Sid's personality held to the more superstitious belief that cats are sneaky and cautious and secretive. In his general demeanor Sid was all of these. As a yellow-eyed solid black cat, it is presumed he felt compelled to be.

Visitors to the couple's apartment were greeted by two cordial, head-butting felines, Sid's roommates. Sid was nowhere to be seen. But after five minutes, an alert guest could feel two slanty eyes upon him. A careful look about revealed Sid disguised within the surroundings like ET in the closet, peeking at the newcomer, watching surreptitiously, curiously.

One Saturday morning when Sid was five months old, the apartment smelled of cleaning solutions as Karen cleaned house. The windows were open, inviting a fresh breeze to waft through from the creek that skirted the rear of the complex. Sid had just finished a heavy play session with his feathers on a string and was enjoying an intermission on the windowsill. He lounged full length against the screen, his shiny black coat dusting the sill.

Diane Arrington

Sensational buttery eyes blinked out from his black face like two caution lights in the night, watching out for camouflaged frogs in the green grass.

Housecleaning included washing the cats' food bowls. All cats were permitted free access to dry food which remained in their bowls at all times. The three ceramic bowls sat in a row on the kitchen floor, lined up neatly against one wall.

Karen picked up the dishes and spilled the brown, mousehead-shaped kibble onto a paper towel. What appeared on the towel surprised her. It was a paper clip. Since a bulletin board hung on the wall above the bowls, Karen passed off the find as happenstance. A paper clip could have easily dislodged from the collection of papers, notes and recipes above and fallen into one of the dishes.

A week passed. The following Saturday Karen's housecleaning ritual was the same. This time when she dumped the food bowls, there was a penny among the kibbles. This raised a question in her mind, but a penny could also have fallen into the dishes, she supposed.

The week following that, a bobby pin fell onto the paper towel. Karen thought it strange, but her life as an elementary school teacher did not permit much time for sweating the small stuff.

Finally, on the fourth consecutive Saturday there were two more odd items in the food. This time it was a headless nail and a thumbtack. Not a push pin, a real metal thumbtack, the kind today's kids have never laid eyes upon. Neither Karen nor Keith had used this style thumbtack in years. Karen wondered where on earth it could have come from. Keith had his office at home, but still he did not use thumbtacks.

Now Karen was concerned. An item so small could easily be swallowed by a cat. How were the items finding their way into the cat food? They could not have been contained in the bag from the store because the items appeared in only one food bowl.

Seventh Sense

Over the next few days Karen began to observe the bowls more closely. She discerned that each cat ate from the same dish each time, an oddity in itself among free-fed cats. Karen also noticed that Sid always ate from the bowl on the right. The following week when Karen emptied the bowls she discovered a tiny gold safety pin and a piece of scrap metal. The oddities came from Sid's dish.

The couple's detective work over ensuing weeks revealed that, without exception, Sid's bowl was the one to contain the strange items. Putting the pieces of the puzzle together, they arrived at the truth: to their utter astonishment, Sid was actually collecting items from around the house and stashing them at the bottom of his food bowl.

Over eighteen months following their enlightenment, Sid became more inventive as he went along. Increasingly bizarre things appeared in Sid's dish.

Sid liked money. Pennies and nickels were found frequently, occasionally a dime showed up. Never did a quarter appear. A quarter may have been too heavy for a cat to transport or was never left lying loose for cat-snatching. There were safety pins of all sizes. There were thumbtacks and nails, but never plastic push-pins. There were needles and there were straight pins. The items were, without fail, metal of one kind or another.

At first Keith and Karen were concerned Sid would swallow one of his metal goods, but he was apparently more interested in hiding the objects than eating them. No emergency incidents occurred, and over time the couple came to trust that Sid would not ingest his trinkets.

Humans think of tin foil as metal, but it seemed Sid did not, as none was ever found beneath his kibble. Apparently the objects were required to have a certain size, weight and feel in order to be considered suitable for stealing. And, of course, items had to be small enough to fit in his mouth and his food dish.

There was the back to one of Karen's earrings, but, though many cats are known to steal jewelry, never the earring itself or jewelry of any sort. No items of human value were ever found. Human trash, kitty treasures.

There was the broken tooth from a metal comb, pitted with age. There was the metal pull from a broken zipper, the broken clip from a pocket pen, and two unused staples stuck together. There was a tiny silver ring, perhaps from between the two halves of a ballpoint pen. There was a headless galvanized screw. There was a pop top from a soda can minus its tongue, and the rusty tongue from a small metal buckle, cat-collar size. And there was a curious and sizable collection of mangled bits of things unidentifiable. All metal, all buried in Sid's food dish.

It seemed to Karen and Keith that, with the exception of one play session a day, all Sid ever did was sleep. Did he spend his nights searching for his riches? Did he regularly patrol the nooks and crannies of the apartment, or did he come across the items at random? And why only metal and no other substance?

Why would Sid hide his finds underneath his food? To the human mind, a better place would seem to be under the couch or in his bed. Sid must have trusted his two companions to never eat from his dish. Did they have a silent agreement among them? This would have to be assured in Sid's feline mind before he decided on the best place to stash his stuff. Were the other cats aware of his activities?

Secreting and hoarding things is not unusual in today's domestic cat. Collecting metal and concealing it with food is.

Keith and Karen never witnessed Sid collecting or carrying any odd items. They had by deduction been able to discover who was doing it, but no one will ever know why. This is one piece of the mystery that will always remain a mystery.

Whatever their weird cat's motivation, Keith and Karen simply learned to live with it and tolerate Sid's exceptional behavior as standard — for Sid. They were, however, forced to shift their lifestyle slightly to accommodate Sid's fetish. Working at home, Keith learned to take care not to leave metal items around. Paper clips and spare change were kept in covered containers. Karen guarded her jewelry box and kept the earrings attached to their backs.

There was one thing Keith and Karen could rely on: whatever the contents of Sid's food dish, it was always half food, half metal scrap.

Sid the scrap collector.

Diane Arrington

Docktale 5
Zoe

It is a common mind game of today's domestic dogs, conning other dogs out of their prized objects. Most often, however, the scheme involves using the owner's attention as a ploy. Zoe's story is the rare occasion when a dog invents a completely new way to accomplish the goal.

A Blue Heeler blend, the mind of Zoe was startling. It is heartwarming to know she was once on death row at the SPCA in Dallas. It was a blessing to Zoe, to Helen, her family and all of those who ever had the pleasure of experiencing Zoe that Helen must have seen a spark in the dog's dark little eyes. She adopted Zoe and took her home.

Zoe, a small, mottled black-on-gray mix with shiny black ears, seemed to understand everyday conversation between and among humans. She responded appropriately to the most passive human request. She "helped" with everything around the house, including painting the walls. Zoe had many occasions of unusual and mysterious behavior. Her chicanery with her dog roommate on a day in March 1999 was just one of them.

It was a familiar scenario. Experienced dog owners have seen it on many occasions: one dog tricking the other dog out of his chewie or bone. But Zoe invented a new way to con Pookie Bear, a black Chow-Chow with a nice, roomy mind.

Zoe lay on the carpet watching Pookie Bear chew dreamily on a bone. Zoe had a chew bone of her own, but as a matter of course, she wanted his. As was customary, she barked in his face a few times, each bark carefully timed a couple of minutes apart, asking him not-so-politely to give it up. This didn't work. Pookie

Seventh Sense

Bear had absolutely no reason to give up his bone, particularly when asked rudely.

So Zoe lay quietly for a minute, scheming.

Then, all at once, Zoe leaped up, ran to the window, placed her spotted paws on the sill and looked out. She perked up her ears, tipped her head, increased her respiration and wagged her tail furiously.

Pookie Bear thought he fell down on his Alpha duties of notifying one and all of anything unusual occurring outside the front window. He sprang up and ran to look, absent-mindedly leaving his bone on the floor. Victoriously, Zoe turned and zeroed in with practiced accuracy on Pookie Bear's prized chew bone.

When Zoe had polished off the bone, Pookie Bear was still standing at the window, wondering what was out there. Nothing was.

In breaking down Zoe's thought process, it dawns on the human mind that Zoe actually *invented* behavior. She had to *pretend*, even to the point of increasing her respiration. She had to know what, of all the things she could choose to do, would be a strong enough incentive to trick sweet Pookie Bear out of his bone.

Zoe's behavior is just one more canine mystery humans are at a loss to explain.

Diane Arrington

Chapter 16
Scruffy

Although it happens with a certain frequency, it is nevertheless uncommon for dogs to do what Scruffy did. An Australian Shepherd and Border Collie mix, Scruffy's behavior offers strong evidence that, upon occasion, dogs choose families and not the other way around.

He came to the first driveway on the cul de sac. It didn't seem right. Neither did the second one. But the third one, the third one was the right one, he just knew it. He could feel it.

It was the year 1993 in August, the hottest month in Texas. He dropped his weary body down by the iron gate. His leg hurt. His ribs hurt. It was so hot. He made a dog wish for some fresh water to drink. Things would get better soon, he knew, because he had found the right place. Trying desperately to ignore the scores of fleas beneath his fur, he rested his chin in the brittle grass to wait, and dozed off.

He dreamed he was in a field. It was not a field of green, lush grass and rolling hills, but a field made of kibble. There were miles and rolling miles of luscious nuggets, as far as he could see. In the very center of the food field was a huge pond of icy clear water. He could see all the way to the bottom, and he could drink his fill of it.

In his dream he splashed joyfully into the water. It was freezing cold against his tummy and his pink tongue. He drank and swam to his heart's content, using his long tail as a rudder, soaking his thick black hair to the skin. Refreshed, he climbed out of the water, shook himself all over and began to gorge. He was just beginning to get full when he heard the sound of car tires on a gravel road. The sound was nearby. Then he realized the sound was not in his dream, it was real! There was a car, just the one he'd been waiting for.

Diane Arrington

The car drove halfway through the gate, and stopped abruptly. A woman emerged from the car. He was glad it was a woman because he was terrified of men. He struggled to his feet and put on his best, most submissive, most enticing behavior. He knew just how to look pathetic. He limped up to the woman, a limp that was suspiciously exaggerated. The woman took one look at him and walked away, up the driveway. Scruffy stayed where he was, near the car. He waited, wagging his tail hopefully.

Soon the lady returned with a bowl of fresh, cold water. She held it low and he followed the water into a field a few yards away. The lady stopped and put the silver bowl down on the ground. The dog staggered over to it. It was his first water in days, and he drank gratefully, filling his gut with the precious crystal liquid.

The woman moved slowly away. Her body language made him suspicious. He knew she was going to leave him. Water or not, he followed her back to the car. She turned and again lured him back to the field. He again went to the water, but would only drink if she stayed with him. She did not. He followed her back to the car.

The woman raised her arms and said *go on, go on*, tried to shoo him away. He was not fooled. It was clear to him that she did not really mean for him to leave, not like the others. He skittered off, but sidled up to her again, begging with all his might for comfort.

At last the woman threw up her hands. He had won! He had made her give in. She let him get into the car, and gave him a ride to the doctor.

Although the doctor was a man, for some strange reason the dog found he wasn't frightened of this man. He knew the doctor wanted to help. The man had to cut and crack the burrs away from the dog's fur. The nice doctor-man found the cracked ribs and injured leg where the bad man had kicked him. The doctor comforted him and petted him and fed him biscuit treats. Soon the man made him go to sleep for a while. When he woke up, he didn't know why, but he felt better. Calmer, sort of. He noticed something seemed lighter under his tail, but since he didn't know the significance of this he wasn't worried. All Scruffy knew was that he felt much, much better.

Barbara, the name he had heard the doctor call the lady, took Scruffy, the name he had heard the lady call him, with her away from the doctor. Scruffy was overjoyed. It was a lusty tail wagging the dog all the way home. Everything had gone just as he had planned it, except for one thing: Scruffy had not expected Mr. Chow.

Mr. Chow was big and strong and very bossy. At first he did not want Scruffy in his yard. He guarded his food and toys selfishly. He bit Scruffy and pinned him to the ground. But Scruffy displayed all the submissive behavior he could muster. He had to endure a few pretty hard bites from Mr. Chow until Mr. Chow finally got the message. It took Scruffy weeks to win the big dog's favor. But at last Scruffy made Mr. Chow realize he wasn't after his food and toys, he only wanted to live with him.

Soon Mr. Chow and Scruffy were cohorts in crime. They ran and tumbled and played wild and wonderful games. Together they terrorized the family cat, which of course was the most fun of all. Scruffy was happy in his new home. It was all he had hoped for.

But it was apparently not what Barbara and her husband Bernie had hoped for. A few months later, just before Christmas, Scruffy found himself inside a strange car with a strange woman, driving away from Mr. Chow and Barbara and Bernie and the cat. He and a woman named June were riding out into the country. Maybe it was just a vacation, Scruffy thought to himself.

June's house was small, but the land was big. There was a mare in the pasture, and Scruffy made friends with her. There were some dogs in the field next door and he ran up and down the fence with them. June was very nice, too. She petted him and threw the ball and the stick for him over and over again.

Diane Arrington

But after a few weeks Scruffy grew restless. This home was nice, but vacation was over. He had chosen his home, and this wasn't it.

One night when it was still cold outside Scruffy dug a hole under the fence. He squeezed through and roamed a bit, sniffing the air intently and looking for Mr. Chow; he was nowhere to be found. Scruffy went back to June's, back under the fence.

A few days later Scruffy went back to the same hole he had worked so hard to dig. It was blocked up with bricks! June must have done this. Scruffy didn't mind. He knew humans often did this sort of thing. He dug a fresh hole and escaped out again. He trotted the country roads, scenting and sensing direction. The time wasn't right. He went back. Several times over the next several weeks he tried and gave up.

Finally one night it did feel right. Scruffy said goodbye to the other dogs and his mare, left June's and struck out for home.

Being on the road reminded him of six months earlier. He couldn't understand why people acted so mad when they saw him. He wasn't doing anything he knew was wrong, just looking in their cans for something to eat and along their curbs for some water to drink. After all, he had been traveling for what seemed to him a very long time. Did they not understand he was tired and hungry and savagely thirsty?

Still, they waved their arms and kicked at him, even turned the hose on him. He found a copse of trees in a quiet field to sleep. No one bothered him there. The murmurs of nearby cattle triggered something in his ancestry. The sound was like a lullaby. He slept deeply.

The next morning Scruffy moved on. He had a close call with a speeding truck about five blocks long. Scurrying to avoid the deafening noise, he stepped on a broken beer bottle thoughtlessly and shamelessly tossed from a drunken cowboy's pickup truck. He stopped near an abandoned barn to lick the blood from his paw, then continued on. He had to keep going despite the pain. He had to get home. It was springtime and not too hot, so he could make pretty good time.

Scruffy somehow knew he had to go west before he could go southwest back to Barbara's. He crossed railroad tracks and highways, traveled roads and crossed fields. For one part of the trip he followed along beside the railroad tracks. He slept where he could when he could. He found pools of stagnant water to drink from, but after a freak rain shower the water was fresher. When it rained he slept under cars, porches, sheds, tractors. He ate what he could find, though it wasn't very much. He found some wild carrot tops in a field, and even, just by luck, caught and downed a field mouse.

As Scruffy neared home, he knew it. He had found this home before and knew the landmarks. Just down this busy street, over the railroad trestle and into the neighborhood. Just a little farther, now, and he would be home.

Three months and thirty miles away from June's, Scruffy again laid his weary body in the darkness by the familiar iron gate.

Sunday dawned brilliantly. Barbara came to the gate to get the newspaper. Scruffy heard her coming and struggled feebly from dead-tired sleep to greet her. He waggled his undocked tail and seemed to say, *See, I came back to you. Aren't you proud of me?* Barbara seemed shocked, which confused Scruffy. Isn't it a natural thing for a dog to return to one's lost pack? Mr. Chow, of course, was thrilled to see Scruffy back. The same could not be said of the cat.

The most mysterious aspect of Scruffy's returning home, when one considers the lay of the land, is how he knew which way to go. Just east of Dallas, Texas lie two nearly interlinking lakes — Lake Ray Hubbard to the south, and Lake Lavon to the north. These are long, north-south lakes with only a small strip of land running east-west between them.

June lives east of Lake Lavon. Barbara lives west of Ray Hubbard at a third lake, White Rock Lake. Scruffy had to know to cut west between the two lakes or be forced to swim across

Diane Arrington

huge Lake Ray Hubbard in order to get back home. Across the small strait of land is the only possible way Scruffy could have traveled. But how did Scruffy know that? Dogs don't read maps, and certainly dogs don't stop to ask directions.

Also curious, why did Scruffy not make the trip to Barbara's sooner? He did not lack opportunity. Why did he escape and then go back to June's so often before he set out on his trip?

Humans cannot answer these questions. Though there are many very good, very reasonable theories, research has not determined with any certainty precisely how animals return to homes of old and what instincts are utilized to do it.

In this dog's behavior there is only one thing we know for certain: Scruffy's name belies his sagacity. After a second set of hardships, and for the second time, Scruffy was home at last.

Seventh Sense

Chapter 17
Abbe

It was with eternally childish imagination that Abbe demonstrated her mysterious ability to solve a problem. She showed a resolve to have her own way that might be found in an impudent human child. Her reasoning ability exists in many dogs and, though it should not, takes humans by surprise.

Abbe wore the look of a dog in permanent distress. It was somewhere around the eyes. It was not *in* her eyes. Perhaps it was the blueness of her irises with the encircling black eyeliner. She resembled a charcoal cartoon, one of a dog who has just received the news that Spike, the neighbor's bullish Bulldog, discovered and dug up the deer flank she had concealed safely beneath the back bushes. A *what do I do now* look, it was. But it was only a facade. At any given moment, Abbe knew precisely what to do.

The random-bred dog as a group is willful and deft of thought. These dogs learn early in life how to use their bulk and density to their own advantage. To her breed relatives Abbe held true, though she was redeemed to a certain degree in her obedience training. She actually agreed to learn and perform Sit, Stay and Down. Heel and Come When Called, however, were a different matter. Her owners didn't know if she was stubborn or stupid. Actually it was neither. Abbe simply saw no reason in the here or the hereafter to perform either exercise, since sniffs were what she was here after.

Why heel when she could be far out in front grabbing the smells before anyone else does? After all, is a dog's world not one of discovering new odors? Why on earth would any self-respecting dog not want to take all the leash she can get? And, most absurd, why go over there when all the best smells are over here, right under her busy nose?

Abbe appeared to follow the same reasoning when it came to a dog's all-time favorite pastime — chewing. Abbe was selective on this issue. Chews and fake bones were okay with her, but slippers were so much better — smellier. However even slippers can sometimes disintegrate too quickly between one's teeth.

Books. Books were the best as far as Abbe was concerned. They last. You can really get your teeth into them. The pages are fun for tearing into tiny pieces and then spitting out on the rug, but the bindings are superior. To Abbe, the smelliest books were the ultimate. That would be cookbooks. Well, not *just* cookbooks. Antique, one-of-a-kind cookbooks from Italy and Germany and France. She could not see why a dog with any dignity, any discerning dog, would not prefer these over the hundreds of dry medical textbooks on her owner's floor-to-ceiling shelves.

But Abbe's truly clever behavior was still to come.

There was a big, ugly, orange vinyl chair in Abbe's house. Fifteen years short of being classified an antique, a remnant of the sixties when orange furniture was approvingly considered far out, it sat in a corner of Abbe's family room. It was Abbe's unique use of this chair that confounded everyone in her household.

The chair resembled a disc three feet in diameter. The back rest circled three-fourths of the chair's circumference. The seat cushion was cloth, soft, plushy and huge. Just Abbe's size and just right for napping. It was a swivel chair, but the agile dog had an easy time hopping into it without losing her balance. The problem was, Abbe was not allowed on the furniture. This rule included the orange chair.

Abbe went through life asking '*why not?*' As with Heel and Come, she saw no reason to stay on the floor, and no reason why she shouldn't sleep in the perfect chair. It fit her better than it fit anyone else. Dogs like to sleep with their backs against something. Her own bed was not as big and had no backrest.

Diane Arrington

Why not? The chair always faced into the room, inviting her, welcoming her, beckoning to her. In Abbe's mind it was the epitome of convenience.

Abbe was told numerous times as many ways to get down and stay down off the chair. She and her owners had argued back and forth about it. Abbe persisted. Owners persisted. It had become an issue in the household.

But not to Abbe. As events would unfold, she presumably got fed up with the nagging.

One day Abbe disappeared. Her owners searched everywhere. They called and whistled and clapped. No response. They shook the biscuit box which always brought her running. Not this time. They opened the fridge, another Abbe-magnet. No Abbe. They ran the can opener. Still nothing.

They went outside and checked the fence to see if Abbe had dug out underneath. She had not. They searched the streets of the neighborhood. No luck. They went back inside and shook their keys, as Abbe was always a sport for a car ride. They heard nothing but the sound of — snoring? Deep, heavy, ecstatic — yes — snoring.

They followed the sound into the living room. They noticed the orange chair oddly facing the wall. And in the orange chair, not oddly, was Abbe, enjoying to the fullest a deep, delicious nap.

Time after time of being told no had sunk in. At long last, Abbe had reached the understanding that getting caught was the wrong thing, her mistake. So Abbe simply turned the chair to face the corner so she would *not* get caught. In their search for her, the family had crisscrossed the family room time and again. The high back rest that encircled most of the chair had made her invisible from any distance and at any angle in the room.

How was Abbe able to deduce that she would not be seen if she turned the chair around? This was not a one-time incident, so it did not happen by chance each time. She repeatedly pulled this trick on her owners. After the first time, she must have wondered how they found her so quickly each time.

Also, how was Abbe able to place the chair so precisely facing the corner? Did she know that if it were placed even one foot off square she would be seen? Because she placed the chair so precisely so frequently, chance can again be ruled out.

Alone in the family room, sleep tugging at her brain, Abbe must have glanced furtively about, making certain she was unobserved. Did she then reach up and turn the chair with one paw? Both paws? Or did she first hop into the chair and use a clever canine foot against the wall to push off and turn herself around?

The most intriguing aspect of Abbe's mystery is how precisely the chair was angled to the corner. It is possible that as canines evolve and become increasingly more domesticated, they gain a more acute spatial understanding of man, his life, his mechanical objects.

In the end, months later, Abbe in her persistence wore her owners down. The big, "stupid" dog got her way after all. The ugly orange chair in the corner was surrendered to the dog.

Abbe's Chair.

Diane Arrington

Chapter 18
Q

The animals humans keep as pets unknowingly give them comfort. Whether it is their warmth, their soft touch, or, most likely, their unconditional love, it is why we keep them in our homes. Q offered solace in a way that was mysteriously aware. It was not unknowing, not inadvertent, but intentional and, deliberate — and so subtle as to test believability.

She was fuzzy and frisky as a kitten, a virtual vegetable as an adult. Named after a cotton swab, by the age of twelve years Q-Tip had taken one hundred five thousand, two hundred eighteen hours of sleep. As a result, she will probably live to be 87 or so.

She was immaculate snowy-white cotton candy. If you could catch her awake, you would see slanted, lime-green eyes, but mostly she was all white, long-haired — and asleep. On the rare occasion when she did move, the cat-fur bloomers she sported were visible beneath a luxurious, fuzzy-caterpillar tail. A feline leukemia survivor, she was hearty, healthy and probably too mean to die.

When younger, the elegant feline worked as a print model. Perhaps this was the genesis of her conceit. For many years she could be seen on calendars and in magazine ads, the picture-perfect house pet draped across a designer bedspread or cuddled among the pillows on a graceful formal sofa. Q had learned to come to a whistle, stay, sit and a few other skills. But over the years she lost these, or otherwise abandoned them as futile. Sleep, not work, became her obsession.

Q would permit one to pet her only if one's hands were clean. If the hands were not clean, she would stalk away, supremely insulted. With an indignant glance back in your direction she would flop herself down and bathe noisily and dramatically from ears to toes. If you caressed her in the wrong place or didn't stroke her fur just the right way, she would bite you. Mainly, she just wanted to be left alone. She knew what she wanted, and did not choose to discuss any options. Q did occasionally purr. She could purr with the best of them. If you talked softly to her she would curl her paws dreamily and purr like a motorboat. But Q did not meow; she yelled. When she wanted something, Q yelled at the top of her lungs.

Generally speaking, Q was not a particularly domesticated cat. She was indecisive at best, rude and unaffectionate at worst. Not the kind of cat one regarded as having lots on the ball. And yet, upon occasion, Q surprised everyone around her with an unexpected moment of redemption.

She was an indoor-outdoor cat. When outside, Q's timidity kept her from treading too far from the walls of the house — ten feet at most — which was the one and only reason owner Mary felt safe in permitting Q to go outside unsupervised. Q could be completely trusted not to run off or to interact with the strays. She could also be trusted to find a way to hurry back indoors if anyone or anything approached the property, or if she got cold or hungry or thirsty or had to use her litterbox. The curious thing was the technique Q invented, all on her own, to achieve her goal of reentry.

The house where Q and Mary lived was small. From inside the drafty, tiny old house, even with all the windows closed and regardless of her location inside the house, Mary could hear the smallest sounds from outside.

The house had fifteen large windows all around. There were two windows in the office, three in the studio, three in the bedroom, all located on different walls. In the evenings when alone, Mary might be working quietly in the studio at the back of the house or cooking in the kitchen, also at the back of the house. Then again, she could be sitting silently at her computer in the office on the east side of the house. There was a chance, on the other hand, that she might be in bed reading and not making a sound in the bedroom at the front of the house, or she might be watching TV in the living room, also at the front of the house. But then she could always be eating dinner at the table in the dining room on the west side of the house. Not a creature of habit, Mary could be anywhere in the house at any given moment.

Here's the amazing thing. From outside in the dark, Q, the non-domesticated cat, knew exactly where Mary was inside the house at any given moment. When she wanted in, she yelled. But Q did not sit by the door and yell, which would be the logical place for a cat to ask to come inside. The door would open and she would enter, right? Not Q. Q's method was to sit outside the *window* and yell. Eerily, Q would go directly to the window nearest which Mary sat inside. That was where Q would sit and do her yelling, demanding in her own delicate way to be let in.

In a house with fifteen windows, all closed, all curtained and shaded, all lighted equally with nothing but silence inside, the cat went directly to the window Mary was closest to. How did Q know exactly which window to yell at? She did not waste time calling at the wrong window or at the door. If she had, Mary could have heard her. Instead, Q went to the correct window at her first demand.

***

Q was raised with a big, hairy, mixed-breed dog. The dog was two when Q came as a kitten to live with her, and the dog and the cat lived ten years together. The pair must have bonded readily because the dog was the only one to whom Q showed affection.

There came a sad day when the dog passed away. The cat, who in ten years had done nothing but sleep, the cat who never showed affection or solicited attention or appeared to give love to humans in any way, was suddenly a lap-sitter.

She did not, as often happens with grieving cats, wander and search and cry. Never did she look for the dog. It was as though she knew where the dog had gone and honored it as a fact of nature. Certainly, death is more natural to animals than it is to humans, a fact of life to be accepted and dealt with. They move on. Never did Q appear to grieve for herself and her own loss of a buddy. Instead, Q appeared to read her owner's suffering.

What Q did was to sit near, next to or on her grieving Mary and purr. For weeks she could be handled in any manner and did not bite. For weeks she slept very little. She even solicited play, something she had not done since kittenhood. She willingly made physical contact with Mary, something she rarely did, even slept in bed with her at night.

Q continued her strange behavior for a duration of four weeks. Interestingly enough, four weeks was the precise amount of time that passed before Mary's grief began to subside. Then, in the space of a few days, the cat returned to her normal sleepy, standoffish ways.

Was it a conscious act for Q to comfort Mary? Indeed, Mary was consoled. At Q's antics, Mary laughed when she otherwise might have cried. She was distracted from weeping on many occasions by the cat's soothing purr and warmth on her lap. Could it have been Q's sole mission in life to ease Mary's pain whenever it might occur? It is a fact that cats are a medium for human emotions. It is not unusual for a cat to act differently after a death in the family. It is unusual for a cat who had never appeared to be bonded with Mary to suddenly become so. Q makes one wonder if pets are sent deliberately, perhaps assigned, to be comforters, healers, servers, providers, teachers for their human companions.

***

The most startling example of Q's gift for compassion came late on a foggy night in December, 1994. Q was twelve years of age.

That night Mary had a nasty visit from a nasty neighbor over a senseless neighbor dispute. A big, abusive man with a chip on his shoulder and bigotry in his heart stood cursing on her front porch. The "family man" threatened the single woman with harm, nearly putting his fist through her glass storm door.

This upset Mary, upset her in the way any violent confrontation sickens any decent human being. The feeling is physical and centered in the solar plexus, the kind of fear and dread that eats at one's gut like hot maggots.

If Mary should ever happen to show a negative emotion in the presence of her pets they became visibly distressed — except for Q. At any display of poor emotion the old cat remained still, calm and seemingly unflustered. At most she raised one sleepy eye as if to signal her annoyance at having been awakened. She did not run or hide or worry as did the others. The others were so obviously troubled by any negative emotion coming from Mary that she habitually concealed the tiniest personal distress from their awareness. This night she again covered it over and went on about her chores. But, mysteriously, the white cat knew the truth.

Thirty minutes later Mary got in bed, still roiling inside. As she did so Q slept, apparently unconcerned, on the second pillow. What the cat did next is the mystery.

The instant the light went out, Q did not hesitate. She promptly climbed off her pedestal, walked around Mary's head, and yelled to be let under the covers. This she sometimes did on cold winter nights to serve her own heat-seeking purpose, but this time was different.

The solar plexus is a system of nerves behind and beneath the human stomach. Some religious philosophies adhere to a belief that all energy flows into and out of the solar plexus and believe it to be the nexus of all energy flow in the body. Perhaps cats know this.

If she slept with Mary, Q always curled her back to Mary's middle in nesting-spoon position. This night as a first time and a last time, Q faced Mary. She lay on her side and, quite deliberately, pistoned all four paws against Mary's stomach, at the very center of the solar plexus — the precise area of the physical discomfort and Mary's suffering. The cat pressed her

Diane Arrington

paws against Mary and held them there and did not move. Mary could feel the warmth, the comforting flow of energy from the cat's paws. The cat stayed in this position, not moving, not sleeping but purring loudly, until Mary went to sleep, fully calmed.

Was the cat able to sense the negative emotion being experienced by the woman? How did she know at which spot to place her paws? She did not display her four-pawed behavior before the incident, nor has she in the six years hence. This fact makes mere coincidence unlikely. If the cat was not deliberately attempting to convert negative energy into positive, how, then, can one explain her actions? What in the feline composition would account for a cat so apparently insensitive to show such tender caring in times of deepest heartbreak?

These three episodes combined with several other similarly eerie events during the lifetime of this cat have given Mary a new respect for her kitty couch-potato. Who's to say even this cat was not the cat of ancient psychic myth, mysterious and telepathic?

As for Q, she's gone back to sleep.

Seventh Sense

Diane Arrington

Chapter 19
Max

The canine species and its legendary connection to mankind demonstrates a loyalty that some theorize dates back to prehistoric times. Max adds a strange new aspect to devotion and presents strong evidence that canines do share human emotions.

If dogs could speak English, Max would have. When he displayed his odd behavior he was fourteen pounds of hysteria.

Vicki, husband Mac, toddler Justin and infant daughter Jan resided in a mobile home parked in the country with a hundred or so others near Lewisville, Texas. Max was adopted before either child was born. It was not until Justin was walking and Jan was five months old that the feisty Shih-Tzu dog developed an eery, untrained eccentricity.

Max was lucky as a puppy. At age six weeks, the white and black dust mop had only to endure two or three days in a pet store before his new owners took him home in 1989. He had a normal puppyhood and was about eighteen months of age when he first showed his heartwarming display of compassion.

What is strange is that Max, though he had the most common male-dog name in the country, was not commonly a dog one would consider sweet and compassionate. He was happy and gay, but he had the reputed bullish, in-your-face temperament of the Shih-Tzu dog. He had, on one occasion, nipped toddler Justin. This was a reprimand nip over food and fortunately did not turn out to be a major aggression problem.

It is common among Max's breed for the dog to think of others in the family, particularly children, as either litter mates or underlings. In Max's mind the former appeared to be the case.

One gentle day in spring of 1991, in the days before infant audio monitors, Mac was at work and Vicki was alone at home with the children. The windows stood open to a fresh breeze, and the woods behind the trailer were bustling with springtime. The children were napping.

Vicki was at the rear of the long, narrow structure whittling away at the ever-present laundry. Suddenly she heard a strange wailing sound, the cry of an infant. A mother knows her own child's cry the way a leopard knows the spots of her own cub. This was not the cry of her child.

She laid down a pair of trousers and went to investigate. She went quietly, so as not to cause the odd noise to stop before she could determine its source. She tiptoed into the kitchen. The sound originated at the opposite end of the trailer, near the children's room. It was not a sound to alarm her, but a ghostly noise, a soft, high-pitched utterance. Vicki crept through the living area to the mouth of the hallway. She peered around the corner.

There, by Jan's door, was Max. He was positioned Sphinx-like, his tail to Vicki. His posture was focused, ears pointed at the closed door behind which the children slept. The source of the peculiar sound was Max's throat. He seemed to be whining, but it was not the cry of a dog or even a puppy. It was a human cry.

Now that she was closer, Vicki could hear Jan crying in her crib. Max continued until Vicki picked up the crying baby. When the baby stopped crying, Max stopped, too.

This was new behavior from Max. Vicki considered it somewhat odd, but, though pleased that Max had notified her of the baby's waking, dismissed it as just one more of Max's relentless attempts to get to the children's toys which he passionately coveted and wished were his.

The baby had awakened only from hunger. Max did not seem to be notifying Vicki of any particular stress or trauma. After the incident all appeared normal — until several days later.

Justin, in the way of a year-old youngster, found some reason to cry. As his wail rose into the air, Max began an equal lament. It was not a dog howling, not that chilling, awesome cry of the wild. It was a baby's wail, identical to the sound of the toddler. The hair on his head quivered as Max trembled and shook — and wept like a child.

Mac was finally able to convince Justin to stop. When he did, so did Max.

Initially Max was not triggered by each instance of crying from the children. It began gradually, every third or fourth time, then escalated to every second time. It was not long before Max was bawling every time either of the children did.

After each episode Max did not look for attention. He did what dogs do when relaxed; went for a drink, scratched, chewed a toy. The two young parents' nerves were frayed, trying to assuage two, now three.

The baby cried, Justin cried, the dog cried. All or any combination sat and cried together. With a worried look upon his hairy, pushed-in face, Max lay on the floor, shivering and crying. The chorus continued, its pitch elevating, until a parent could get it stopped. Max did not start everyone else. Rather, the dog's hysteria was triggered by an infant human voice. The sympathy reflex, perhaps.

During a crying incident Max behaved as though he didn't know what to do with himself. He agitated. He sat. He laid down. He sat again. He cried and moaned and carried on until the humans stopped crying. He mimicked human voices. He may have regretted that he could not imitate the sniffling.

When Justin cried, Max imitated precisely his pitch and tone. When Jan cried, Max adjusted the timbre to match hers exactly. Most interesting, Max refused to stop the strange, wailing noise until everyone else did.

Max's motivation is unknown. Mimic behavior makes up a large part of an animal's learning resources. But it does not seem that Max was simply mimicking the children. He appeared to be truly distressed. His unnatural sounds were accompanied by trembling. A dog rarely trembles falsely. The two facts together indicate Max was experiencing real anxiety in some form.

One might hold that Max was merely seeking attention, but this was not the case. While it was true Max saw the babies receive parental interaction for crying, Max did not look for attention when he cried. The behavior was executed with an attitude of reflex, as though it were an involuntary reaction to the sound of sibling distress.

To a dog's ear the sound of a human child's cry closely resembles the strains of a howling wolf. Some might suggest that Max's wolf instincts to answer the howl were triggered. But Max did not howl. He did not assume the muzzle-to-the-sky caricature, and he emitted a sound not like a wolf, but the precise sound of a baby crying.

Perhaps the most intriguing and peculiar thing of all about Max's strange behavior was his uncanny ability to imitate so precisely the sounds the children made. The canine throat is without the vocal dexterity of the human larynx. How was he able to reproduce the sounds with such accuracy, to hear, translate and reproduce a human vocal? It is beyond physiology.

Vicki knew only one thing. Once Max had developed his new, annoying habit, until the kids grew up or Max gave it up, she would have to mollify, at a minimum, one crying baby and one literally crying dog.

Diane Arrington

Chapter 20
Katie

Katie shows an uncanny ability to comprehend the spoken word without visual cues, to reason out spatial concepts, and proves through her behavior that dogs do, indeed, possess the animal kingdom's fabled "sixth sense."

Katie. Humanoid. Golden Retriever of the century. Born to a litter of six in 1988, she was the only female. But woe befalls he who lets this fact fool him into thinking that puppy Katie could not hold her own. She was, indeed, the Alpha dog of the plump, wiggly bunch.

So, too, could Katie hold her own against any form of obedience training whatsoever. She grew to an gargantuan 105 pounds. Partly due to her strong will, partially to her remarkable size, not one of many trainers could override her steely determination to be a couch potato. She was too smart for anyone. Owners Dennis and Barbara ultimately succumbed to her iron will and, within reason, permitted Katie to live life any way she chose in their home in Shrewsbury, New Jersey.

Fleshy and robust, Katie was white-gold. Her luxuriant feathers shimmered pearly white. By the time she was four months of age she had alarmed everyone; the vet, the groomer, the kennel — not to mention her owners — were confounded by Katie's keen ability to mentally navigate the two-legged world.

Katie had a special communion with her toys. She liked to take her toys along with her through life. She liked Chewman the best. He was her imaginary living playmate. Katie thought Chewman liked it outside the best. At least three times a week she treated Chewman to a ride outside for some fresh air and a little fun getting killed in her "jungle," the spacious, dark,

Diane Arrington

deliciously cool pocket beneath the low, spreading branches of a mammoth blue pine.

One stormy, snowy Saturday afternoon in November 1994 Barbara was in the kitchen preparing chicken casserole for dinner. Outside the window a blanket of wet snow covered the ground. Katie was enjoying the weekend with her family home from work for two days. She traded her precious time among Barbara, Dennis, and her toys.

Barbara cleaned, cut and chopped at the kitchen counter. Soon Katie sauntered into the kitchen toward the back door with Chewman pinched lovingly in her mouth. This ritual indicated her plan to take him out. She had never before been denied this simple pleasure, but the weather outside was frightful.

Without addressing Katie directly, without looking at Katie, without turning from what she was doing or using Katie's name, Barb spoke to the chicken: "You can't take Chewman out right now." An offhanded remark and nothing more. Barbara was not often surprised by Katie's unusual personality, but what Katie did next surprised even Barb.

Suddenly, without breaking stride or even changing pace, Katie executed the smoothest U-turn and walked calmly back to the living room, still holding Chewman in her mouth. Katie did not hesitate, for once did not argue, just heard the words and understood.

Dogs understand humans by means of their expert ability to read body language. They read us, our bodies, our faces. Or, they understand words frequently spoken in context and followed consistently by certain of our behaviors. Since Barb did not address her, how was Katie able to understand a full sentence that she had never heard before, particularly when it was not spoken to her? How could she not only know the statement was meant for her, but so accurately interpret its meaning? And why did she not argue the point as was her invariable habit? These questions have no answers in the limited human mind.

Seventh Sense

***

At Christmas 1992, Katie was four. That year Santa brought her a giant rawhide chew. This chew had to be a dog's dream. At least two and one-half feet long, it bore knots the size of softballs on either end, tied right into the rawhide. When she saw it, Katie's beefy brown eyes literally glittered. She looked as if she were about to cry. The two next things she did with the chew almost made her owners cry.

First, Katie wrapped her teeth around one of the knots and tried to pick up the toy. She could not. The chew weighed perhaps five pounds and was a burden even for Katie's powerful jaws.

Puzzled, the big Golden retriever loomed over the prize, staring it down as it lay passively on the hardwood floor. She thought for a moment, the canine equivalent of scratching her head. Standing stock still, she studied the chew visually for perhaps five seconds. Her brown eyes studied it up and down, from one end to the other. Suddenly, Katie seemed to arrive at some form of doggie decision. What she did next was a most ingenious thing.

Without further hesitation, she reached down and grasped the chew at its very center. She lifted it successfully, balancing the long stick perfectly. At least a foot of length stuck out from either side of her proud golden face. Then Katie laid the chew down, and again picked it up successfully. The dog was practicing, flexing, testing out her theory: *If you lift it by the middle you can carry it. It's easy. Just put 2 ½ pounds on either side of your head.* Who says dogs don't reason? Katie does.

Katie beamed over her new gift. Now that she knew how, she carried it around with her most of Christmas day, like a child with a brand new toy. When the humans left the den for the kitchen, Katie deftly and proudly picked up her new chew and eagerly followed.

Diane Arrington

But Katie hit a snag. What she did about it was even more amazing than learning balance.

As she tried to enter the kitchen, Katie was abruptly brought to a halt. She discovered with dismay the chew was longer than the doorway was wide. The knots hit the door jambs on both sides and prevented her from passing.

Katie looked confounded. Apparently thinking this could not be, she backed up a few steps and tried again. Again she was prevented from following the humans into the kitchen. Driven equally by an oral fixation and an obsessive need for human companionship, Katie stubbornly refused to release her grip on the chew stick.

The dog stood with the chew in her mouth, thinking hard and eyeing the doorway. Her ears looked perplexed. All at once, what was initially canine confusion turned like the darkness to the morning dawn of light. The gleam of challenge crept into Katie's eyes. Her next thought was beyond all human supposition.

Amazingly, on her third attempt to fit through the door, Katie actually tilted her head sideways! With the chew slanted upwards, she was able to pass freely through the doorway. With a look of smugness at what a clever dog she really was, Katie walked into the kitchen waving her thick tail victoriously. She was pleased with herself and her one small personal success.

How could Katie know that to tip the chew vertically would enable her to get through an opening too small? Most dogs would drop the chew and drag it through. Not Katie. It was trial and error, true, but how was Katie able to find the right solution, to resolve a spatial conflict, in so few trials? No one knows.

***

Katie's most impressive mystery of all occurred when she was only sixteen weeks of age. It was The Mouse Incident.

Katie's two-story home faced south and had two doors leading outside, the front door and the side door. The side door was located on the west end of the house. On the opposite, east end of the house, beyond the garage and the farthest point from the side door, lived a cat in the house next door.

Nikki, an expert mouser, was permitted outside on demand. The two met the day Katie came home. During the puppy's first two days in her new home Nikki trained Katie. He did not run from her but instead smacked her when she got too close. As a result, Katie never did chase Nikki. The cat kept the dog at bay like a boxer controls an opponent.

Due to the placement of the garage at the east end of Katie's house, no windows or doors existed on Nikki's end. Katie could not see or hear the cat from inside her own house, even if Nikki was outside. In fact, there were no windows anywhere in the house low enough for Katie to see outside.

It was a sunny day in early spring. The weather was warming and the snow melting. Dennis opened the side door to go out, not thinking of or watching for puppy Katie because she was nowhere in sight at the time.

But Katie, ever-aware of an open door, materialized from nowhere. The puppy bolted, suddenly and inexplicably, through the door. True she was wild, but this was in itself unseemly behavior for Katie. The bigger mystery was where she was going so fast.

Without so much as a glance right or left, Katie literally flew off the porch, her tail sailing straight out behind her. She hit the ground running. Startled, panicked, Dennis sprinted after her. Katie sped straight from her side door around the front of the house to Nikki who was sitting at his gate next door. In his mouth he clenched a live mouse. Making expert use of the element of surprise, Katie snatched the mouse directly from the cat's mouth and raced away.

Katie's radar took everyone by storm, particularly the cat who sat stunned and mouseless. He had not a moment to react or even get a better hold on the mouse. Katie ran away laughing,

Diane Arrington

chewing the poor mouse like gum as she went, puppy joy and the spring breeze ruffling her golden hair.

The cat had been at his own gate, beyond the east side of Katie's garage. How did Katie know the cat was there? She knew better than to chase Nikki. It was the mouse she wanted. But how did she know the cat had a mouse?

When you consider the distance Katie had to travel — down the steps, around the corner and along the front of the long house, past the garage and to the cat at his gate, a total distance of about one hundred feet — and consider that Katie had no humanly-conceivable way of knowing the cat was there or that he had a mouse, her behavior boggles the mind. It is uncanny. Barb wants to know if dogs can smell around corners.

For the dog of the century, it is the mystery of the century. It can only be a result of a sixth sense, an enigmatic canine psycho-phenomenon.

Incidentally, Katie routinely exhibited a similar sixth sense when she was downstairs, outside, and Dennis was upstairs, inside, trying to silently open the popcorn. If you want to see a dog with a purpose, witness Katie at this moment.

Seventh Sense

Diane Arrington

Chapter 21
Buddy

Buddy's physical appearance was not the only unusual thing about him. This young dog displays an odd behavior made even more strange by its one-time-only blush in and out of his life and the life of his owner.

Picture a golden bear cub. The eight-week-old Chow and Golden Retriever blend found himself at a flea market in Texas, and so did Connie Baldwin.

It was February of 1991. Connie was shopping a new oriental rug for her apartment, not a puppy. She strolled the aisles, hunting just the right rug. Happenstance took her down an aisle containing a small pen. The pen contained a litter of seven-week-old puppies. In an atmosphere of busy shoppers and noisy children, not a sound came from the pen. The puppies were fast asleep. Well, six were. Six football-sized blobs of black dreamed puppy dreams in a heavenly tumble of fleshy puppy warmth.

But the seventh puppy, the single golden one, sat apart from the rest. He was fully awake. His small black eyes watched quietly as the humans passed by. His tiny ebony nose twitched as he scented each one, right from where he sat on his plump little behind.

Connie paused to watch. *Cute*, she thought to herself. *Very cute.* But Connie lived in an apartment and could have no dog, no way. Her complex did allow pets. *But all that responsibility,* she thought, *all that housetraining. It would be too much. No way. Absolutely not. No.* She moved on.

But thirty minutes later Connie's undoubtedly coincidental wanderings again took her past the pen. Still the golden bear watched while his brothers and sisters slept unaware. He was nothing but two black eyes and a black nose set in a pleasing mass of shapeless amber. His ears, too short for his rounded head, could barely be seen. This time their eyes met, the girl and the dog. The little pup stared at Connie. She gazed back — and was taken in. She asked the lady attendant if she could hold him.

As the attendant lifted him over the pen to Connie, the puppy extended his chubby paws and seemed to reach for her as would a child. From a distance, through racks of cowboy hats, belts and used baby furniture, Connie had seen others at the market hold the puppy. He seemed to hang disinterestedly in their arms. But when he found himself in Connie's arms he contentedly cuddled against her, even clung to her. Then he reached his face to hers, and, with all the delicacy of a rutting moose, stuck out a miniature black tongue and gave her a kiss on the cheek. One whiff of that sweet puppy breath and Connie plunked down $25. She and the rug and the little yellow puppy were home in an hour.

Connie officially name her new puppy Buddy-Boy, but as the months passed he acquired the shortened version, Buddy. Over the following ten months Buddy undertook more than his share of the usual puppy biting, chewing, unruliness — and stealing. It was his stealing that led to his strange, deep-night behavior.

In his first year Buddy ate and grew and ate and grew some more. He ingeniously taught himself how to use his nose to open the trash compactor. During the night while Connie slept he habitually opened it out and helped himself to its contents.

This is characteristic, almost classic behavior for larger Dogkind. Dogs are opportunists. Even when dog food is abundant, if a large dog happens upon human food or anything that, however remotely, resembles food, or anything bearing human food residue, he eats it. Upon the spot it is consumed, quickly and efficiently. Which makes what Buddy did even more strange.

It was just before Thanksgiving, mid-November 1992, when Buddy was eleven months old. Something woke Connie in the night. In a sleepy stupor she made her way through the apartment

Diane Arrington

to the kitchen for some water. On the floor near the refrigerator lay an empty bread wrapper. She picked it up. It was not torn or chewed, but Connie had an immediate mental impression of what had happened.

While Connie slept, her big dog had been surfing the counters. To his dog delight he happened upon a fresh, full loaf of bread just sitting there, unguarded. There for the taking. He must have pulled it to the floor, opened it and ate it on the spot.

Connie stood holding the empty wrapper. She looked at Buddy in the darkened kitchen. He returned her gaze, wiggling his thick tail and grinning. Then he stuck out his tongue.

Connie does not hit animals, and it was really too late for a scolding. The deed was done. She went back to bed.

Three nights later Connie was sitting on the couch watching TV. Buddy lay nearby on the carpet doing his dog things. He cleaned his feet, idly chewed an old flea bite, attended to personal hygiene and then tried to lick Connie's feet.

Suddenly an idea entered his dog mind. He stood up. Without looking at Connie, he walked across the room straight to a pile of huge decorative pillows stacked on the floor. As Connie watched, Buddy used his muzzle to rummage around beneath the pillows, moving his square head this way and that. At the exact moment Connie began to wonder what he was up to, Buddy emerged with a slice of bread. He promptly wolfed it down. It struck Connie as odd, this stray piece of bread, but she remembered the empty wrapper, mentally dismissed the incident and returned her attention to the TV.

But then Buddy turned and walked purposefully to the couch. He rooted under the cushions right beside Connie. He shoved his nose deep into the white couch, nearly burying his own head. He surfaced with another piece of bread. He ate that one, too.

Now Connie's curiosity was aroused. She got up to investigate. While Buddy watched, guiltlessly wagging his tail at the prospect of some new activity, Connie lifted the pillows from the floor. Beneath them was a second slice of bread, a bit mangled, but as yet uneaten or even nibbled. She investigated further. She found three slices of bread tucked inside the fireplace. Two had been stuffed into her brass-potted plants with some dirt scraped over them. One slice of bread was tucked into the stairs, and another was hidden beneath the stairs. She found two pieces of bread cleverly buried beneath a pile of dry cleaning on the bedroom floor.

And the couch. She pulled off the cushions and found a gold mine. Eleven pieces of bread were crammed between the seat cushions, back cushions and down the sides.

All tolled, Connie found nearly a full loaf of bread. This could mean only one thing: Buddy had eaten little if any of his pilfered loaf of bread. Instead, he had hidden each single slice in a different location around the apartment.

What possessed this dog? He is a *dog*. He is supposed to *eat* what he finds. It was not uncommon for Buddy to shop the counters and comb the premises for anything edible while Connie slept. But whatever he found he ate. Why, on this single occasion, would Buddy override his natural instinct and stash instead of eat? Could a dog know that eating that much bread at a single sitting could make him sick?

It could be hypothesized that Buddy was already full when he found the bread. But according to Connie, Buddy was a dog who was never, ever full. If given the opportunity, he would eat until he exploded.

Buddy may have spent an entire sleepless night finding just the right spots to secret his prizes away. He must have worked by scent only, since dogs do not see clearly in the dark.

Bread in a wrapper is a tight fit. How did Buddy remove every last crumb from the wrapper without inflicting even the tiniest toothmark upon the plastic? How long did Buddy intend to leave the bread hidden? And what mental mechanism caused him to decide just when to go for a snack? Is the thought process the same as in humans? If left to their own devices, would dogs snack while watching videos?

Diane Arrington

Most intriguing of all is not that Buddy hid the bread, but that he concealed each piece in a different spot. Buddy considered each slice a separate treasure. To Buddy, each one was a prized morsel — a serving.

Connie did not reward Buddy for his heroics; much to his dismay, she threw away the stashed bread she did find. Anguish must have been his as he watched her slip it down the disposal. *After all that work, all that brilliant and clever ingenuity...*

Only one thing is certain. Humans think of a loaf of bread as one item. Dogs don't.

Seventh Sense

Diane Arrington

Chapter 22
Amos

Amos shows a pure and gentle respect for life itself. His uncanny instincts and resulting behavior defy human scientific logic. His actions offer proof that the canine mind is, indeed, a rare and loving thing.

It was a glorious early morning in April 1991 before the spring time change. George Coleman awoke not with the alarm clock, not with the dawn, but from the odd fact that his Golden Retriever Amos did not deposit gritty saliva on his face at 6 a.m. as usual. George glanced at the clock. It was 6:40 a.m. Concerned, he kissed his wife Celeste on the forehead and climbed from bed. He headed down the hall to start the coffee and find out what Amos, ever the clown, was up to this time.

Amos was a dog torn between two loves. He loved his family and wanted to be inside the house with them, playing ball and scratching his back on the carpet. One of his favorite things was when George and Celeste tried to give him a training session. Amos was plenty smart and could learn easily; he simply chose not to. Instead, he eagerly rose to the challenge of distracting humans with his silly antics. He made them laugh until they gave it up. He thought Sit-Stay was the most fun. It thrilled him to go limp while they both tried in vain to pick his 85 pounds up off the floor and put him back into his Sit. Mouth agape in something suspiciously resembling a grin, big tongue hanging, Amos put on an air of total befuddlement. *Sit-Stay? Why, whatever do you mean?*

But Amos also loved Cat. Cat was a feral female Tortoiseshell who had taken up residence a few weeks earlier beneath the back porch. Amos and Cat played Chase, Hide-and-Seek and took naps together in the warm spring sunshine. Cat seemed to like Amos, too, and seemed perfectly happy living outside. The family provided her with a heated mat under the porch when the nights were cold, and made sure she had a constant supply of fresh water and food.

Indoors, Amos was notorious for gobbling cat food at every opportunity without conscience. Curiously, though he adored the rich cat kibble which was kept in plain reach for Cat on the porch outside, Amos did not eat Cat's cat food. He seemed to understand and respect the fact that it was hers. Could he possibly have known she needed nourishment very much right then?

Amos assigned himself the task of dividing his attention equally between his family and Cat. This made him a very busy dog. He was constantly running back and forth from the house to the yard through his dog door. He wished Cat could live inside so that all his loves could be in one place and he could have a nap. But evidently Amos also enjoyed staying busy, as he would soon prove.

George and Celeste did not mind Cat living under the porch, in fact they enjoyed making things nice for her. There was only one problem: before they could arrange to have her spayed, she dropped a litter of kittens. This explained why she had quite suddenly come to live with them — she needed a safe place to have her family. The place she chose was under the Coleman's back porch.

Amos, of course, was thrilled. The prospect of seven new playmates captivated him. He couldn't wait until they got big enough to chase. He spent hours lying with his head in the dark under the porch and his rear in the sun in the yard. His tail was perpetual motion as he watched Cat nurse and bathe and clean up after the tiny naked things. He wished she had more time to play like before, but he didn't mind. He seemed to understand she was a bit preoccupied. Likewise, Cat did not seem to mind the dog breathing all over her kittens.

The sun peeked through the trees to the east as George came down the hallway. Still Sleepy, George entered the kitchen and

Diane Arrington

stopped short. He rubbed his eyes. He could not believe what he was looking at.

In one corner of the kitchen, on the cool tile floor, lay Amos. This in itself was not unusual. What was unusual was that Amos was surrounded by seven squirming four-week old kittens!

The huge golden dog was anxiously losing his battle to keep seven four-legged satellites no bigger than his snout gathered into a cluster. He licked their tiny bodies. He nudged them and tumbled them to their backs in play. He nuzzled them gently to his belly, the way he had seen Cat do. He could not seem to figure out why they did not all stay against him the way they did with her.

When George walked in, Amos looked up at him with pride in his eyes. He pounded his tail against the cabinet, but did not rise to greet his owner. He seemed to say, *Forgive me for not getting up. Got a job to do here. You understand.* George thought Amos had the look of a dog in seventh heaven. He had never seen his dog happier.

George was so stunned, he could only mutter three words: "*Well I'll be.*" He rubbed his hands over his face. "*Well I'll be*," he repeated, unable to think of anything else to say. Where was Cat? What was Amos doing with her kits? And how did they get into the kitchen?

George went immediately outside to search for Cat. He and Celeste searched for her the entire day, but she had mysteriously disappeared. To this day they still have no idea what became of her.

Amos knew, but he wasn't telling. He also somehow knew the kittens could not stay outside by themselves and survive. So, during the night, he held true to his retriever breed. He crawled under the porch and, with his soft mouth, gently lifted a kitten and retrieved it into the house through his dog door. He placed it tenderly on the floor in the corner, then dashed out to get another one. He brought it in, carefully placed it next to the other one and raced back outside for the third. Seven trips Amos made.

Seventh Sense

Once he had them all inside, they couldn't get away. They were his.

How did Amos know Cat would not be returning? The kittens had been under the porch four weeks. Three of those weeks he watched Cat nurse her babies. During the fourth week he must have watched her leave many times during the night or day, to hunt and capture birds or lizards for her brood. He had never attempted to steal her kittens in her absence. It was not until he knew Cat would not return that Amos adopted her kittens.

Amos was a neutered male dog who adopted a litter of a different species and attempted to mother them. Male wolves in the wild participate in the raising of cubs, but to a limited extent. They teach hunting skills to the youngsters in the form of play, and only occasionaly share nursery detail. What resource did Amos have to learn mothering skills except by watching Cat? Are these skills preprogrammed, even in males?

Why did Amos not harm the kittens? They were, after all, things small enough to eat in one gulp. In many regions inhabited by wolves, mice and small mammals are a significant food source. By all wolf logic, his ancestry should have instructed him to devour the kittens, but he did not.

Amos is a hero. He saved the kittens from certain death. How? Amos was the only one in the family who could fit under the porch to capture the kittens. He somehow knew he should. He did, and Amos the Golden Retriever kept the tiny kittens warm and alive until help was at hand.

Diane Arrington

Docktale 6
Louie

Louie, a silver long-haired kitten eight months of age, lived in a house with two litter receptacles positioned one on either side of the commode in the bathroom.

One day Louie stepped into the first box. He dug his hole and poised above. But something about the trench wasn't right. Louie broke position and tried again, scratching earnestly about in the pan. Still it didn't suit him. Even an ardent third try did not measure up.

Frustrated, Louie leaped from the box. He dodged behind the commode to the second box and hurriedly hopped in. In this pan Louie's small sterling face looked pleased and relieved. He had gotten it right on the very first try.

But what Louie did next was a wonder.

Without covering, Louie dashed back into the first box to energetically cover what he had actually installed in the second box.

There's no sin in a bit of kitten confusion.

Seventh Sense

Diane Arrington

Chapter 23
Star

Every so often there is born into this world a dog with extraordinary capacities for deciphering mechanical human contraptions. How do they do it? Three examples are Star, Gus and aptly-named Houdini.

Star was beautiful and smart and a gigantic dog at that. This two-year-old Neapolitan Mastiff may have had a brain the size of a cantaloupe. Whatever her brain size, she made good use of it, mostly to take advantage of everyone around her.

She was not wooly, but she was wild. Star learned early how to use her thick self to get her way. She was as dominant as they come, which of course indicates her superior intelligence. Star decided what she wanted and she got it — whether by canine wiles or brute force.

The family of Star drove a utility vehicle. They bought it for Star. The only other vehicle she would fit into was a schoolbus. Since buying a bus was not practical, they purchased a utility vehicle with a large cargo area to hold the dog.

Star was vehicle-compulsive. She found a ride on four wheels irresistible. Any vehicle would do. Show her an open car door and discover the meaning of the shortest distance between two points.

Star's love for riding may originate in the same emotional wellspring as does the human love for carnival rides. To the wolf-descended dog, it might seem strange to find the ground moving beneath your four paws, turning and bouncing and stopping, then starting up again. From a dog's point of view, the only other way to see so much scenery in a short amount of time would be to run full speed for a full day. And of course wind forced up your nose may perhaps be the strongest thrill of all.

Seventh Sense

Star's owner Ann wanted Star to ride behind the back seat in the cargo section. This was, after all, why she purchased a $35,000 vehicle. Just larger than her dog kennel, the area was the perfect size for Star. It kept her safe, and kept the seats where the family sits clean and free of hair and doggie toenail gashes. Making Star ride in back also kept to a minimum Star's jowl emissions which the wind stretched into strings against the sides of the van.

But making a dog like Star ride in back was not as easy as it sounds. Star much preferred, indeed insisted, on riding in front with her head and chest and front legs and paws hanging out the passenger window, ears flapping in the breeze like the WWI Flying Ace.

In the world today it would have been a simple matter to install a safety screen between the back and front seats. This would not only have kept Star in back, but would also protect Ann from 2500 pounds of flying dog in case of a sudden stop. At the time, however, the screens were hard to find, and this option was not available to Ann.

Each and every time Star went in the car, without fail, a battle of wills took place over where Star would ride. Ann insisted Star ride in back. Star insisted Star ride in front. Worse, when Star did win the battle and ride in front, Ann was forced to ride with the passenger window open. If she did not open it immediately upon motion, Star morphed into a lap dog, stretching a sandbag-sized thorax across Ann to achieve the wind at the driver's open window. If the window was closed, as in cold weather, then peering out over the steering wheel was a suitable enough thrill for Star.

One thing which worked in Ann's favor was Star's impossibly huge size. With the rear seat up, Star could not fit between the roof and the seat backrest to get into the front. But here is where Star's wiles worked in her favor, and her mysterious dexterity first appeared.

Diane Arrington

One day while transporting a large load, Ann had occasion to fold flat the rear seat. The huge dog, standing in the extreme rear of the vehicle and grumbling about it, looked on.

The next day Ann put Star in cargo as usual, folded the back seat up to keep her there, and took off for the market. Moments later Star was next to her in the passenger seat, looking smug. She pawed at the window. Ann looked in back. The seat was folded down flat. Thinking she might have dreamed she had put up the seat, Ann stopped the car. She fought the reluctant dog into cargo and put up the rear seat.

Moments later Star was next to Ann in the passenger seat, looking priggish. The rear seat was down. Ann thought the locking mechanism of the seat must be broken. Again she pulled to the curb and stopped the car. Again she put up the rear seat. It locked into position. It was not broken.

For the second time the small woman risked a hernia muscling the powerful and uncooperative dog into the back. This time she watched in the rear-view mirror as she put the car in gear and pulled away.

While the car was motionless, so was Star. Motionless and innocent. But as the car pulled away from the curb, Star went into action. With an oar-sized paw she pressed the release button the way she had seen Ann do the day before. Then she pushed the seat forward with her chest. She stepped smoothly to the front, walked between the bucket seats and into "her" chair, looking conceited. She pawed impatiently for an open passenger window as if all this back and forth were perfectly unnecessary. She knew where she wanted to ride and had made it completely clear. *Why in the world not?* she seemed to ask.

Star needed only one careless demonstration to know how to get her way. From that day forward the war was on. Regardless of what Ann dreamed up to keep Star in back, she was unsuccessful.

Star had observed and learned. The vast amount of information a dog can assimilate by means of simple observation is awesome. Still, how was she able to manipulate a clumsy dog paw so adeptly?

But there is an even bigger question. Since the strong-willed dog had been unwilling to learn anything else in her two years, any of the civilized things like Sit, Stay or Come, what made anyone think she would be taught something as abstract as Stay In Back?

Diane Arrington

Chapter 24
Houdini

Houdini offers proof that dogs not only make decisions, but can follow an intellectual course of action initiated by observation and learned by imitation.

Houdini was a dog one might regard as untamed. He and his human counterpart, eight-year-old Edward, were impetuous and uninhibited. Their personalities were identical. As dogs go, Houdini did not hold to the traditional concept of the Standard Poodle as sophisticated and elegant. It is true he was beautiful, but because he seemed so goofy, his intelligence came as a surprise.

Even as a very young pup Houdini was difficult to contain. The fluffy black Standard Poodle puppy the size of a basketball seemed able to get past the most elaborate of puppy enclosures. He perceived any cardboard box, baby gate or wood paneling devised to keep him confined a mere obstacle course, just one more entertaining challenge for him to delightedly meet and overcome. Perhaps these early challenges nurtured his future skills. As Houdini grew, he grew increasingly more talented. Much to his family's dismay, he began with baby gates and worked his way up.

Houdini's cavernous home was equipped throughout with horizontal door knobs conducive to canine control. Commonly installed in new and remodeled homes today, they were brass and shaped like a slender S on its side, parallel to the floor. Operation took only a simple push downward with one hand — or paw. It was relatively simple for any dog who has a mouth, is tall enough to reach, and smart enough to figure it out.

One late winter morning in January of 1994 the family's nanny Madeline was having tea in the kitchen. As she scanned the daily, a stealthy draft crept round her ankles, then her knees.

Diane Arrington

Her quick investigation found the terrace door wide and the cold streaming in. Outside was Houdini, poking idly about the garden. Madeline assumed the one to leave the door open had been Edward. It had not been Edward. Houdini had just graduated from baby gates to doors.

Many dogs today know how to manipulate these door handles. The mystery is precisely how dogs, in this case Houdini, learn to manipulate the handles at the very first incident. Dog often learn things quite by accident. They may be pawing at a door when suddenly it opens. From this they learn, and one occasion is all it takes.

No such accident happened with Houdini. From what could be determined Houdini, on only one occasion, happened to be watching Edward as he opened the door. Houdini learned by *watching*. One simple observation and he had it.

It was amusing to see the long, lanky dog with puffs on head and tail, a dog curly-black and shiny one would expect to find in the atmosphere of the Westminster Dog Show, in action as he undertook to demonstrate his unique skill.

While at play in the den, Houdini would interrupt his own play and trot purposefully to the garden door. No human was near; the dog was alone. With his magnificent head and long, close-shaved black muzzle he reached up, grasped the gold door handle in his teeth and turned it down. He backed up as he pulled the door open, and hurried out to potty. Once business was complete, he rushed back inside, anxious to resume his play, eager anticipation on his young Poodle face.

Once he had acquired his new skill, Houdini used it to let himself out for purpose of elimination. This made life nicely convenient for his busy owners. But there was a down side. The door did not close behind him. As winter turned away, the house filled up with flies and mosquitos, bees and wasps as Houdini practiced. And it got worse.

In the beginning, if someone closed the door in his absence, Houdini asked to be let back in. As he stood by, observation taught Houdini that the door handle worked the same from the outside as it did from the inside. It wasn't long before he was letting himself in the door, too, whenever it pleased him.

There are occasions in any dog-owning household when the dog must be put outside. Houdini, too, was occasionally sent to the garden, only to let himself back in directly. It became necessary to lock the door behind the big dog, so enamored was he of his new-found freedom. A door to Houdini had becomes nothing more than a paltry hindrance.

Houdini knew no impediment. His amazing skills just kept coming.

For his next trick Houdini deciphered round doorknobs. Glass knobs were the easiest, with their octagonal shapes. These knobs existed on virtually every interior door in the house. Family members found themselves in all states of embarrassment — changing clothes or in the bathroom — when unexpectedly the door opened and in walked the dog. He would admit himself whenever the mood moved him or his Poodle brain struck upon a particularly worthy reason, like to get petting from someone sitting in the bathroom.

One day from across the yard Houdini waved goodbye to Madeline as she left through the side gate. To open the gate, the human finger pulls a trigger-like mechanism that lifts the cross bar from its locking slot. One observation of Madeline's operation of the latch was all the big, smart dog needed.

The wrought iron latch in the wood privacy fence would be a stumper for a wolf. Not for Houdini, Circus Dog. It was necessary for Houdini to bite the latch and hold on, then step back and draw the heavy gate open far enough to slip through before it automatically fell shut. Somehow, with tooth and jaw, he reasoned it out and cavorted the neighborhood at will. To Houdini's delight, the neighbors would dutifully walk him home, time and time again.

If the neighbors didn't bring him home, the gate had no exterior mechanism for Houdini's reentry into the yard. This fact may have slowed him down, but it didn't stop the amazing

Diane Arrington

Houdini. When he'd had his fill of roaming and wanted back in, it took him only a few occasions to devise an ingenious plan for meeting his goal. He decided upon throwing himself physically against the gate. Again and again he threw his shoulder into it until the latch popped or the family heard the ruckus and let him in, whichever came first. Houdini seemed annoyed that he could not reenter at will. With an indignant glance in the butler's direction he would canter by, then meet his water bowl face-on.

By the time Houdini was six months old, he was freely letting himself in and out of all exterior doors, all interior doors and both garden gates.

How was Houdini able to figure out so many different means of exit and entry? How could a canine, limited by the absence of hands and fingers, manipulate so many mechanical objects? How was he able to conceive the idea of doing things for himself when it came to barriers? Who says canines are dependant on humans? Not Houdini.

Houdini's door-opening talent was an hysterical thing to witness. It was clear he knew precisely what to do. As startling as the child whose very first words are spoken in a complete, grammatically correct sentence beginning with a capital and ending with a period, Houdini didn't waste time biting or chewing at a knob or a latch to work it loose. He didn't mess around getting it just right. There was no need. With the deportment of a human being he walked up, reached up, and did it. It is uncanny, and it is a mystery.

Houdini. A puppy aptly named.

Seventh Sense

Chapter 25
Gus

Gus may take the cake for great and mysterious escapes. By the time he was eleven months old, he had everything figured out.

This close-haired moose of a mixed breed was all legs and brain cells. Mostly black, some brown, some white, he may have been a cross between a Labrador and a Great Dane. His owner Tiffany happily shared a small one-bedroom apartment with the big dog. To this day she marvels at how quickly Gus learned to open every vertical door in the apartment, including the folding louvered doors on the closets. All the doors had smooth round knobs, yet Gus was able to decipher how to get his teeth around them and pull or turn to accomplish his primary goal: never permit a closed door of any kind to remain closed. The only two doors Gus was unable to open were the bathroom door, which locked from the inside, and the front door, which locked from both inside and outside.

But turning door knobs with his teeth and opening folding doors was all just elementary to this clever canine, as Tiffany would soon learn.

At the rear of the apartment were tall, floor-to-ceiling sliding glass doors which opened onto a tiny enclosed patio outside. Because she lived on the ground floor, Tiffany always made it a habit to lock these doors in her absence.

One day Tiff arrived home to find Gus napping dreamily in the warm sun — outside on the patio. Gifted Gus had discovered how to open the heavy door and simply let himself out for a sniff and a wink. But Gus did not just learn how to open the heavy door, he had learned how to unlock it, not a simple matter even for the human hand. The latch was located behind the handle and had to be slid up vertically with a good measure of force. How was a dog able to manage the tricky lock with only a tooth-lined muzzle to work with?

Since Gus was a destructive chewer, one can only imagine the dilemma the dog's unusual skills created for Tiffany. It was necessary to contain him to prevent his chewing, but Gus could not be contained, not ever. It was spooky, his confounding ability to escape. There were times when Tiff was convinced some human had stolen into the apartment and deliberately freed Gus from confinement.

The single place inside the apartment from which Gus could not escape was the bathroom. But in his frustration at not being able to fulfill his open-door policy, he demolished the bathroom door frame. It had to be replaced at Tiffany's expense. The only option she had left was to crate poor Gus all day while she was at work. Tiff purchased a sturdy, airline-approved plastic dog kennel.

Many dog owners are familiar with these portable kennels. The wire doors are tricky. The latch must be squeezed, pinched together vertically from top down and bottom up simultaneously, in order to pull two vertical steel bars from their slots at the top and bottom and free the door for opening. Each must be depressed simultaneously and held together while at the same time the door is pulled open. This latch was on the outside of the cage door, and the cage door was made of three-quarter-inch stainless steel mesh.

Gus may be only the second or third dog in history to do what he did next.

Upon the first morning of his confinement in the crate, Tiff put Gus in, said goodbye and left the apartment. At the car she discovered having forgotten her car keys and reentered the apartment.

Gus met her at the door. He smiled and waved hello with his obnoxious bullwhip tail. He had decoded the latch from the inside, and he did it in less than sixty seconds.

Jaw power was no problem. This Gus possessed. But how was Gus able to decipher an intricate latch mechanism that can

Diane Arrington

be difficult even for humans? How did he manage to get his teeth through the mesh and operate them so precisely as to hold the latch together and push on the door at the same time, all from *inside* the crate?

Further, how did Gus decipher the code so quickly? He had never even seen a crate before, had no previous opportunity to work on the puzzle. Is it possible he watched Tiffany close it and was able to reverse the process in his mind?

It was frustrating enough for Tiffany that her lummox of a dog was winning the game, but the cavalier approach he took was infuriating. He never sulked or acted ashamed, nor did he seem proud of his accomplishments. To Gus, escaping from any configuration of barricade or confinement his owner could devise was simply something he did. A part of his life. A job. An entertaining job. To Tiff, the situation was something akin to bicycling uphill on ice.

Is Gus closer to the wolf or closer to the human in evolution? It is necessary for a wolf in the wild to release himself from any entrapment that would potentially interfere with his survival. Indeed, wolves have gone on record as having gnawed through their own legs to freedom when caught in the vicious leghold traps used by inhumane hunters. But doorknobs and louver doors and sliding glass doors and intricate cage latches? By all accounts, Gus looks like a dog. By all accounts he does not think like one.

If random breeding and evolution are working together to develop in the dog a brain closer to man's, a brain more suited to surviving technology than surviving in the wild, this makes the activities of Star and Gus and Houdini easier to accept. Perhaps it is a powerful combination of unknown forces enabling mysterious behavior not only to begin, but to continue its progress to increasingly more difficult and intricate tasks.

Whatever Gus's enabling force, humans cannot know it. What we do know is that Gus was a happy camper, secure in the

Seventh Sense

knowledge that his open-door policy, temporarily at least, would remain in effect.

Diane Arrington

Chapter 26
T-Bone

In recent years, increasing numbers of cats are exploding the old myth about cats hating water. Indeed, among cats in general, water seems to be a growing fascination. T-Bone's bizarre activities involving water could be more accurately described as obsession; he fully shatters the wives' tale. The stories in this book describe unusual behaviors. T-Bone is an exception. His story describes, pure and simple, an unusual cat.

The plaintive sound of a kitten's distress call is designed by nature to carry long distances. It serves to reunite the wayward kitten with its mother. A lost kitten knows only that his Mom is missing and he needs another one. He trumpets his pleas for love and protection until they are found.

Carl heard the sound coming from beneath a huge dumpster in the parking lot of an apartment complex. In the clear dark of an early April morning he traced it to the smallest kitten he had ever seen. Its eyes were barely open. It looked like a baby rat crouched beneath the mammoth steel receptacle. Frightened and alone, the three-week-old kitten shivered against the cement curbing.

Barely able to see in the dimly-lit parking lot, Carl watched in amazement as the tiny mouth, seemingly incapable of any noise but a peep, opened to emit the hearty cry of a mature young cat. When it sensed Carl's nearness, the kitten fell silent. It did not run. With smokey, unfocused eye slits the tiny feline struggled to look upward in the man's direction.

Carl, a big, gentle man, stood motionless. He strained to hear answering calls from the kitten's family. He reasoned that if the mother was simply out hunting food, her distress upon returning

Diane Arrington

to find her kitten gone would be overwhelming for her. He did not wish to inflict that hurt upon the mother cat. He waited and listened. He heard only the rusty-gate sounds of hidden locusts and the distant cadence of roadway traffic. The sticky Texas morning was quiet.

Carl gently lifted the kitten. Instantly its tone transformed from boisterous hollering to tiny, pleading peeps, sounds much more suited to a creature so fresh from the womb. Carl was unable to resist the powerful human instinct to protect those smaller and more helpless than ourselves. He rescued the tiny orphan foundling and took it home.

Carl's wife Ann received the miniature kitten into her hands. As she did so, it snuggled lightly against her chest. It purred quietly, as if it knew it was safe.

Or, more likely as things turned out, the cat was a con artist from the start.

So it was that on April 9, 1989, Carl and Ann Mason became proud though reluctant surrogate parents. Perhaps it was the kitten's separation from his mother before weaning, his absent litter experience, that made him the way he was. At that moment the young couple could not have known what they were up against.

The black and tan tabby possessed a nose too broad for his face, giving him a strong resemblance to a seasoned ex-boxing champ. Black stripes swept back from his fat nose and across his cheeks. Another stripe streaked down his back, breaking into perfect black diamonds when it reached his tail. Carl and Ann named the kitten T-Bone after a favorite musician.

It was necessary to his survival to bottle-feed T-Bone. Cradled on his back in the crook of Ann's arm, the kitten ate hungrily. He slurped, swallowed and purred simultaneously. He kneaded the warm towel in which Ann swaddled him. T-Bone would not accept any nipples made for baby kittens. No baby stuff for him. Instead, T-Bone insisted on the big nipple made for human babies.

From the very beginning, T-bone liked everything big. He liked Carl's big hands, he liked his big pink nursing towel, though he probably wished it had been a more macho color. He refused to settle for anything but the big nipple, and he had an enormous appetite. T-Bone the cat would bottle feed for the next five months.

He would also learn new things with lightning speed.

Food Obsession

T-Bone loved his food. Only at mealtime did his kitten fur seem to stick cartoonishly straight out from his body. He learned the hum of the microwave meant food. Whether or not it was his dinner inside, the sound always triggered an eager, bounding flight to the kitchen. Other kittens too small to jump to the counter would politely mew their request for a lift. Not T-Bone. T-Bone screeched his demand. Once up, he rubbed soft, skinny cheeks over and over against the beloved oven, purring his unpracticed kitten purr and squeaking like a mouse in labor.

Within only a few days the kitten learned the beige and blue flower print loveseat in which Ann or Carl fed him was the Food Chair. When either of them sat in that loveseat, feeding time or not, it was T-Bone's signal. He would charge across the room, claw his 24 ounces straight up the side of the couch and, in his unsteady baby way, stagger into whatever lap and assume Nursing Position.

Most fascinating about T-Bone's bottle feeding was that he learned to hold the pint-sized bottle with his own tiny paws and literally feed himself. On very quiet nights, one could hear soft gurgling sounds as T-Bone filled his own tummy. Lying all alone on his back by the fire, sunk deep in a huge blue pillow, he clutched the bottle to his fuzzy, baby-fur chest. Like a human baby, his little chin worked rhythmically at the nipple while glassy, half-closed eyes gazed off into space and slid in and out of focus.

Occasionally in the evenings after he had already been fed, T-Bone would launch an impassioned campaign for a second feeding. Strategically, he would yowl and beg at the top of his lungs as if he had not in his lifetime eaten a single meal. Upon garnering no response to his desperate pleas, he would climb into the love seat, roll onto his back, throw his legs apart and expose his belly. Like a human child throwing a tantrum, he'd toss back his head, muster up his most pathetic sobs and extend small paws to the sky, begging his beloved bottle.

That T-Bone could not fix the bottle himself was a good thing. As it was to be, T-Bone grew and grew some more, well past the average ten-pound cat. Eventually he would develop into an enormous eighteen pounds. As an adult T-Bone resembled a small cougar, complete with broad nose, golden eyes, black whiskers and swinging belly.

After four weeks on a bottle, T-Bone began to look for other, more interesting things to eat, things he could chew. One night the fridge went on the blink and froze everything inside. Ann was on her knees, removing spoiled goods and salvaging what she could when she heard a crunching sound behind her. It was her kitten T-Bone, chowing down on a frozen head of lettuce.

Bath Roll Obsession

Having lacked the normal visuals of a healthy litter experience, there were certain feline behaviors that T-Bone never did engage in. He did not hiss. According to Ann, on no occasion did he ever assume the defensive arch-and-puff body language. Kitten play, however, another product of a normal infancy, was not missing from T-Bone's repertoire. Many of the games he invented were instinctive, the rest were purely original.

Spider Man was played most often in the wee hours of morning. T-Bone discovered he could leap from the bannister, fly through the air over the stairs and stick into a cedar wall. As though his paws were made of Velcro, eighteen tiny rivets

Seventh Sense

locked him in. From there he would proceed vertically up the half wall. When he got to the top he would recline on his chest like a cougar on a limb, his chin flat and two legs dangling over each side.

Bathroom tissue is a common favorite for play among kittens and puppies — in moderation. But once T-Bone discovered this delight, it rapidly became an obsession.

One rainy afternoon in early November of 1989, Ann returned home to pastel streamers coating most everything in the house. It was the first time, but it was not to be the last. She stood in awe at the extent of the mess.

Apparently while his humans were away and the other cats were sleeping, T-Bone grew bored. He had either discovered the roll in the bathroom or dug it out from inside the cabinet. Either way, a visual image of T-Bone in action is impossible to avoid.

With Pure Joy on his face he took the loose end in his mouth. Eyes wide and sparkling, ears all aglow, tail flying straight behind him, he streaked from one end of the house to the other. Top to bottom, up the stairs and down again, he covered nearly every square foot of the apartment with paper. From what we know of T-Bone, he would not have been satisfied until the roll was empty and he was panting like a dog.

One night in October 1989, when T-Bone was about six months of age, Carl came in from work, climbed the townhouse stairs, tossed down his keys and wallet. In the bathroom he discovered T-Bone had discovered the toilet. There was T-Bone, perched on the toilet seat, rump high in the air. He had one front paw down inside the commode and was tapping energetically at a full roll of bath tissue bobbing in the water. This was only a hint of things to come.

When it came to the bath roll, kitten T-Bone was an opportunist in the truest sense of the word. Like a lion stalking prey, he lurked quietly in bathroom shadows behind fixtures, awaiting his opportunity to capture the fat, moth-like object that broke down perfectly in the kill. When one of the humans forgot to hide it from him, he was conveniently there to snatch it.

Diane Arrington

Though it nearly outweighed him, he always managed somehow to drag it to the toilet and throw it in.

First, he soaked it in the toilet. Then with brand new, half-grown teeth, he pulled the paper off in hunks. These he left in the water. Once he had completed the task of ridding the cardboard roller of its paper burden, he fished it out of the toilet bowl and took it to bed with him, dripping through the house as he went.

T-Bone was also obsessive about the cardboard rollers. These were apparently friends of his. Any roller would do, but that it be sopping was a requirement of a close friendship. Once thoroughly soaked, the rollers routinely became his sleeping companions. Most often he selfishly took them to bed with him, never minding that his bed was also Carl and Ann's bed. Other times he deliberately carried his prizes across the mattress to one of his people. He would proudly present the cherished, water-logged gift, plopping it down on the sheet, unselfishly giving them an opportunity to love it like he did.

Because of the cat, the family was consuming far too much bath tissue. Ann and Carl tried desperately to keep the tissue away from T-Bone. If it was on its holder set into the tile wall, T-Bone only unrolled it all over the house. They tried hiding the roll inside the vanity cupboard. Knowing it was in there, it took T-Bone less than five minutes to figure out how to open the cupboard door and reclaim it. The couple was eventually forced to lock all bath rolls inside the medicine chest high above the sink.

By now T-Bone's obsession with the toilet had begun to replace his obsession with food, and led him to his most bizarre activities of all. It was his obsession combined with his total lack of reaction to the only two water baths he was ever given that, in retrospect, joined him to his future.

Seventh Sense

Commode Obsession

It wasn't long before T-Bone was dropping toys other than the bath roll into the toilet. The plastic rings from milk bottles were a favorite. He repeatedly carried them in his mouth from the kitchen where he found them up the stairs to the bathroom. Once he got one upstairs, he threw it in the toilet to watch it float. The next several hours were spent using tiger-striped paws to dip it out, only to drop it in again and repeat the challenge.

The idea of a quiet evening with a book or a game of cards was elusive if not impossible with T-Bone as a pet. Whether Carl and Ann tried games, television or company, a background of splashing and gurgling noises coming from the bathroom was omnipresent. As far as T-Bone was concerned, no one else was present, so pure was his focus.

One day Ann brought home a new makeup brush. The brush promptly belonged to T-Bone, no discussion. Of course, he tossed it in the toilet. But this toy presented a new problem: this toy did not float. This fact would teach T-Bone to not object to getting wet.

The brush sank straight to the bottom. The five-pound terror huffed and snorted and marched around the seat, wondering how to get it back into his possession. It was almost nap time, he had no bath roll, and he was incapable of sleeping alone.

Ann watched secretly as T-Bone experimented. He stepped one front paw gingerly on the sloped side of the bowl. It was cold, but solid. With his back feet still behind him up on the seat, he plunged his other striped arm shoulder deep in the water. He swirled and groped for his imaginary fish. It remained still and uncaught at the bottom of the bowl. For a cat, a hunter, it was a perplexing situation. But T-Bone would not give up. In everything he did, T-Bone was relentless.

Diane Arrington

T-Bone inched farther down the side of the bowl and tried again. Still he could not reach his prey. He decided to take his back feet off the seat and stand inside the bowl. He discovered he could then reach the toy and easily brought it out, victory vibrating his whiskers.

After a few days' practice, T-bone had perfected his fishing technique. He gradually grew comfortable with standing completely inside the toilet bowl. Back paws on the slope and front paws on the very bottom of the bowl placed him fully neck deep in the water.

Thusly, T-Bone spent much of his kittenhood wading in the toilet.

Every so often T-Bone was forced to emerge from the toilet water for bothersome chores such as eating or sleeping. On occasion he licked himself dry, most often he did not. This may not have been a problem except that he preferred to sleep on Ann's pillow.

Ann and Carl agreed T-Bone's bathroom activities were amusing. They had not been particularly serious about putting a stop to his water sports. From a practical standpoint, however, particularly in the colder months, it was getting old. They asked themselves why their cat couldn't just chase strings and play in bags and boxes — dry ones — like any other normal kitten on earth. An hysterical, psychotic friend suggested they simply flush the toilet during one of his fishing expeditions.

The couple's attempts to get T-Bone to cease and desist his watery games were many, all futile. If they closed the bathroom door, T-Bone yelled until the neighbors complained. They had already tried keeping the toilet lid down. T-Bone fussed and thundered and physically launched himself against the toilet until the lid was lifted. In the end, T-Bone's controlling behavior regarding any interference with his obsession forced the couple to allow the cat to play at will in his own private pool. People own cats because they're warm and soft and cuddly. T-Bone was neither. Eighty percent of the time, T-Bone was soaking wet.

Water Obsession

Events unfolded at the Mason Water Park until one evening the unthinkable happened. While Ann was bathing, T-Bone discovered the bathtub. It frightened Ann to see the dawning look of discovery creep into his eyes as he watched her bathe. She had seen that earnest fascination on his face before and knew where it usually led with T-Bone.

It began gradually. At first T-Bone sat safely on the flat white rim of the tub. For a few nights in succession, T-Bone only watched quietly. Was he planning his strategy? The cat's oversized juvenile ears pricked forward reflexively at the smallest sound of splashing water. A few nights later T-Bone began to pace back and forth along his ledge of safety. He begged to lick the suds off Ann's fingers. Gradually, the kitten became more active on his ceramic platform. He paced and sat — and repeated this. Soon it was not an accident that each sit required a sneaky tail-dip in the water. With its tip wet and the rest fluffy, his tail resembled a scorpion's stinger.

Several baths more and T-Bone was bravely dunking his chubby paws. He tested the water. He swiped at the ten wiggly things sticking up from the water near the faucet. Could this be a fish he should trap and eat? When his paws got slippery, T-Bone took a time out. He sat down and, with each paw in turn, spread razor-tipped toes like an eagle's claw to lick meticulously between each.

As the evenings passed, T-Bone grew more and more courageous. Ann began to dread her baths, but she knew from past experience that closing the bathroom door was not an option. Before long T-Bone was plunging both forearms arms into the water, groping for the bottom. When each bath was over, T-Bone emerged from the bathroom soaked and matted, chin to ribs.

The curious thing about T-Bone's water obsession is that if he really is a cat, why did he seldom lick himself dry? He could walk away unconcerned, dripping water throughout the house. It was simply not a problem for T-Bone to go to sleep soaking wet.

After six or eight weeks of company in the bathtub and six or so long months of living with a cat like T-Bone, Ann longed for a simple bath in the peace and safety of her own sound mind. The couple had already seen that obsessive behavior ruled T-Bone's life. Despite this fact, Ann tried again to close the door while she bathed. As expected, on the opposite side of the closed door T-Bone complained at the top of his lungs. He threw himself against the door. He bellowed his jungle cry, the one that worked so well when he was three weeks old. He broke the humans down and finally got his way. Again, T-Bone's behavior forced Ann to open the door just to put an end to the racket and salvage sanity. Once T-Bone had discovered the bathtub, a bath in peace was just not to be.

One evening in February 1990, at the age of ten months, T-Bone's daring almost reached its peak — almost.

Ann was trying to relax in a bath with her constant companion in his customary position. She lounged back and rested her heels on the ledge of the tub beneath the faucets. T-Bone extended one tentative paw and tapped on her shins. Nothing happened. He pressed harder. Still nothing. He placed both front paws on her shins, tested his weight, and found they held. Ann didn't dare move. Then, unbelievably, the cat ventured out and stood fully on her legs. Curious as to how far he would take this new exploration, Ann let T-Bone walk her shins.

Soon T-Bone the cat was taking great pride in his admirable sense of balance. He strutted arrogantly up and down the rails. His tail whipped and spun, helping him to keep his footing. Ever after a new adventure, T-Bone stopped, crouched, and shot one arm shoulder-deep into the water, seeking the bottom from this new and different angle. Ann envied the absolute concentration of which the young feline mind is capable. The cat was driven.

Finally, one Saturday night in spring of 1990, T-Bone's courage crested and he achieved his ultimate.

Seventh Sense

T-Bone was now about eleven months old and weighed eleven pounds. Ann was drying off after her bath. T-Bone had spent his usual recreation hour with her in the bathroom. As was customary, he was sitting on the edge of the tub watching with fascination as the water gurgled down the drain. Ann was brushing her teeth. Suddenly she heard a splash behind her. Her heart leapt and she whirled around. She was thunderstruck. Without provocation, T-Bone had deliberately launched himself into five inches of soapy water.

T-Bone was immersed in water and suds nearly to his shoulders. He swirled up and down the tub. His black and tan diamond-studded tail floated behind him. Verbally trilling his delight, T-Bone was fairly smiling. His chest, soaked to the skin, puffed like a peacock in spring. He purred hugely to himself. He had finally found the bottom. T-Bone's obsessions had peaked.

And so it became nightly ritual for T-Bone to go swimming. Not the first cat in the world to swim, but certainly an unusual event among cats.

As time progressed, T-Bone's interest in water did not remain confined to the bathroom. At parties he discovered the quickest way to the ice cubes was to knock over the glass. Water's water, even when frozen. T-Bone often snoozed aloof on the kitchen floor, sound asleep with his elbow in his water dish.

***

As T-Bone grew to adulthood, his interest in full-submerge swimming waned. He moved on to other obsessions. He began to love biting guests in his home. He found he loved to lick stamps. He began to love the taste of human toothpaste. He still loved frozen lettuce. He hated the house-call vet.

At last contact with T-Bone's family, the main thing on T-bone's mind was T-Bone himself. His size alone demanded that those around him follow his instructions carefully. He was like many cats, reclined on one elbow, eyes shut on the world, lost in

Diane Arrington

some ancient aristocratic haze. But T-Bone's black-tipped tail signaled ominously to all who passed they'd best continue on.

    The big cat had been the life of the party at the Mason house. In adulthood he tamed down a bit, but the Masons weren't holding their breath that T-Bone had completely pulled out of it. With a cat like T-Bone, you never know. You just never know.

Docktale 7
Sugar

Sugar was a white Shepherd mix of some sort, a puppy. Wild as a hare, frisky and happy as a lamb in spring, Sugar did surprisingly well in beginning obedience class, with one exception. Although Sugar heeled perfectly well in three directions, Sugar refused to heel going west.

Heel Sugar to the north and one would find her walking perfectly at the left leg. Heel her to the south and Sugar walked calmly at the calf on a slack leash. Heel her to the east and Sugar was equally cooperative.

But turn to the west and the 30-pound dog would trail the leash-holder like a water skier. At class, at home, in the park or on the other side of town, some mysterious Force lying somewhere to the west seemed just too much for Sugar.

What was it that made Sugar unable to help herself when traveling west? It's a mystery.

Diane Arrington

Chapter 27
Lolly & Cubby

Lolly shows an instinct for discerning and a continuity of thought that is spooky only because it happened in the canine mind. Through her propitious capability for logical, linear thinking, she displays a nobility most often associated with humans, not dogs.

It was 1990 in Garland, Texas. A man brought his two-year-old pet dog to a veterinarian for her annual shots. During the appointment the man suddenly began to pat his pockets, exclaiming that he had forgotten his checkbook. He would run to the car and get it, he said. The man left and never came back, leaving his dog behind. No one knows why he abandoned her, and no one could have known what a heroic spirit she would turn out to be.

***

Deb could hear the screams from two blocks away. She ran frantically towards the sound. There is nothing quite so pathetic as a puppy's screams of fear and pain and confusion. It is a primal cry of agony spawned by trust gone wrong, faith betrayed, forsaken honor.

The big, gnarly man held fast the four-month-old puppy so that he could not flee, could not escape the crushing blows of a heavy car chain and repeated, rib-shattering kicks with the man's heavy, steel-toed boot. The man would show the dog who was boss, he told Deb.

Deb reached out her hands to the puppy, a handsome Shepherd-Husky cross. In his face she saw raw, heartbreaking terror.

Diane Arrington

"*You want him, take him,*" the man spat, "*he ain't no good for nothin' anyway.*"

Deb did. She took him to the vet where his physical wounds were tended. She took him home to heal his emotional wounds. It is impossible to fathom the absent heart of the human being capable of rendering such pitiless beatings upon an innocent new puppy, but especially this puppy; Deb discovered he had been blind from birth.

Five years passed. For his resemblance to a bear cub, Deb had chosen the name Cubby for the dog she had rescued. Cubby grew into an 85-pound cream puff. He sported the wolf-like Husky mask, pointed Shepherd ears far too big for his head, and a big, thick, waggy tail curled high over his back. He was frisky and loving. He was immensely loyal, as rescues often are. He loved to swim in the pool. Four of those five years Cubby swam daily and he swam strongly.

His green, empty eyes looked in your direction and, though he could not see you distinctly, he wagged happily at your nearness. Because sight had never been his, and because he was a dog and dogs take things as they come, he did not lament his blindness.

It is possible that residual effects of early abuse interfered with Cubby's development. Perhaps he somehow contracted the canine equivalent of dementia. By the time he was five, Cubby was aging fast. Arthritis had already crippled Cubby's rear legs and hips. He rose and walked stiffly. For the large majority of the time the gentle, affectionate giant maneuvered the world by means of a keen, enigmatic radar. Other times he wandered the yard, lost in his own mind, appearing to forget where he was.

While Cubby's blindness had always been, his arthritic pain came and went. He had bad days, but he had more good days. To that point the veterinarian opined Cubby was not in so much misery as to be put out of it. Still, Deb and her roommate Wanda did not know how much longer he would be with them.

It was then, when Cubby was five, that Deb and Wanda found Lolly.

***

Deb stood in the window at the vet's office watching the man drive away and gaping in disbelief. How could someone keep and feed a dog for two years and yet love her so little as to heartlessly abandon her? Deb looked into the dog's eyes. They were soulful eyes, the eyes of an intelligent canine watching the door anxiously for her owner's return. Marked like a Doberman with a Labrador coat, floppy black ears and a Shepherd snout and tail, she was adorable, sad, and now, homeless. Deb's big heart could not avoid taking her home to live with Cubby.

Deb named this rescue Lolly. As the next 48 hours would have it, Lolly permitted Cubby to think he was in charge. Upon their first introduction Lolly seemed to instinctively understand that Cubby could not fully fend for himself. Instantly she began to care for him. In the way of a true Shepherd she herded him, guided him to things he needed like the water dish and the back door. Cubby had no problem finding the food.

When Cubby underwent one of his spells and seemed to forget where he was, Lolly, ever the sharp lookout for Cubby's welfare, somehow managed to be handy when it happened. Caringly she went and got him. Gently she herded him back to safety. Lolly could not rest that night until Cubby had gone to bed.

Though she didn't let on that it was so, right from the beginning Lolly designated herself Cubby's Keeper. Deb and Wanda couldn't believe how quickly Lolly adopted this task as her own. Two days had barely passed when newcomer Lolly revealed her noble spirit.

It was a bright, hot, summer Saturday morning. Lolly had been with them only two days. Deb and Wanda were busy cleaning in the back of the house. Loud music floated into the kitchen where Lolly sniffed the fresh air through the screen door

Diane Arrington

which overlooked the swimming pool. Cubby was outside. With veteran radar, Cubby was able to sense where the edges of the pool were and stay clear. He rambled around the pool area, living by his nose and ears.

Lolly watched Cubby through the screen. Even though they had just met, she rather liked the old guy. She longed to be out playing with him instead of locked inside. They might even swim together in the pool.

Suddenly Lolly's ears perked forward. As she watched, Cubby seemed to enter one of his spells. He appeared to become lost. He staggered slightly. He was too near the edge of the pool. His weak back legs began to lose balance. All at once Cubby lost his footing. His hips and rear legs slipped into the water. Feeling himself sliding backwards, Cubby desperately tried to catch himself with his front paws on the edge of the pool. He could not. He vanished over the side, plunging into the deep end of the pool.

Though a strong swimmer in his early years, Cubby's now-arthritic hips made swimming almost impossible. His sightless eyes would never find the steps. He was doomed. With his back legs of little assistance, he splashed and struggled gallantly with his front paws trying to keep his head above water. Cubby was becoming increasingly vertical in the water, an aquatic position all dogs know is certain death. Watching from inside the kitchen, Cubby's Keeper went berserk.

Like a dog possessed, Lolly screamed and barked and trembled. She clawed frantically at the screen door, but it was latched with a hook located too high up. Even standing on her hind legs, she could not reach it. With the vacuum cleaner roaring and the stereo turned up, the girls did not hear Lolly's screams.

Cubby was silent, absorbed in the panicky pursuit of self-preservation. His moonstone eyes were filled with panic. He choked and clawed at the slippery sides of the pool. The stairs were at the shallow end. In the deep end was only a vertical metal ladder to carry humans up and out of the pool. It was impossible for him to climb. He sank and resurfaced, sputtering and frantically snorting water from his square white snout.

Lolly leaped to her hind legs and pushed hard on the screen. It stayed latched. She threw her compact 45 pounds at the door again and again, but the latch would not break. Finally, while Cubby struggled to keep from drowning just a few yards away, Lolly dug with all her might at the edge of the screen where it attached to its wooden frame.

At last Lolly broke the screen free. With all her might she pushed until it tore away from the frame. With her strong muzzle she pushed hard at the hole. She literally dived through the screen, tearing it open as she went. Free at last, she dashed to the pool and to Cubby.

While a white-hot Texas sun blazed down unconcerned, Cubby's old Husky face grimaced with the effort of staying alive. Lolly positioned herself at the edge of the pool inches from Cubby's head. Then, curiously, she began to bark.

It was a rhythmic, repetitive barking. She barked loud, short bursts, and with each bark she dipped and bounced on her front legs. Cubby heard. Surprised, perhaps relieved, he turned his blind face in Lolly's direction. Then, miraculously, he turned and swam towards his new friend.

Cubby swam toward the sound of Lolly's voice. As he did so she backed away, little by little, a foot at a time, never permitting him to reach her. She stayed inches ahead of him, barking loudly in his face. Each time she moved he adjusted his watery path to swim toward her sound. Bit by bit Lolly backed her way toward the shallow end of the pool. Bit by bit Cubby followed.

Lolly barked Cubby all the way to the shallow end of the pool. But that wasn't enough for Lolly's guardian heart.

Deb and Wanda finally heard the commotion. A glance through a window summed up the situation in one panicked instant. They raced to the kitchen, only to find Lolly's escape attempts had bent the metal eyelet, locking the hook in its eye.

Wanda ran for the pliers as Deb watched helplessly through the screen.

Cubby had made it to the shallow end. Still, he floundered aimlessly, unable to locate the stairs. Seeing this, Lolly leaped into the water. She swam strongly and quickly to Cubby. Though both dogs struggled in the water, Lolly somehow managed to grab Cubby's nylon collar securely in her teeth. Cubby outweighed Lolly by 40 pounds, but Lolly was determined. Her muscles strained to swim backwards. Her black-brown paws flailed underwater. Ever so slowly, Lolly pulled Cubby along until she had dragged the huge dog all the way to the steps.

But that still wasn't enough for the valiant Lolly.

Cubby located the steps with his front feet, but he didn't climb out. Now Lolly swam around behind him. She barked furiously, almost scolding, urging him to climb the stairs. Cubby hesitated. So Lolly swam full force into him from the rear. With her shoulder, she literally pushed the old dog up the stairs and onto the safety of the pool deck.

Cubby emerged onto the pavement. He shook his exhausted, sopping self. Lolly climbed out and shook too. Then she sniffed Cubby and licked his muzzle, seeming to ask if he was all right. He wiggled his soaked tail in her direction, as if to thank her. Just then Deb and Wanda pried the hook apart and hurried to rescue Cubby, but the deed was already done.

Lolly had not even been a member of the household long enough to complete a bond with Cubby, yet she had saved his life. But then, all dogs are distant cousins and cousins, it is supposed, look out for one another.

How Lolly knew what to do will always remain a mystery. By what sense did she know Cubby was in trouble? Having been in the house a mere two days, and having not yet been in the pool, how did she know where the shallow end and the steps were? How did she know that the shallow end meant safety for Cubby? How did she know to take the rescue as far as literally pushing him up and out of the pool? Most amazing, how did

Seventh Sense

Lolly know that barking would be the only way to save Cubby and that if she barked Cubby would even follow the sound?

When performing acts of heroism, both humans and dogs put into action every last shred of capability, every fiber and faculty available. Lolly somehow knew that Cubby was blind and the heroine relied on the only sense she knew could save him — his hearing.

As for Lolly, the abandoned one, Cubby's Keeper, Sentry of the Century, she thinks it's no big deal. All in a day's work in the life of a superdog.

Diane Arrington

Chapter 28
Manor

Manor's actions are reassuring evidence of lucid problem-solving in the canine mind. He identified the problem which interfered with the goal, then adapted his own behavior to provide the solution and achieve the goal. The goal, of course, is universal among dogs. But in visualizing how to attain it, Manor shows uncommon creativity.

Perhaps he was royalty in a past life, perhaps he was manor-born that Wednesday in 1990, but his name was Manor. A classy, happy, rough-coated Jack Russell Terrier, he was a mere two years of age when he first developed an extraordinary skill.

The Jack Russell Terrier is sophisticated, wise and intelligent. He dislikes being demeaned. He will give you what you give him. His need for intellectual stimulation and challenge is great. For this reason, many of this breed do not do well as the pets of families disinterested in or too busy to educate the dog. This is proven, at least in part, by Moose.

Moose received no education and little stimulation within his original family. He was permitted to run loose with no challenges, no functions to perform and no limitations on his lifestyle. As a result, Moose was a frightful behavior problem before he became Eddie on the popular TV series, *Frasier*.

All of this explains why but not how Manor developed his clever technique.

Because inbreeding among Jack Russell Terriers was at the time kept to a minimum by responsible breeders who collectively avoided for years registration with the American Kennel Club, the demeanor among individual dogs remains fairly true to form. When Manor reached a year of age his owners did obedience train him. However his need for discourse did not continue to be met over the long term. I is for Inventiveness, and Manor chose to invent his own form of challenge.

One of Manor's favorite dog jobs was Squirrel Patrol. Perched on his owners' bed like a king on his throne, the small, brown-on-white bullet-shaped dog monitored the yard hour upon hour. From the second-floor window at the rear of the family home, Manor's bright brown eyes watched for the tiniest movement in the yard or trees. The bed was an infinitely convenient place from which to watch, as a nap could occur at any moment without warning. Spring and fall were Manor's favorite seasons. That was when the bushy-tailed sources of entertainment were the busiest. It was spring of 1992 when the sagacious dog first showed his true colors.

At first glimpse of one of his quarry things, Manor sprang to action. He flung himself off the bed with a crash, raced across the floor and threw himself down the hardwood stairs like a rock down a washboard. Nails clicking like a machine gun, he careened around the turn at the foot of the stairs, somehow managing not to slip on the waxed wood floor. He raced down the hallway, crashed full force through his dog door and exploded into the yard like a hair missile. Manor was yet unaware his endeavors were clearly overheard from outdoors. All the commotion, of course, sent the squirrels scurrying.

In the yard the little power-packed dog stopped short. He raised his muzzle to the sky. He gazed into the trees with a puzzled look upon his small face. He stood in the quiet yard and tipped his head, wondering where everybody went. Birds twittered and a breeze rustled leaves high in the trees. Manor mustered up a half-hearted bark or two anyway. He sniffed the base of the tree where he was certain he had sighted the squirrel. Why had it vanished? He simply could not have gotten there any faster.

Manor carried out his hysterical, overdone Squirrel Patrol daily for almost three weeks. Then one day one of his owners,

Seventh Sense

Charlie, happened to be in the room when he noticed Manor behaving strangely.

Manor spotted a squirrel through the window. But this time, instead of catapulting off the bed, Manor executed an odd, deformed sort of slide, like the yolk of an egg sliding from counter to floor. This accomplished a surprisingly soft landing. Traveling fast but quietly as possible, Manor raised himself onto his toes in the most bizarre manner, his compact little body strangely contorted. In this way he scurried on tiptoe down the stairs, around the corner, down the hall and up to the dog door. There he came to a full stop.

With his white, black-whiskered nose, Manor gently nudged open the flap and effected a one-eyed peek outside to be certain the squirrel was still there. It was. Sneakily pushing through the flap with his nose, Manor let the flap run along his back like a whale swimming beneath kelp. One stealthy paw after the other, Manor poured himself slowly through the opening like sap oozing from a tree. He was almost out. With one careful, pointed back toe he eased the flap closed silently behind him. In every instance he used his right rear paw to do this. The instant he was certain the flap was closed securely without slapping, Manor bolted to action.

He charged the tree like a Rottweiler, thinking what a huge dog he really must be to be so scary. Of course the squirrel would scream and run. When he had cleared the yard to his satisfaction of the pesky nut-colored invader, Manor trotted back to the house with smugness in his gait. He reentered the house normally, not sneaking. Through the dog flap he went. He pitter-pattered up the stairs to once again resume his cozy post, most certainly all The Hero.

It took Manor less than three weeks to abandon his earlier, hopeless method of chasing squirrels and teach himself a new one. After all, the satisfaction came in watching the squirrel flee in terror. So one day he figured things out. He pulled all his nerves into a bundle and learned to sneak through the dog door so as not to warn the squirrels.

Diane Arrington

It is fascinating that Manor learned, without instruction from any resource but his own brain, a concept as abstract as being quiet. How did he do it? Even more comical is watching the small Jack Russell literally sneak through his dog door. But most intriguing of all is that Manor was a tornado one day and a silent, speeding canoe the next. Both questions could be asked. What took him so long to figure it out (weeks)? And How was he able to resolve the problem so quickly (overnight)?

It was Manor's self-assigned challenge, Squirrel Patrol was. Whether he had been mentally working on his personal problem for the full three weeks or three days or three hours, Manor's behavior exemplifies adaptive intelligence in its purest form, and adaptive behavior at its most refined.

Seventh Sense

Diane Arrington

Chapter 29
Chuckie

It is most fascinating to trace the thought process of this tiny kitten during this incident. There is mounting evidence that even young animals can reason. Chuckie reasons out not just one thought, but an incredible series of seemingly complicated mental maneuvers.

Chuckie was rescued as an infant into a home with one female owner Angela, two adult dogs and one other adult cat. Born in the wild, Chuckie was a creamy tan-on-white tiger cat with amber eyes and ears that were much too large. At the age of only four weeks, Chuckie showed signs of being a person in a cat suit.

One night in summer 1991, just a few days after his rescue, Chuckie perched on the back of the couch. Angela stroked him and spoke softly. She reassured him that his new home would be perfect for him. As she spoke, he looked directly and deeply into her eyes. He watched her lips as if actually listening to and hearing each and every soft-spoken word. Suddenly golden eyes in a tiny kitten face shifted and followed one of the dogs as she moved across the room twenty feet away. This was a kitten whose eyes had been functional only two weeks. For a four-weeker to exhibit this kind of keen awareness gave Angela a clue as to what she was up against with this little guy.

As he grew, the infant fireball learned quickly how to get what he wanted. How he decided what he wanted is as yet unknown.

Chuckie was a free spirit. He insisted on being permitted all the liberty he might have in the wild, all the freedom he felt he deserved. For example, closed doors were a tremendous bother. They interfered with his self-imposed immunity to house rules.

Chuckie simply could not tolerate being denied access of any kind to any place, including the outdoors.

So, the instant he was tall enough, Chuckie learned to stand on his hind feet and use his front paws to turn doorknobs. He was a sight, stretched to full length, his buff-and-orange rib stripes separating with the reach. As soon as the latch cleared, his weight pushed the door open and he was in, just where he wanted to go. If the door happened to open towards him, Chuckie simply cleared the latch with his paws first, tugged a bit, then dropped quickly to the floor where he tucked an upside-down paw under the door and pulled it open. Chuckie always got his way.

The self-reliant youngster's most amazing demonstration of intelligence occurred when he was a mere eight weeks of age.

After Angela taught Chuckie to reliably come when called, he was routinely permitted free access to an enclosed back yard. His kitty door was an open rear window which could be closed to keep him inside in her absence. Angela also wanted to teach Chuckie to find his way home should he ever become lost. To achieve this, Angela had carried Chuckie along on daily walks with the dogs ever since his rescue at the age of three weeks. Chuckie particularly enjoyed these journeys nestled in the comforting arms of his owner, ten stories above danger. He seemed utterly fascinated with the unique, sky-high view of life in the great outdoors. Rain, snow, wind or moon, he got his nightly rides.

One evening Angela chose not to take Chuck along on her walk. She and the dogs prepared to leave the house. Chuckie crowded the door in anticipation. Because he seemed always to understand what she said, Angela had fallen into the practice of talking to him as though he were a person. She explained to him he would have to stay home, just this once. Chuckie looked shocked. He must have understood he was being told no, being denied a fond pleasure. He became agitated, and a battle of wills ensued.

Diane Arrington

Chuckie squawked. He yelled. He threw himself to the floor. He pushed and fussed and insisted on going with. Angela struggled with her headstrong kitten, unnerved at the cognizance coming from a kitten. She managed to squeeze through the open door and get it shut before the small kitten sneaked through. Chuckie huffed and blew and gave her a look as she left him and closed the door.

Outside on the porch Angela breathed relief, thinking she had won the argument. The dogs milled about as she zipped her jacket.

But she had won the battle and not the war. Fifteen steps later Chuckie met them on the front lawn! Behind his whiskers he wore a smug expression. Victory was his.

The moment the door had closed with him on the wrong side, Chuckie knew exactly where to go. He bolted for the open rear window. On tiny kitten legs he cleared the distance through the house from the front door to the back window. He leaped through. He raced along the back of the house. Eyes wild with the challenge of meeting the goal, he vaulted the fence, careened around the corner, dashed full speed down the long driveway and appeared in the front yard — all in less than ten seconds. At Angela's admonitions, he flipped his skinny tail. During this walk, Chuckie carried an extra flaunting bounce in his gait.

How could this kitten the size of a shoe with a brain the size of a grape have known what steps to take in order to achieve his goal? Not only did he know what to do and where to go, he knew he had to hurry. Most house pets would throw themselves at the inside of the front door, at the object of their frustration. Not Chuckie. Chuckie reasoned. Somehow he knew going in the *opposite* direction of the front door was the only action he could take that would provide the most immediate solution to his dilemma: how to go along on the coveted walk.

In the end Chuck got his way as usual. But from that night forward, things changed. Chuckie was permitted to join the family outings, but only on his *own* four paws. And as was customary with this happy little kitten, Chuckie loved his walks anyway. He simply found a new way to challenge himself, like climbing every last tree along the way and thumbing his nose at the dogs on the ground.

Diane Arrington

Docktale 8
Murphy

Murphy, a six-month Golden Retriever, loved watching the birds in his back yard. This was his obsession, exact center of the yard was his post.

Murphy did not try to catch the birds or bite them. It seemed the birds simply provided for the puppy his own private dog video. Nor did Murphy lie down. Hour upon hour Murphy stayed in a sitting position, eyeing his feathered friends.

During the winter of 1993, Murphy's hometown of Dallas, Texas experienced at least one ice storm. It rained then froze, icing over the grass and ground where Murphy customarily positioned himself to observe his birds. Suddenly, on this day, Murphy had a problem: an icy behind.

In the afternoon of the same chilly day, Murphy's owner returned home to a sight that made him laugh. Murphy was at his station as usual, but rather than sit on the cold ground, the dog was sitting on a welcome mat.

Murphy had found the mat by the back door. The puppy had dragged it across the yard and positioned it dead center on his post. The mat was not bunched as though Murphy had been playing Kill and it landed there incidentally. The mat was neatly spread out flat, a perfect insulation for Murphy's chilly sitter.

Some say dogs don't use problem-solving and lines of reasoning. Murphy did. He recognized the fact that he had a problem, and he ingeniously took the appropriate steps to solve it.

Seventh Sense

Diane Arrington

Chapter 30
Ralph and Steve

Ralph and Steve undertake a behavior for which there can be no known origin in the primordial mind of the wolf. There is no behavioral explanation, no physical explanation, no environmental explanation. Its cause lies locked inside the minds of two canine pals.

Ralph and Steve were two Australian Shepherds. They were not littermates, but they were virtually joined at the hip. The two dogs did everything together. At the age of one year, they played Keep Away, Wrestle, Tug, Chase, Tag, Bite Me — every game imaginable. If they could have tossed the frisbee to one another they would have.

Ralph and Steve competed strenuously. For toys, for owner attention, to be first in line on a walk, to ride in the front seat in the car. They tried their best to beat each other through doorways, and, like an old Laurel and Hardy routine, sometimes got jammed in.

Ralph and Steve took safety in numbers. They seemed fully aware that their owners were at a disadvantage when they both acted up at once. In terms of obedience and dignified, mannerly behavior, they were an impossible duo. "The boys" were out of control ninety-five percent of the time. But there was one aspect of life together in which Ralph and Steve displayed remarkably controlled behavior, particularly for a couple of dogs who appeared to have no sense of civility whatsoever.

Owners Jerry and Jen were of the wise opinion that two dogs are better than one. This is true where social animals are concerned. It is immeasurably more tolerable for two dogs to endure together a life with two-legged pack members absent ten

Seventh Sense

hours a day than it is for one lone dog. Ralph and Steve were adopted within a week of each other.

Shortly after the adoption, Jerry and Jen mail-ordered two personalized food bowls for Ralph and Steve. Made of heavy pottery, they had flat bottoms to prevent puppies from tipping them. The bowls were a handsome grey with royal blue rims. Their names appeared across one side of each bowl, Ralph on one bowl, Steve on the other, elegantly scripted in blue. It wasn't until the dogs were several months old that the couple noticed an unusual behavior regarding their pets' sustenance.

One Saturday morning Jerry had taken Steve to the vet. Ralph was home alone with Jen. Both dog bowls sat empty on the kitchen floor. Jen was washing up the breakfast dishes.

"*Here Ralphie,*" she called. "*You can have these left-over eggs.*" She scraped a plate absent-mindedly into one of the bowls. The dogs lusted after table scraps like cats after tunafish, and unfailingly inhaled the precious tidbits. But on this particular morning, Ralph only gazed longingly at the tidbits with his blue eyes. Then, without eating, he sat down.

"*Go ahead, Ralph, they're for you!*" Jen encouraged him.

Ralph stood up and whimpered. He looked at Jen with a confused look on his juvenile face and sat down again. He sniffed at the eggs, but would not eat them.

Jen was concerned. This was new behavior for Ralph who, under normal circumstances, ate like an anaconda. In the blink of an eye he would scoop up anything on earth that landed nearby, whether or not it was edible. Now he did not. Jen thought he was sick.

Ralph stood again and sniffed at the scraps a second time. He seemed to want the food but something, some mysterious force, prevented him from lapping it up.

That's when Jen noticed she had scraped the plate into Steve's bowl.

"*Oh, excuse me,*" she joked Ralph. "*Poor dear. Did I put it in the wrong dish?*" She dumped the food from Steve's bowl into

Diane Arrington

Ralph's. The food instantly disappeared into Ralph's stomach. This was Jen's first indication of a weird behavior developing.

The couple began to watch Ralph and Steve's eating habits more closely. They searched their memories. A few weeks hence they realized the truth: each dog refused to eat from the other's bowl.

Jerry and Jen experimented. They turned the bowls so the names weren't visible. The dogs chose the correct dishes anyway. They washed the bowls in the dishwasher thinking the scent was how they determined which bowl to use, and 140-degree water and sterilizing soap would remove the scent. Could happen, but the dogs still knew which bowl was which.

Then Jen and Jerry tried switching the bowls. They put Ralph's on the left and Steve's on the right. The dogs weren't fooled. Jerry and Jen tried separating the bowls and placing them on opposite sides of the kitchen. Ralph and Steve circled momentarily, then settled on the correct containers. Dreading the possibility their dogs could read, the couple tried covering the names on the bowls with masking tape, but Ralph and Steve would not be had.

Nothing would make Ralph eat from Steve's bowl or Steve eat from Ralph's. It seemed either dog would starve before he would eat from the wrong dish. Each dog seemed to think if there was no food in his own dish, there was no food at all.

How Ralph and Steve hit upon this imaginative idiosyncracy is a mystery. Why they continued is an enigma.

How did the dogs decide the very first time who would belong to which bowl? Did they have a conference, a meeting, during which they reached some mystical agreement undetectable to humans? If the method by which the dogs identified the correct bowl was not by scent, not by sight and not by position on the floor, then by what method was it? What in a dog's universe would motivate them to eat only from one bowl? It goes against all canine survival impulse.

Seventh Sense

The only experiment the couple did not try was to completely replace the bowls with new ones. Why bother? Indeed, it would be far too unsettling if Ralph and Steve did the same thing with the new bowls, too.

Diane Arrington

Chapter 31
Sampson

For many millennia burying has been a daily ritual for today's cats and their ancestors. What Sampson didn't seem to know is that burying is a behavior associated with consumption and digestion. Sampson displays a related behavior that is unique and impossible to explain.

It was winter's last gasp and Helen Barstow of Irving, Texas could barely bring herself to leave her warm place by the fire. With a good book and the cat in her lap, things just didn't get any better. And the fire. What is so hypnotic about it? At fire we are the free-spirited beasts of our ancient past.

But present-day cat, a handsome tuxedo, was stirring and singing for his supper. With a small sigh Helen tore herself away.

The Troll doll is a relic of the sixties, but is still around today as a child's toy. One of these three-inch cave man replicas had been left at Helen's house by a grandchild the previous June. Her cat Sampson had discovered it that very day and, ugly though it was, had adopted the Troll as his very own. For unknown reasons he preferred the Troll to all other toys. Looking like Sylvester finally nailing Tweedy Bird, Sampson ravaged Troll nightly. Nevertheless, the hearty Troll retained its eternal grin.

By now Troll's flaming orange hair was tangled and matted. Bite marks covered its arms and legs. Every night it was flung high into the air, pounced on, rolled on, pawed, clawed, bitten and dragged by the hair. Still, the prehistoric beast kept smiling. It could not know it was in for an even more insulting experience, again at the paws of Sampson. Helen did not expect the odd break in routine that eventually occurred.

Diane Arrington

After dinner that night, as it was every night, Helen knew Sampson would manage to schedule into his daily feline agenda some practice Stalk-and-Kill with poor Troll as his target, as usual. She could count on this nightly activity like she could rely on the sun rising and having to scoop the catbox in the morning.

Cat creatures are habit creatures, and every night for almost a year Sampson interacted with Troll. But on this particular night, Sampson did not play with his darling pet. Instead, Sampson lay strangely inactive on Helen's bed.

Sampson was characteristically an outgoing cat, always buzzing, rubbing, talking or something. He was a very busy cat, particularly at bedtime. But this night Sampson acted guilty, as though he were hiding something. Helen's husband Elliot also noticed Sam's strange behavior. The couple dismissed it as just one more inexplicable feline mood swing and turned out the light.

As for Sampson's hiding something, he was — or had.

The next morning Helen went to scoop Sampson's two boxes. Sampson was one of those cats who most often used one box for one thing and the other for the other. Oddly, though, on this particular morning, one of the boxes had not been used for its usual function. Helen was dumbfounded at what she found.

Instead of finding Sampson's leavings, Helen found one brown plastic foot and a clump of orange hair peeking out from beneath the clay granules. To Helen's amazement, Sampson had buried Troll in his litter box! The box was clean except for the doll.

Since the box was clean and had not been used since she changed out the litter the previous night, Helen extracted the doll, shook it off and dropped it on the rug in the den where the horrid thing stayed most of the time.

Sampson's demeanor returned to normal. That very night he abused Troll as always, though Helen thought he played a bit more enthusiastically than normal. Perhaps he had missed the strange-looking critter while it lay buried overnight in his litterbox. Sampson's white-tipped tail flipped and puffed, his whiskers stood straight out from his cheeks and his willow eyes dilated as, for the predestined thirty minutes, he tossed Troll in the air, attacked it and avidly mauled it with tooth and claw.

A few days passed status quo. Then, quite unexpectedly, Helen again found Troll implanted, again in a fresh, clean litterbox. She pulled it to safety, shook the clay from its hair and gave it back. Sampson seemed to love seeing it again and played with it passionately.

A few days later, the cat again assigned Troll to its place beneath the clay.

Over the ensuing few months, Sampson's strange behavior became a regular and annoying ping-pong game between human and cat, burying, rescuing and re-burying Mr. Troll. Sampson entombed his chum, Helen shook it off and gave it back, only to find it once again mysteriously dispatched a few days later.

Sampson never put the doll in a dirty box. Helen and Elliot never saw Sampson carry or bury the doll. Exactly when he did it was Sampson's secret.

Soon the incidents became commonplace enough that Helen could tell when Sampson had temporarily disinherited Troll even before she discovered it in his box. Sampson's behavior changed. He grew quiet and reticent. He lacked his usual luster. His behavior was in sharp contrast to his normally ebullient nature, but she was unable to discern whether Sampson was guilty or lonely. It could have been either or both.

Did Sampson, like a human, tire of Troll's stupid grin? If he had lost his affinity for his comrade, would he have been willing, even eager, to play with it as usual between interments? If Sampson had somehow developed a dislike for Troll, why did he never bury it in a dirty box? This might have been the ultimate feline insult to an item distasteful to a cat.

Housecats are fed like royalty, precluding their need to hunt. Human hands wash, brush and groom them, providing them even more spare time. It is true that domestic cats have little to do but devise methods by which to entertain themselves, their tactics

Diane Arrington

very often annoying to humans. Could this have been Sampson's motivation? Was it simply an inventive device for his own entertainment?

Or, did Sampson truly aspire to rid himself of his partner and then find himself confused that it continued to reappear? Were he endeavoring to destroy the Troll, how disorienting it must have been to find it couldn't be killed. This raises the question of why he did not disown the doll every night, but randomly instead. What ancestral link told him which nights to bury it? And what made him "hide" it in the first place? Why Troll and not another toy, his feathers or fake-fur mouse?

A mental image is unavoidable of Sampson, the black-and-white beauty boy, carrying the ghastly flesh-and-flaming orange Troll to his cat litterbox. He may have set it aside, or he may have held it in his mouth and dangled it by the hair while he dug its grave in the sand. Did he place it into its gravelly grave with tender loving care, or drop it brutally from high in the air before deft and industrious front paws neatly covered it over?

Sampson had never before buried odd items in his box. His odd habit of burying Troll was episodic. When Helen was forced to endure one of Sampson's episodes of burying Troll repeatedly in the space of a few weeks, she could not help but imagine how much simpler life would be if Troll were to accidentally stumble into the fire.

Seventh Sense

Diane Arrington

Chapter 32
Amy and Arnold

The behavior of these two cats shows a remarkable connection between two like species that is very nearly human in nature. It is impossible for humans to predict yet fascinating to see what behaviors, locations or, in this case, objects animals will associate with their love for one another.

Amy and Arnold were littermates. Whelped together, weaned together, adopted together, raised together — and as in love as any two of a species who were altered could be.

Mutual grooming between two cats is a sign of a perfectly-balanced relationship, and a heartwarming thing it is to the human eye. Without provocation, orange tabby Arnold would approach Amy, most often while she was flat on her side in repose. He looped an indiscriminate front leg across her Tortoiseshell shoulders and pinned her to the couch, carpet, bed or whatever other surface she happened to be meditating upon at the time. With green eyes at half mast and quick, sure, loving strokes he washed her face, her ears, the top of her head.

Amy's ochre eyes closed in a heavenly look. She stretched her head back, exposing her throat for him, the ultimate act of feline trust. He purred, she purred in a mixture of love sounds that could be heard across the room. As he began to clean her ears, she tipped up her muzzle and kissed his cheek. Then the two adoring cats would attempt to groom each other simultaneously, twisted together like a live, orange and black pretzel. Soon they would fall asleep, together in a rumbling, dreamy jumble of fur and kitty friendship.

Arnold and Amy played fervently together like two crazed things out of control. They chased and thundered through the apartment at night, Hide-and-Seek and Attack, Pounce-and-Kill and Boo-Cat. These games are not unusual for cats, but few display the one extra ingredient of adoration these two did, which is where their mystery begins.

Arnold loved an odd thing, wax bubble gum wrappers. He stole them wherever he could find them. No one can say what it was about them he was so strongly attracted to — the taste of sugar, the waxy texture perhaps — but Arnold was obsessed. He carried them in his mouth at every opportunity.

His twenty-something owner Judy found the wrappers on his bed, on the carpet, in her bed. Arnold even stole the waxy things back out of the waste can. Arnold would get busted with head, shoulders, arms and chest deep in the receptacle, back feet on tiptoe, shopping for his prized goodies. Rarely did a day pass that Judy did not see Arnold with a wax bubble gum wrapper in his mouth.

Arnold wanted desperately to share his finds with Amy, but little Amy remained aloof and unimpressed with the objects. When he presented a wrapper to her with pride in his ears, she gazed at him with golden-eyed doubt. She took one look at the mangled bit of trash and promptly exited the area, leaving Arnold looking confused and hurt and wondering what to do next. He could not understand why she was not simply thrilled, and routinely became visibly upset over her lack of interest.

Each time Amy refused him he threw himself onto his back. He kicked his feet in the air, indulging himself in either a tantrum or an impassioned plea to return and play with him. Then he stopped kicking and looked sideways after her. For two or three moments he waited for her return, flat on his back, legs spread, orange belly to the sky and wrapper in his mouth. But momentarily spacey Arnold became distracted from his distress by the challenge of juggling the wrapper on his paws in the air above his face without dropping it into his eye. His tantrum was over.

Diane Arrington

It was a Thursday night in August of 1993 when Arnold contracted an illness that required a three-day stay at the vet. What Amy did in his absence surprised and mystified Judy.

Judy left Arn at the vet on a Friday morning. When she returned home, Amy met Judy expectantly at the door. When Judy walked in without Arnold or his carrier, Amy looked befuddled. For forty full minutes she sat staring hopefully at the door. She appeared to anticipate Arnold or his carrier or both to come through just any minute.

Amy finally gave up her guard at the door, but the rest of that day and evening she did not sleep or eat. She paced. She cried. She looked everywhere for Arnold. She checked and re-checked all of Arnold's hiding places. She kept sniffing at his bed. With a tiny paw, she tried to lift it and look underneath. She repeatedly returned to the front door through which Arnold had left and never returned.

Late Friday evening Judy was in bed reading. Amy jumped onto the bed with something in her mouth. Judy was astonished to see what Amy carried. It was a wax bubble gum wrapper!

Neither Judy nor Amy slept much that first night. Throughout the night Amy continued her anxious search for her beloved brother. Saturday morning Amy declined to eat and opted instead to continue her visual search and sound track, calling wretchedly for Arnold. Much of Saturday she spent calling with her mouth full of Arnold's gum wrappers. Judy did her best to comfort Amy, to no avail.

By Sunday Amy was beside herself with worry. She was obsessed with Arnold's absence. She still had not eaten and had slept little. She spent the entire day with a bubble gum wrapper in her mouth. She did not play with it. She simply carried it from room to room throughout the apartment. She set it down, sniffed the air and called for Arnold, then picked it up and carried it to the next room, reenacting her distress in each room.

Judy was glad to see Monday morning. As she left to pick up Arnold, she discovered a strange thing. Just inside the front door, like the Reese's Pieces in the film E.T., Amy had piled at least a dozen bubble gum wrappers. The wrappers were heaped into a mound at the very spot Amy had last seen Arnold.

What was taking place in Amy's mind? She had never shown an interest in gum wrappers before Arnold's disappearance. By what process was she able to choose the one item with which Arnold was so fascinated to act out her anguish?

It appeared to Judy her cat was using a form of reasoning. Amy seemed to think if she showed an interest in the one thing Arnold loved so dearly, if she placed not one but many at the door, Arnold would somehow be lured back to her through that very portal. It even appeared that Amy, like a human would, blamed herself for Arnold's disappearance. She had, after all, refused to participate in his enchantment with the useless clutter.

The obvious love and friendship between the two cats was profound. That Amy connected the gum wrappers with Arnold is fascinating. How she made the three-way connection between her grief, the wrappers and Arnold is a mystery that will never be solved.

Diane Arrington

Chapter 33
Piffles

Wolves in the wild hide edibles to preserve them for later consumption and/or conceal them from competitors. Like their ancestors, domestic dogs also occasionally hide items. This practice is most often associated with food items in high-density populations. Piffles displays a little bit of both preservation and concealment, but her motivations are mysteriously clear. She may not have the most imaginative name on the books, but she would ultimately prove to possess a most imaginative mind.

It was winter in Houston, 1969, back in the days when retail stores still sold puppies by the dozen. Three and one-half Wire-Haired Fox Terrier puppies sat like monkeys in a cage at Foley's. The puppies were eight weeks old.

At feeding time the three big littermates pounced on the food and shoved the little one aside. Moments later, when the food had disappeared, the dwarf female climbed into the empty food bowl.

Just then owner-to-be Elizabeth happened by and could not avoid noticing the plump puppy-in-a-dish carefully eyeing the people who passed by her cage. The youngster appeared to be shopping. *Not you, not you, nope, not you either.* But when she spotted Elizabeth, she seemed to say, *"You! Come here!"* Elizabeth did, and took the small puppy home.

Piffles, the half-puppy, grew into half a dog who was difficult to train, a Sherman tank on walks, and a complainer who muttered and grumbled under her breath when forced to do things she didn't choose to do. From this she developed a habit of "talking" to Elizabeth. She may have been only half a dog, but the other half must have been human.

Diane Arrington

In the evenings Piffles perched herself on the arm of Elizabeth's chair. With her fuzzy face only inches away from Elizabeth's, the loquacious dog looked straight into the woman's eyes and chattered her teeth. This of course brought a verbal response from Elizabeth. Piffles chattered more, then stopped to permit Elizabeth time to talk. Elizabeth talked, Piffles listened. Then Piffles threw her head back and again clacked her teeth, afterwards stopping to "listen." This interchange could persist for twenty or thirty minutes, the dog telling the woman all about her day.

In view of her early experience, Piffles was understandably obsessive-compulsive about food. On one occasion Piffles, being the opportunist all dogs but especially terriers are, nosed open the refrigerator door and efficiently cleaned off the bottom shelf. She did not chew the containers of leftovers she found there but managed to carefully open each one without damage. When Elizabeth discovered the mess, only one edible item remained spilled in a glob on the kitchen floor: a half-cup of leftover spinach, not to any youngster's liking after all.

Piffles loved cocoa. On frequent occasions she surreptitiously absconded one single packet of the delectable, chocolatey stuff. In her mouth she carried it high onto the bed where the other dogs she lived with might not discover her. With her teeth she ripped the treasure carefully, so as not to spill a nip. She ate thoroughly, rejoicing in every last particle of dust. There on the bed, her curly white coat visibly standing out with joy, she licked the foil package whistle-clean, and smacked her lips in satisfaction.

On certain previous occasions in her life together with Piffles, Elizabeth had seen the little dog attempt to bury food items in the carpet. Dog biscuits, chew sticks and such, all unsuccessfully, of course. Invariably one of the other, larger dogs wandered through the room and, to Piffles' dismay, her meticulously camouflaged treat was history.

Seventh Sense

After eighteen months in a multi-pet household, Piffles devised the perfect solution to perpetuating her eating disorder.

On a Saturday in early spring 1970, the sun was shining brilliance. Outside, cheery birds heralded the coming of warmth and longer days. Elizabeth had spent the morning cleaning house. After her work she had just stretched out on the bed for a short nap when she heard a soft, almost imperceptible noise in the room. It came from near the closet door. It was the kind of noise one senses rather than actually hears. Quietly, Elizabeth raised up on her elbows to look. What she saw surprised her.

It was Piffles, and she was sneaking. Slightly crouched, the little dog entered the room slowly, walking step-by-step on soft dog paws. She tiptoed to the closet door, clearly unaware she was being observed. The stubby dog could not see Elizabeth above her, watching from the bed. Stealthily, Piffles looked first to one side, then the other, then over her shoulder at the bedroom door.

Satisfied not a soul would witness her cleverness, Piffles nosed open the unlatched closet door. She disappeared inside. Elizabeth could hear the little terrier rummaging around in the depths of the closet. She waited.

After a few moments Piffles reappeared — with something to eat. She quickly chowed down, the way a human compulsive eater sneaks a midnight snack from the fridge. Her mustache literally quivered with pleasure, and with her pink tongue she licked from it all lingering evidence. She glanced back at the closet, then skipped hastily from the room with a smile on her face, as though she had gotten away with something incredibly sinful.

Unbearably curious, Elizabeth rose and scouted inside the closet, a carpeted area about eight feet square. Stashed safely away in the far back corner, behind shoes and bags and long dresses hanging from the rod high above, Elizabeth peered into the dark corner. What she found there pushed the limits of human believability. There, in the darkness of her closet, Elizabeth discovered a pile of food items expansive and varied enough to keep a dog Piffles' size alive for three months. Containing particulars from seasons earlier, it was an unbelievable stash.

The most interesting item was from the previous Christmas, a gift pack containing six different varieties of dried fruit. Elizabeth remembered receiving the gift, but could neither pinpoint nor recall its disappearance.

But Piffles could, and had known exactly where it was. She, personally, had hidden it months earlier in the closet. From it she had just consumed a powdered sugar date.

Piffles' cache contained milk biscuits, Snausages, potato chips, taco chips, loose kernels of popped popcorn, a cellophane-wrapped sucker, a stick of Juicy Fruit chewing gum. There was some regular dry kibble and a piece of cat dirt covered in clay, evidently swiped from the litterbox at some point in the far distant past. There was a lemon peel and a piece of butterscotch candy. Chew strips of all kinds were sprinkled in to complete the mixture, along with many, many items unrecognizable.

That Piffles managed to successfully smuggle and conceal so many items may not be an insurmountable task for a clever dog. But why did she not eat the items when she found them? She readily consumed other items on sight. By what mental mechanism did Piffles decide which items would make for good storage? How was she able to hide her stash from the other dogs who most likely possessed a sense of smell superior to hers? Did she use distraction to trick them away from the area should they chance to come near her secret zone?

Most mysterious of all is the mechanism that dictated to Piffles' canine mind when to steal an opportunity to have a snack. Was it intellectual, a simple decision as a human would decide to enjoy a particular activity? Was it visceral, determined simply by the fact that she was hungry? Or was it circumstantial, influenced by the presence or non-presence of others, dog or human?

Seventh Sense

When you consider the planning, the scheming, the divisiveness required from a mere dog, Piffles' behavior is fascinating. Her motivation is not the mystery. The mystery is her clear awareness of the necessity for secrecy. Mysterious as well is her capacity for attention to detail in order to successfully pull off her caper month after month after month.

From this story one supposes that even a dog can overcome all odds in order to satisfy an addiction.

Piffles. A dog with an eating disorder, and a dog clever enough to devise a plan to support her habit.

Diane Arrington

Docktale 9
Obie

Obie, a luxurious though skittish silver Persian cat, was having problems using his litterbox correctly. In fact, he wasn't using it at all.

One day Obie was cat-napping in his favorite place, crammed inside the 8x8x8-inch sink at the wet bar. Thirteen-pound Obie was a comical sight jammed into the tiny stainless steel compartment. The sink appeared to be stuffed only with cat hair. No head, paws, tail, ears or whiskers were distinguishable.

Husband-wife owners sat in the same room, fifteen feet away, discussing Obie's behavior problem. In the spirit of pure facetiousness, Mike said, "*Let's box up the blue cat and send him off to your mother's.*" He was, of course, referring to Obie.

What happened next was eery.

Suddenly, like a jack-in-the-box or a gopher popping out of his hole, a shocked face appeared from the nest of fur in the sink. Obie took one horrified look at Mike and bolted. He leaped to the floor and tore across the house for the laundry room.

There Obie hid behind the washer, trembling and terrified, refusing to come out for several hours. He dropped his hair in gobs, a sure sign of extreme feline anxiety, and even skipped dinner, a First Event for hefty Obie.

Mike had not used Obie's name. How had Obie understood a threat that was only implied? How did he know it was meant for him? Can a cat possibly know what color he is? Most intriguing, how was Obie able to recognize as peril such an abstract concept, that to box him up and send him off to Grandma's would be a bad thing?

Or had some wayward, vicious flea simply nipped poor Obie under the tail at that precise moment in his life?

It's a mystery, a mystery that took Obie almost a full day to get over.

Seventh Sense

Diane Arrington

Chapter 34
Rosie

Rosie was an unusual bird. All parrots are unusual in the sense that they are able to speak human language despite what that race considers limited vocal abilities. Rosie, however, had a capacity to mimic that far exceeds the capacity of even the most advanced human technology. Rosie took her talents to the extreme, far beyond human tolerance for a pet bird.

Rosie was four. Her vivid color and plumage were outdone only by an edgy sense of humor. The Double Yellow-Headed Macaw was purchased in a pet store at the age of six months and taken to live with two dogs, a cat and one other parrot.

Rosie didn't say much the first year in Anna's house. It was at the end of that year that Anna discovered why Rosie may have been up for sale. Turns out Rosie wasn't shy, she was watching and listening — and learning. Like the late-speaking child whose first words are multi-syllabic, Rosie shocked everyone.

One day when Rosie was eighteen months old the phone rang in the kitchen where Rosie's cage was kept. Housekeeper Maria was alone in the house. She answered the phone, and got a dial tone. Later, it rang again. Maria answered. No one was calling. Three times that day Maria answered the phone to hear nothing but a dial tone. Two days later the phone rang twice before Anna picked it up. She reached to answer it. BZZZZZ, said the earpiece.

A week later on a foggy April morning Anna was in the sewing room of the huge, sprawling house, just off the kitchen. It was 10:15 a.m. Anna's husband Frank was away at work. Maria was laundering clothes in a room on the opposite side of the

Seventh Sense

kitchen. The house was quiet as all the animals napped. Or so the humans assumed.

Suddenly, from her sewing room, Anna heard the squeaky door leading from the garage into the kitchen. She reminded herself for the hundredth time to ask the houseboy to oil it. She thought it odd for Maria to be in the garage.

Then the door slammed. Maria thought it certainly could not be quiet, shy Maria who would never in the world let a door slam behind her. Then Anna heard her husband's footsteps. It was odd for him to be home in the daytime. She started to call out to him but heard him whistling, a constant practice of his. Anna came from the sewing room with a frown and a smile, at once worried something might be wrong and pleased to see Frank in the middle of the day.

But Frank was not there.

Anna checked the garage. Frank's car was not there. She asked Maria if she had heard Frank come in. She had. The two women looked at each other, then at Rosie. On her perch inside her elaborate cage, Rosie was silent as snow. She shifted her weight on her scaly feet and returned their gaze with an innocent one of her own. *Moi?*

A few days passed. The following Wednesday Anna was reading in the den. She heard the back door squeak open and she heard it close. She heard Frank's footsteps. She heard him whistling again. But this time Frank called, *"Anna? You home?"* Then silence. The absence of sound. No keys, no parcels, no more footsteps.

Anna headed for the kitchen with an expectant smile. The smile faded abruptly. Frank was not there. Maria and Anna entered the main kitchen simultaneously. It was empty except for Rosie. Again the two women exchanged eye contact. Again they looked at Rosie. This time Rosie exploded in laughter. The laughter, however, was eery — it was Anna's laugh in Anna's voice.

As the weeks went by Rosie began to imitate more things in her environment. The phone was her favorite. To watch humans pick it up and answer it seemed to give dear Rosie a satisfying sense of power. She played this trick on the family six, seven times a day. Even Frank was fooled into answering the phone.

Rosie imitated the beep of the microwave. She mimicked the soft, squishy sound of rubber-on-rubber as the refrigerator door opened and closed. She copied the rusty squeak of the oven door. She imitated the voices and the laughter of all humans in the house. She imitated the dogs barking and the cat meowing. Rosie cloned any sound she could get her voice on.

Like a rotten child, Rosie antagonized her family nearly every day month after month after month. Often it was funny, occasionally it was curious, mostly it was annoying. Eventually Rosie found she could not only torture humans with her skills, she could also torment the dogs.

Using either Frank's voice or Anna's voice, Rosie called the dogs into the kitchen. They came running. Then Rosie sat smugly silent in her feathers, gazing down her beak on two dogs looking quizzically about the kitchen, their tails waving confusion.

Other times when the dogs rushed obediently to her call, Rosie laughed hysterically at them in her own voice. Still other times she told them sternly to sit, which they did. After a few of Rosie's more creative days, the dogs were exhausted by mid-afternoon — because Rosie could throw her voice, too.

She threw her voice to the bedroom, calling the dogs in Anna's voice. The eager, obedient dogs galloped full speed the eighth-mile all the way to the back of the looming house. Then the evil bird called them from the kitchen in Maria's voice. They turned round and ran like lunatics all the way back through the house to the kitchen. This not only wore them out, it ruined their training. They stopped coming when called because it never paid off.

But Rosie's ultimate was her tormenting of Shadow, a stunning but pitifully shy German Shepherd. Shadow was so fearful he was even afraid of the family cat who had never mistreated him in any way. It was speculated that Shadow's shyness may have been caused in part by Rosie confusing him daily for a year. The poor dog never knew what to expect next.

It was a summer afternoon when a trainer was at the house working with Shadow. By this point in time Rosie's imitations were raucous and rude and undisguised, carried out almost with an air of pride.

The trainer finished with Shadow and permitted him to return to the kitchen, his safe haven, for a water break. Shadow drank, but at that moment the cat walked in. Shadow spotted her out of the corner of his eye and dove under the kitchen desk, water still streaming from his mouth. The big Shepherd crouched there, trembling, jammed behind the chair, to let the cat pass.

And then the unthinkable happened.

At that moment Anna heard it, Maria heard it and the trainer heard it. Rosie said clearly, in her own voice, *"Awk! Shadow afraid! Shadow hiding! Ha ha ha ha!"*

With four simple words, Rosie astonished a household. That her observations were a fortuitous coincidence of timing is too remote an idea to entertain. Rosie identified both Shadow's outward behavior and his internal motivation for that behavior.

How was Rosie able to identify the *dog's* emotions? She observed his behavior and accurately identified his cause of action — in English. And how does a parrot know what "hiding" is? Infant parrots do not play hide and seek as puppies and particularly kittens are prone to do. What in Rosie's natural ancestry, what in her intrinsic behavior, would have taught her to recognize and identify "hiding" as it is defined in the English language? Rosie had not been trained in any way. Her expressions were purely spontaneous, and it boggles the human mind

For a parrot, a celebrated imitator, to copy the human voice or laugh or whistle is feasible. But how was Rosie able to imitate other sounds so precisely? How was she able to fool a wife into thinking she had heard her husband's voice? Even for a parrot, the ability to imitate the full tonality of today's electronic phones

Diane Arrington

so accurately it fills a room, so convincingly it fools the human ear and even the brain into actually answering the phone is almost impossible to believe. The squeak of the garage door, the rubbery whisper of a refrigerator door, the heavy, metallic sound of the oven door, the footsteps — these sounds have low tonalities that are more vibration than actual, reproducible sound, at least with parrot vocal equipment.

And why did Rosie do it? Was her motivation conscious manipulation, or simply the entertainment of choice for an intelligent bird like Rosie? No one can say until Rosie does.

The only thing Anna's family knew with certainty was that life with Rosie would never be dull. They knew they would be challenged forevermore to separate reality from Rosie's recreation.

Seventh Sense

Diane Arrington

Chapter 35
Gretchen

The canine grasp and understanding of the spoken word is seldom assumed outside the context of dog obedience training. Gretchen's story suggests language is one aspect of canines the human race might be well-advised to consider more seriously. Throughout her life Gretchen showed an uncanny ability to not only comprehend but internalize the most off-handed human remark.

On a searing Friday afternoon in Texas, Mara, Terri and six-year-old Gretchen greeted their friend Josey at the door. Come in, come in, do have a seat. Smiles and hugs passed warmly, and refreshments were presented.

"*Gretchen,*" Mara spoke, "*this is Josey. She'll be staying with you while I'm away this weekend.*"

Young Gretchen looked at Josey, smiled, walked directly to her and put her head in Josey's lap. Not so amazing for a six-year-old, except that Gretchen was a dog.

Every day across the world dogs are either taught or learn by exposure and repetition the human lexicon. In any language, in any country, in many situations, dogs are seen to recognize and understand frequently-used phrases without having been taught them in the atmosphere of operant conditioning.

Every dog owner has seen evidence of this ability in their own dog's response to such phrases as "*want to go out, go for a walk, time for your bath, where's the squirrel, go in the car, get your ball, go to your bed.*" Family pets frequently understand and act on these suggestions. These situations occur daily at the very least. The use of repetition, the same words and the owner's

Seventh Sense

same ensuing behavior all explain how dogs learn the meaning of the words and phrases. It is not a mystery that they do so.

Gretchen, however, appeared to understand new word combinations. A casual word, a random phrase, a chance encounter with a brand new situation — Gretchen seemed to grasp human concept the first time out. This is the mysterious and unexplained of Gretchen's behavior. She appeared to interpret thoughts and ideas with the same subtlety and discerning as would a human being.

A muscular Chesapeake Bay retriever, Gretchen was an exceptional dog both in terms of learning capability and cognitive adaptability. She did well in obedience class, but breaking down her iron will without crushing her marvelous spirit was the tricky part.

One of the qualities humans love so very much about dogs is the delightful sense of humor which thrives inside nearly each and every one of them. Except Gretchen. When it came to her personal agenda, she had zilch, zip, nada. Gretchen wagged her tail plenty — for greeting, for play, for excitement — but she was a serious dog who seldom smiled. She was not stoic, just a bit cranky upon occasion.

It should be noted that Gretchen was not without redemption. While she may have had no sense of humor on issues she deemed important, she occasionally seemed to think it was hilariously funny when her owner asked her to Sit or Stay. Often, when she did not see any particular reason for the request, she put her nose in the air, opened her mouth wide in a wise, gaping grin — and refused to obey.

Gretchen's owners, roommates Mara and Terri, frequently enjoyed recreational camping. When they went, the dogs were rarely left behind. One Labor Day weekend in 1990 they were packing the camper for a three-day trip to the Arkansas foothills.

While carrying tents, sleeping bags and lanterns from the house to the truck, the girls laughed and joked in the spirit of vacation. The other dogs, Gretchen's roommates, milled about the driveway and house, participating in the activity and excitement. Not Gretchen. The worried dog trailed Mara as though tied with a two-foot rope to her ankle. Mara joked with Gretchen, trying to cheer her.

"*Aw, Gretchen, I'm so sorry. You can't go this time. You'll have to stay home all by yourself.*" It was innocent teasing without a hint of ill-will in her inflection. But Gretchen was not a dog who appreciated sarcasm.

She looked at Mara, a startled look of surprise in her deep brown eyes. With barely a hesitation she spun around, raced to the truck, leaped in through the open passenger door and scrambled into the back seat.

Mara followed her to the truck and peered in. Gretchen sat centered in the back seat, equidistant from either exit door. Her yellow ears were pinned down. Her heartfelt eyes were huge with worry. She whined softly and looked into Mara's eyes. Mara explained that she had only been kidding and asked her to come out. Gretchen wasn't buying it. She only trembled and cried and stayed put.

Gretchen refused to come out of the camper for any reason. No amount of persuasion or food bribes could convince the unhappy Retriever to move from her spot. She was not about to be left behind. It was hours before the trip commenced, but Gretchen stayed glued to the vehicle she knew would carry her humans away.

Mara and Terri at first thought Gretchen's response to their innocent teasing was funny, so unexpected and overdone was it. But Gretchen was not amused. She just sat and shook and cried. She would not even stand up on the seat until the entourage departed.

The words that produced such an emotionally-fraught reaction from Gretchen had on no previous occasion been spoken to her. She had had no previous occasion from which to learn these words were threatening. Gretchen's behavior proved, without question, that she had understood the meaning of the words. It is curious why she understood the first part, however, and did not seem to understand the apology.

Similar incidents of clarity were common in life with Gretchen.

One of Gretchen's favorite games was, as one might expect of a Retriever, retrieving. With the aplomb of an Olympic athlete, Gretchen fetched any item her owners were kind enough to throw for her. By far her favorite was a frisbee flung far out over the water. She delighted in pitching herself in the water, no matter how chilly, and swimming mightily for the brightly-colored disc. Her powerful tail ruddered her through the water like a well-oiled canoe. Her muscles rippled and her coat glistened liquid gold as she pulled herself ashore. She dropped the frisbee, shook herself dry with gusto, and stood flexed and ready for another run.

That same Labor Day weekend at the campgrounds, Terri played frisbee with Gretchen. The other dogs tried to play, but Gretchen was the fastest and the strongest and always got there first. Possessed of a competitive spirit, Gretchen seemed to take pride in being best at the game.

At one point Gretchen lost sight of the frisbee. With the sunlight bright and her vantage point low in the water, the big dog could not see the flat saucer floating on the surface. Behind her from shore Terri shouted, "*Gretchen! Look left!*" Gretchen immediately looked to her left, swam directly to the frisbee and retrieved it forthwith.

Directional commands, like obedience commands, are taught to dogs every day. Taught. It's a time-consuming human undertaking and an abstract lesson for the canine mind. But it is customarily a learned response, acquired after weeks of repetition and reward.

Gretchen had never been taught directional commands or any similar command at any point in her life, nor had she been given such commands, even off-handedly. Yet she understood and proved it through her behavioral response.

Diane Arrington

On all three occasions Gretchen interpreted accurately and acted upon, without hesitation, the context of human words. How did she know what the words meant? How was she able to ascertain an appropriate response? Her owners had not a clue, but these startling enigmas in Gretchen's behavior, her ability to discern and interpret human vocabulary, continued to occur for the whole of Gretchen's life. One thing was certain. Einstein Gretchen kept her owners well on their toes and watching their words.

Seventh Sense

Diane Arrington

Chapter 36
Kate

Among canines, digging is a natural though often unacceptable instinct. It originated with wolves in the wild many thousands of years ago. Today's domestic dogs have their reasons for digging, too. Kate's reasons resemble the wolf's only in the most remote and distant way.

She was all girl. She was pretty, as her name implies, and she seemed to know it. She used her chocolate-drop eyes the way any woman would. She flirted. She begged. She was shy one minute, bold the next, funny still the next.

Kate's gold-white fur dripped like icicles off her tail and haunches. She weighed thirty-five pounds, and was smart as a whip. She was so perfectly feminine and sweet, it didn't occur to observers that she was actually a dog. But Kate was, and she possessed the most basic of instincts which she took to mysterious extremes.

At the age of six months Kate was dumped at a Dallas shelter by her first owner. She narrowly escaped death because Susan adopted her in the nick of time. But a few weeks after Susan took her home, after Kate got comfortable with her new surroundings, Susan discovered why Kate may have been abandoned. It wasn't enough that she was already upsetting the trash, jumping and chewing destructively. Kate started digging.

Digging is a dog habit of which there are many kinds with many reasons and causes. Spot-digging resembles golf divots and takes place over a wide area, as if the dog were searching for buried nuts, seeds or grubworms (Squirrel Dog). Cooling holes, generally the size of the dog doing the digging, are shallow and located under brush or against a building (Hot Dog). Construction Dogs dig ditches, areas large enough to install a swimming pool, and China Dogs dig deep, narrow post holes. Kate chose to combine the latter two.

Kate dug holes not only large in circumference, but holes two and three feet deep. An occasional glance out the rear kitchen window would often provide the looker a glimpse of Kate's elegant tail sticking straight up out of the ground like a golden willow sapling. Kate dug holes big enough and deep enough to bury herself. Her reason for digging the holes is Kate's mystery.

Susan began to notice that when she gave Kate a chew, the dog invariably scurried directly outside with it. She assumed Kate simply held a preference for doing her chewing outdoors. It did not strike her as odd that she never saw the chews again.

Day after day, Susan arrived home from work to find trash spread generously across the kitchen and fresh dirt flung wide across the yard. After several weeks of trying to discover a cause for Kate's digging, Susan eventually happened on an opportunity to watch through the window her four-legged genius at work.

Early on a sweet September Saturday, Susan watched as Kate raced outside with her new chewy in her mouth. The nighttime dew had moistened the grass and dampened the earth. With her small black nose sniffing frantically, Kate eagerly scoured her yard. At last she appeared to decide on the perfect location. She set the chew delicately on the ground right beside the proposed excavation site. Then Kate began to dig.

And dig she did. Deeper and deeper she went as Susan watched. Soon Kate's head was invisible below the surface of the ground. Then her shoulders disappeared. Never did Kate hesitate or take a break. Anyone could have walked right up behind her, so focused was she. She was a dog with a purpose. The minutes trickled by as the earth flew. Through her skinny rear legs dirt gradually piled higher, covering her back feet and swelling to a mound bigger than a Rottweiler. Kate was a digging machine.

Then, all at once, she stopped. She turned and addressed the chew. She picked it up gently, lovingly, in her mouth. With utmost care, Kate held the chew directly over the center of the hole and opened her mouth, deliberately dropping the chew into the hole. The hole was so deep, Kate watched a moment until the chew finally landed, a dog depending on gravity.

Next, Kate became the Earth Mover. Patiently, she began the overwhelming task of moving the mountain of dirt back into the hole. This part of the process took her a good while. Most of the time she moved the dirt with her small muzzle. Occasionally, apparently when rushed, she turned her back on the hole, straddled it with her rear legs, and, using both front paws, pushed the dirt in backwards. Other times she stood beside the pile and swept her paws sideways, scraping and scooping the dirt the way a human would, one hand at a time. Gradually the crater shrank.

When Kate felt the job was complete, she used her dusty black nose to tidy up, actually patting down the fresh dirt on top. Making sure the job was done to her satisfaction, she stood back to admire her work. The whole process took twenty-six minutes. Then Kate turned away. Tail wagging high and proud, she scampered across the yard and burst through her dog door — only to beg another chew.

Because Kate was not always careful about filling in the holes, Susan was eventually able to discover the most mysterious thing of all. With some sleuthy investigation and much digging by hand, Susan found why Kate dug her gigantic holes. True, she buried chews and bones in the holes. But more often Kate dug holes the size of Rhode Island to bury tidbits no bigger than a zygote.

Susan could understand a dog burying a chew, of course, or a bone. It's instinct, she knew. A biscuit, okay, or a meat-scented nylon bone. But Kate dug holes expansive enough to bury a goat in order to inter a bit of foil no bigger than her dewclaw. She excavated a gargantuan pit in the lawn only to drop in a meat-soaked piece of string with the dimensions of an inchworm.

Kate buried the tiniest treasures, and almost anything qualified as a treasure. A pecan, a peach pit, a Wheat Thin. The corner of a paper towel, a chunk of pizza crust equal in size to a

AA battery, a pea-sized wad of plastic wrap, a broken bit of Styrofoam from the grocery meat department. Anything with food potential got buried deeply and well. These miniature things Kate honored by digging to China.

Nature provides animals with an efficiency borne only by those who survive. In the wild, the perilous fight for survival puts one who spends too much time at any one task at risk. The shallowest indentation or depression serves to hide the largest carcass. Where did Miss Kate miss the train?

Why would Kate think it necessary to dig such hulking huge holes to bury infinitesimal items, tidbits the size of a watch battery or a computer chip, barely large enough to be held between human thumb and forefinger? When you consider what a dog's mouth can do to a flea, it may not be surprising that she could handle the items without losing them.

But why would articles that to the human mind are senseless bits of nothing take on such strong significance to Kate? Puppies have an interest in things wee, but they grow out of it. Could it be that the treasures were not truly treasures but served only as an excuse to excavate? Was hole-digging simply a form of exercise, entertainment or general recreation for Kate? And how did Kate decide when the hole was large enough, when to stop digging and drop the item in?

Our questions won't be answered until Kate learns to speak English. What is known is that Kate met a bit of foil the way she met life itself, with inimitable enthusiasm.

Diane Arrington

Chapter 37
Noel

If all living things are kindred, why not humans playing fetch and dogs playing golf? To at least one dog in the world this makes perfect sense. Noel's mystery lies both in what she does and in where she may have gathered her idea of the most perfect form of self-entertainment. Was it strictly imaginative, born of her mind and nothing else, or was it from watching TV? Therein lies the mystery.

Noel was a smart-looking black-and-tan Yorkshire Terrier puppy just over a year old, and a fancy, lively, busy thing she was. She lived in a luxury high-rise with her two owners, Joan and Larry. Noel seemed to look at you not with her eyes, but with her exquisite eyelashes. Originally a Christmas puppy, she was a round-eyed, sweet-faced electron. She had a cavorting style to her walk, sassy as a circus dog. She was an avid fan of the Indianapolis 500 and liked to pretend she was a contestant, speeding through the house around furniture and through table legs at 120 mph. Indy Dog.

Noel was an only pet. Both Joan and Larry worked days, outside the home. Except for her confinement to a bedroom during the day, Noel was given free reign over humans and surroundings. She was the typically spoiled Yorkshire terrier who had little need for legs of her own; human legs took her where she wanted to go.

Noel was hyper-reactive to external noises, which made her a noisy dog. She had no concept of how small she really was. Like her terrier cousins, Noel was fearless. Beneath her topknot tied with a little red bow, she fiercely stood her ground against the toughest Bulldog or largest Great Dane she might encounter in hallways or elevator. She did not imagine she might be

Diane Arrington

perceived by such large dogs as not a real dog, but simply an hors d'oeuvre. Stretching to her full height like David to Goliath, Noel would bark up at them with all her might. Mighty Mouse in-your-face.

Over her year of life Noel had developed the annoying habits of barking at everything she heard and snapping at her owners when they did things of which she did not approve, such as reaching for her while she was lounging on the sofa or in their bed. At night, Larry was having a problem getting into bed with his own wife. Noel had designated the wife and the bed as her own. He, apparently, was not allowed.

But despite her behavior problems, which to the casual eye might deem her unlikable, Noel was playful and happy. She was not intrinsically aggressive, she was bored. Her problems stemmed only from the fact that she was not getting enough stimulation in her life. She was too smart to be kept as a stuffed toy with no education, limitations or rules to follow.

Noel's behavior program involved the use of a body harness that would not choke her, and a trailing rope to give Larry and Joan immediate control over Noel's barking at people passing by the door. Uncharacteristically for a dog who does not cotton to restraint, Noel fell in love with her harness. When Joan presented the tiny halter the little dog eagerly pushed her head up through it. She wore it proudly, as a nouveau riche might wear her first ultrasuede coat.

Noel's control rope was made of smooth but stiff nylon, one-half inch diameter and about ten feet in length. To keep it from unraveling, Larry had wrapped the end with tape. This made it even stiffer and enlarged at the end, club-like. It was how Noel chose to put the rope and ball to work for her and the novel game she invented that resulted in her fully unexpected behavior.

One night around the Easter holiday Joan and Larry had lots to do. Business was good, and both of them often took work home. Noel was wresting about after a day of being confined alone in her room. One little walk outside at six p.m. had not been enough for energy-packed Noel. She began to pester Joan and Larry to play ball. They dutifully tossed the ball a few times, then quit. It wasn't enough. Noel annoyed them. They threw the ball again for a few minutes. Still not enough. At her third request, they flatly refused.

Undaunted, Noel devised her own game.

She took her rope in her mouth, not in the middle but a few inches back from the end. Because the rope was stiff, this grasp formed a four-inch "club." With her club in her mouth she addressed her ball, a red rubber one the size of a golf ball.

With one great shake of her tiny head and with perfect aim, she slapped the ball with the rope. This projected the ball across the rug, giving her a chance to chase her beloved toy. She flew across the carpet, pounced on the ball, tossed it gleefully into the air, caught it on the fly, dashed it to the floor and dove on it, executing the final coup de grace.

Finished with one round, she turned and trotted back to the end of her rope lying on the carpet. She picked it up and carried it to her ball. Again she grasped the rope in her teeth leaving about three or four inches free at the end. Again she swung her head and swatted the ball with the rope. The ball flew across the rug with Noel in avid pursuit.

Nobody would propel the ball for her, so the ingenious little dog found a way to propel it for herself.

One interesting aspect of Noel's golf games was the accuracy with which she was able to bat the ball. Because Joan refused to believe that Noel was a natural-born golfer, she surmised that Noel had invented the game while alone during the day as a simple result of idle boredom. It was too much to believe that Noel had not had some practice, that the game was the result of spontaneous generation. Noel never missed the ball with the club, never had a whiffer.

It is also curious to note that Noel never attempted to play golf with her tennis ball, which would be too heavy to move with the thin rope. It must be presumed that Noel, through trial-and-error, had discovered that fact on her own, unwitnessed by the

Diane Arrington

human eye. Noel played golf for long periods of time, but only with balls the size of golf balls light enough to be highly motivated by the rope. This ostensibly provided the best chase. In the evenings, after hours of providing her own entertainment, Noel was exhausted and fell out for a well-deserved nap.

Whether Noel was a canine frustrated at not being able to play real golf, or whether she was a famous golfer reincarnated, she chose a convenient form of self-entertainment. Noel and human golfers may after all be kindred spirits, because Noel could play hours and hours and hours on end, hardly tiring, regardless of weather or carpet conditions.

Tiger Woods, beware!

Seventh Sense

Diane Arrington

Chapter 38
Fergie

There is increasing evidence that cats, dogs and other animal species really do understand, if not what humans say, at least what they mean. Fergie is a prime example. After reading Fergie's story, humans might be encouraged to more often try reason in the management of their own pets.

Fergie was a dignified, sophisticated and independent kind of cat who knew what she wanted and made it clear to everyone around her. Fergie was adopted from a shelter as a tiny, fuzzy kitten. The mixed black-and-tan tabby and her owner Kelly had shared a one-bedroom apartment in Plano, Texas for about two years before Fergie displayed most mysterious but thrilling evidence of feline understanding.

Like all cats, Fergie had different voices for different requests, and she utilized each to maximum potential. If she wanted out, she went to the door and meowed, looking back over her shoulder at Kelly. If she wanted wet food, she used a different voice. If she wanted a treat, she used a third call with differing tonal inflections from the others. A new voice announced when it was time for play, and still another combined with soft purring expressed a need for affection.

All this is not unusual for cats. Kelly understood Fergie, but never, until one soft spring morning in 1993, did Kelly imagine that Fergie could so clearly understand her.

Fergie had somehow contracted a urinary tract infection, common within the feline species. Treatment required a ten-day regimen of antibiotics. This is not the most pleasant-tasting medicine on the market, but its administration was necessary to Fergie's recovery.

The first morning, before leaving for work, Kelly tried to give Fergie her pill by opening the cat's mouth and dropping the pill to the back of her throat the way she had seen the vet do so quickly and efficiently. But as any cat owner knows, and as Kelly quickly discovered, medicating the feline is not easy for the inexperienced. Particularly with a cat like Fergie, it was just not that simple for Kelly.

From the very first morning, Fergie fought her medication tooth and claw. She developed a suspiciously sudden case of lockjaw. Her body became stiff and unyielding. Twenty minutes later, scratched and bleeding, Kelly gave up. Fergie did not get her medication that day. Hoping for better luck the next day, Kelly left late for work.

But the second day was an instant replay of the first, and still a third day went by with Kelly unsuccessful at medicating her hard-headed cat. The situation had reached the point of morning ritual wrestling between woman and cat.

Kelly was at least able to get the pill into Fergie's small feline mouth and hold it shut for what seemed like forever. But when Kelly released her grip the pill came rolling out, wet and mangled, ejected by one unhappy cat. One more pill rendered useless, one more day without medication, one more day Kelly was late for work. She had no better luck in the evenings.

Then a strange thing happened.

On the morning of the fourth day Kelly had yet to succeed at getting the medicine into Fergie and keeping it there. Still, she diligently entered combat once again. They were on the bed. Fergie did not run from Kelly; she simply refused to have a dry old pill forced down her throat. She seemed to derive some perverse pleasure in emerging victorious from these daily tete-a-tetes.

Once again Kelly tried, Fergie fought, Kelly gave up, rested, and started again. After ten minutes of struggling, Kelly tired before Fergie. Her concern for her cat's health and welfare finally led to exasperation. She put the pill on the flat of her hand

and extended it to Fergie, showing the cat the harmless little yellow pill.

"*Look, Fergie,*" she panted, "*it's just a pill. Why don't you just take it?*"

Fergie sat perfectly still. She stuck her chin in the air and looked away, her whiskers stiff and unrelenting.

"*Fergie,*" Kelly said evenly.

With golden eyes Fergie looked down her nose at the pill on Kelly's palm. Then suddenly, to Kelly's astonishment, Fergie leaned forward, sniffed the pill and, amazingly, downed it in one gulp.

But that's not all.

From that moment forward, Fergie voluntarily consumed any medication Kelly offered. Years later she continued to cooperate. Kelly had only to put the pill on her hand, show it to Fergie, and Fergie scarfed it up as if it were a yummy treat.

It is obvious Fergie knew what Kelly meant that morning in spring, but *how* did she know? It is not a generally accepted notion that cats can comprehend the human language. Could it be Fergie knew from the start what Kelly intended but was simply holding out for a little respect? Indeed, while sometimes necessary, it must be an uncomfortable, even distasteful experience for a cat to have her mouth forced open, a finger shoved down her throat and her face held shut until she swallows.

The most intriguing possibility of all to consider is whether Fergie could actually have been teaching Kelly, hanging in until Kelly figured out what Fergie was trying to tell her. After all, she did not run from Kelly, and medicating the cat was never again a problem in Kelly's life with Fergie. Was Fergie Kelly's teacher? The traditional method did not succeed with Fergie; a pioneering approach, human style, did.

How distressingly simple it all was in the end.

Seventh Sense

Diane Arrington

Docktale 10
Holly

Holly the Collie deserves a mention for her remarkable abduction abilities.

A canine kleptomaniac, Holly could make disappear one potato chip from the bowl on the coffee table during a party without dislodging a single other chip. No big deal, right? Wrong. Holly actually premeditated.

With the bowl at face level, most dogs would stand and scarf down as much as possible before being caught and stopped. Not Holly. Could a dog possibly know she'd get more by being sneaky?

Holly bore a striking resemblance to Lassie plus forty pounds. She would position herself about ten feet away from the table. With beady amber eyes and a secretive face, the clever dog eyeballed her target. Then she scanned the room full of humans to see if anyone was looking. If anyone was, Holly walked innocently away.

But if Holly discerned that no one was looking, she moved to action. She walked in a way that was consciously nonchalant — not too fast, not too slow — and made a direct pass by the low table. Holly had the expert timing of James Bond. As she sauntered by the bowl full of goodies, she turned her pointed muzzle ever so slightly, latched on to one chip and stayed her course. It was one continuous motion, smooth as honey. Holly never broke stride.

To the casual observer, Holly had simply strolled past the table. But to the avid listener, there came a secret munching sound from the hallway, for that is where Holly paused to consume her ill-gotten gains.

But only a fleeting discontinuance it was. The insatiable dog repeated the process for the duration of the party. If left unapprehended, Holly would annihilate an entire bowl of chips.

Seventh Sense

Holly did not abscond with pretzels, crackers or even taco chips. Potato chips were her addiction.

One wonders if the fact that Holly was a born couch potato had anything to do with her love for potatoes.

Diane Arrington

Chapter 39
Prince

Bred to detect the tiniest scent and trail it, the Beagle is a coursing dog designed to track — on the ground. The Beagle is also a widely social breed, and apparently this instinct, initially at least, overrode Prince's grounded heritage. What made him persist is where his mystery lies.

The year-old Beagle puppy huddled against the damp-gray concrete wall at the back of the cage. He seemed to wonder of his family, the children, the place where he'd spent his childhood. With the loyalty to man instinctive in all dogs, he seemed to pine for the past, neglectful though it had been. This place was noisy and scary. His ears drooped and he shivered.

Two men moved ominously along the aisle formed by the rows of cages, stopping briefly in front of each compartment. The little dog could hear them talking under the deafening vocal staccatos of hundreds of other abandoned and homeless dogs and puppies.

The puppy sat up expectantly as the men approached. The white tip of his tail tapped the cement floor uncertainly as they stopped in front of his cage. They seemed to be deciding something. He heard the word "*sleep.*" Go to sleep or put to sleep, he couldn't tell. But surely they knew sleep was impossible in this noisy, echoey chamber. The puppy was too tired and too frightened even to eat.

What seemed like days but was in fact only hours later, a group of people filed slowly in front of the cells. Humans gaped in at him and poked their fingers through the wire. The puppy stayed where he was, his back pressed against the cold, hard wall.

Then a lady and a man kneeled quietly in front of his cage. They looked directly into his eyes and smiled as if they already knew him. Hesitantly, he got to his feet, his tail held under. Soft, patient voices encouraged him. He tiptoed forward, stopping halfway to scent them, then continued. He allowed these people to scratch his head.

Just then a corpulent, smelly, loud man passed behind the two people. He jerked his head in their direction.

"*That one's gettin' put to sleep this afternoon,*" he stated flatly without stopping.

The couple looked stunned. They looked at the puppy and then at each other.

Suddenly the cage door was opened. Before he knew what was happening, the puppy found himself hugged into loving arms and whisked into a car where he was snuggled into a warm human lap. He promptly and competently fell asleep.

The car ride ended at a big, cozy kitchen. There was a big, soft, cushy dog bed to burrow in. Plenty of food, water, toys and quiet surrounded him. He had no more than 2.3 minutes to marvel at his good luck before delicious sleep overtook him once again.

Ken and Mary Karis of Lewisville, Texas named their new dog Prince. In hindsight they might have named him Jacob.

Prince turned out to be a nosy, comically entertaining dog obsessed with human companionship. He slept on his back in his dog bed with all four legs waving stiffly in the air. He snored like a pig. He spent hours in front of the bunny cage, staring down the Karis' pet rabbit, Linsey. Ken and Mary thought the dog was babysitting the rabbit. Prince knew differently.

Ken and Mary ran a contracting business from their home. At any given time of the day there were five or six subcontractors at the house, picking up or reporting back jobs. The Karis home was an active place. People clustered about constantly. This suited the human-obsessed Prince just fine, and for three years after his adoption he remained fairly normal.

Summer is the time for home improvement. One warm, shady day was chosen to give the split-level home a fresh coat of paint. Prince was four. He was busy burying his newest chew bone beneath a Boxwood bush when, to his delight, six men he recognized showed up. These were friends of his. They called him "Fred" for his appearance and "Regal Beagle" for his tendency to rule the household.

But to the dog's dismay, they filed on past him. With confusion all over his tri-colored face, he watched as one by one each climbed a round-rung aluminum ladder fifteen feet to the roof. Prince bayed and bounced at the foot of the ladder. He stretched his stubby muzzle skyward. It might have appeared strange to a dog to see five men climb into blue sky and puffy white clouds and then disappear. Most distressing to Prince, they had left the ground without him.

High in the air atop the roof the men joked, smoked, and discussed the job they had to do. Suddenly among them was a Beagle. Prince had climbed the ladder after them!

Prince wagged and sniffed them in normal greeting, just as though he had been standing on the lawn. While the men scratched their heads in disbelief, Prince cruised the rooftop, happy to once again be in the company of humans. He did not seek approval nor did he act ashamed. He appeared unafraid, even near the edge of the roof.

Prince was matter-of-fact about his feat of physical accomplishment. To Prince it seemed a most natural thing to climb a ladder to follow your bliss if that's what it took. It was the obsession Prince developed from this random incident that surprised everyone.

The family had been having a mild problem with squirrels on the roof. The arboreal rodents sought the chimney and the skylight over Ken and Mary's bed, presumably to nest.

One summer night as Ken and Mary lay in bed reading, the squirrels were at it again. They heard thumping and scratching on the roof. The sound of investigation. Then clicking, a kind of clawing at the plexiglass bubble-type skylight. All the usual noisiness, and the whining. Whining? They looked at each other. Squirrels don't whine. And they don't work at night.

Diane Arrington

Ken switched on the light and looked up. There, looking in at them through the skylight, was Prince's jowly Beagle face. His ears covered his temples as he looked down upon them in their bedroom. He wrinkled his forehead questioningly. He flattened a tentative paw against the glass and whimpered pathetically.

Someone had forgotten to stash the ladder, which was still leaning against the roof. Prince occasionally slept outside at night, and during that night's security patrol he had discovered the ladder. He had climbed it again. Only he and the gods know why.

Prince grew obsessed with ladder-climbing. He had only one problem, and it was not ascending the ladder. It was that he got stuck up on the roof every time. He could not descend independently and, like a cat stuck in a tree, cried pitifully for help. Since Prince would not be coaxed to the ground, Ken or Mary or one of the others dutifully — and repeatedly — climbed the ladder and carried him down every time.

Human frustration with the situation was intense. Why? Because once he found himself back on solid ground, Prince shook himself in relief, wagged a thank you, wiggled a bit, spotted the ladder and headed straight back up. Day or night, rain or shine, hungry or full, when Prince chanced to find a stray ladder at the roof, he climbed it. He could not seem to help himself. The type of ladder did not matter. Flat step, round-rung, homemade, weak, rickety or sturdy, Prince went up it. Invariably he was stranded and couldn't get down. Invariably someone had to climb the ladder after him and carry him down.

Prince climbed the ladder approximately twenty times in the space of two years, not counting the parties at which Prince's trick was the entertainment of choice. And, it seemed there was always a reason for a ladder. In the summer there were roof repairs and window-cleaning that required a ladder. In the fall there were gutters to be cleaned. Winter meant Christmas lights and chimney-sweeping. In spring there was painting to do and gutters again.

There were days when Prince spent hours stuck on the roof until someone came to his rescue. Many times Mary came home to see Prince wandering or, even more bizarre, napping blissfully unconcerned in the sun — on the roof. Neighbors phoned to roll their eyes and snicker, *"Your dog is on the roof again."*

Why would a dog become so thoroughly obsessed with climbing ladders, particularly when without exception he became stranded away from food, water and grass? Perhaps his ladder-climbing was simply a way to entertain humans. Or, as a normally ground-abiding animal, did he truly enjoy the unusual view?

Perhaps for Prince climbing ladders was a means to a hug while he was being carried down. It is possible Prince believed the roof to be a part of his security zone to be protected by Prince, 21st-Century Guard Dog. It was, after all, enclosed within the perimeter of a territorial animal. Did Prince feel he could better pursue his guarding duties from the high vantage point of the roof?

Whatever Prince's motivations for climbing ladders, humans will never know. As Prince grew older the family tried to wean him from his addiction in fear he would be hurt, but to no avail. Ken and Mary knew that throughout their life with Prince, they would be facing many more festive seasons of preventing Beagle Ladder Addiction.

Diane Arrington

Chapter 40
Chris

The story of Chris is the story of a frustrated owner with no perceptible way out of a dog behavior problem. The only solution rested in this dog's mysterious ability to "read" her owner and understand an abstract human concept.

Chris, a clear-eyed Australian Shepherd was six years old. She was a dog of normal intelligence. In her youth, she caused her owner a few problems with her temper and the excessive use of her mouth. She did not seem exceptionally gifted in any aspect of her life. She loved to run and chase the ball, to herd small dogs and frogs away from her yard. She emerged above average but not blue ribbon from her obedience class. In short, Chris appeared to be a normal dog in every way — not exceptionally intelligent, and not particularly prone to unusual behaviors.

But when she was four, Chris exhibited a behavior that to this day still mystifies her owner.

Each weekend her owner, attorney Stacey Harris of Richardson, Texas, took Chris and her Rottweiler housemate Layla to a certain nearby park for much-needed romping and running. On each of Saturday and Sunday they enjoyed a couple of relaxed hours after an attorney's long work-week schedule.

The park was just two blocks from the house. A creek ran through it. The creek was deep enough for swimming and about thirty feet wide. Both Chris and Layla were passionate in their love for swimming and retrieving anything Stacey might toss into the water.

But upon every arrival at the park, Chris displayed an annoying habit. She plunged into the creek and swam across full throttle, legs pumping unreserved. Once across the creek she lunged up the other bank and charged the picnic area to gleefully mingle with the families and friends enjoying peaceful outings and cookouts.

Suddenly above the happy laughter of a park in summer rose the cacophony of panicked screaming. The dog's "fun" terrorized everyone there, primarily the mothers and children. As they fled in horror from the "mad" dog, Chris became even more excited. She thought they were joining in the Most Favorite Game of Chase, and they were It.

It was embarrassing for Stacey. People complained, some bitterly, a few even shouting crossly at her. She felt her dogs deserved some healthy exercise off the leash after sitting alone at the house seventy hours a week. She was torn between restricting the dogs to leashes or incurring the wrath of neighbors.

If Chris did not cross the creek there would be no problem, the people said. If Stacey could just keep her on their own side of the creek, the people had no issue with the dogs being off the leashes. Stacey must find a way to regulate Chris's behavior. She tried what traditional methods she knew or could discover to keep Chris in check.

Scolding Chris did not work. Putting her on a long cotton line and yanking her back did not work. Her Recall command did not work. Chris came back to Stacey's call, got petted, then streaked back across the creek. Her Stay command did not work. When Stacey released Chris from Stay, she fairly flew down the bank and went anyway. It seemed that the sole purpose of Chris's wild behavior was to greet the people. She was the self-appointed Welcoming Committee. After the deed was done, she swam back across the creek and became the perfect dog. Stacey knew all this, but the terrified mothers did not.

Frustrated, Stacey phoned a local behaviorist about the problem. The behaviorist gave advice that seemed useless: talk to the dog, she said. Stacey was certain Chris was just being a bad dog, that she should know better after all Stacey's efforts. But she was desperate. Nothing she had tried thus far had worked. She already felt guilty enough leaving the dogs alone for so many hours. Running them was of vital importance to her — and to them. She decided to give talking a try.

The next Saturday, as instructed, Stacey sat Chris down on the bank of the creek. She squatted down beside her and put her arm around her. As the summer season carried on around them, Stacey talked quietly to the Aussie's cheek and ear. She explained things to her.

"*Chris*," Stacey said, feeling foolish as could be and hoping no one was watching, "*you have to stay on this side of the creek. I know you are just happy to see the people and that all you really want to do is greet them. But they don't understand. You are frightening them. It is important to me and to your health that you stay over here with me. We could get sued.*" Spoken like a true attorney.

Chris only panted and smiled and quivered with the anticipation of leaping into the water. She appeared not to be hearing a word Stacey spoke. But dutifully, Stacey went on.

"*Chris, if you don't stay over here I will have to put you on a leash and you will no longer be able to run free. Because I love you I want you to be able to at least enjoy this little time we have together freely and untethered. Please, Chris. Stay on this side of the creek with me and Layla.*"

Chris was not listening. Her keen eyes swept the landscape repeatedly, but always focused back on the children calling and playing fifty yards distant. Feeling it was a futile effort, Stacey released the dog.

Chris sprang from Stacey's arms and blasted toward the creek. She leaped into the water, Stacey thought with a particular zeal this time, and began to swim die-hard for the other side. Oh well, Stacey sighed. It was worth a try, wasted effort though it was. She watched the dog's black and white coat disappearing from the bank.

Then a strange thing happened.

When Chris reached exact center of the creek, the precise halfway mark, she performed an abrupt U-turn and swam back to

Diane Arrington

shore. She climbed out, shook off, and, with a wild-dog face, raced away to play Attack Layla. She offered not the slightest glance at Stacey.

Stacey was stunned. Surely this was a coincidence, she thought.

But the next day Chris did exactly the same thing. The dog sprang into the water, swam to the halfway point, turned around and swam back. The next weekend, after a week had passed and Chris would surely have had time to forget her polite new behavior, Chris still swam halfway across the creek, turned, and headed back.

Stacey "explained" things to Chris in the fall of 1993. At last contact, Stacey and her dogs still lived in the same house and visited the same creek. Chris still had not, on any occasion, crossed the creek.

Stacey admits that she far underestimated a dog's ability to hear and understand. Though dogs often appear not to be listening, Chris heard, perhaps even appreciated, Stacey's gentle talk. Somehow, mysteriously, she knew what Stacey meant and abided by the request — permanently.

Docktale 11
French Fry

French Fry, a strange but friendly little Calico cat, was named for her love of McDonald's french fries. Perhaps she should have been named Olive, because French Fry had a serious fetish: olives. She simply adored olives.

Black ones, green ones, pimento-filled, pickled, her attraction was irresistible and unadulterated. For French Fry the allure of a dish of olives was so captivating it became necessary to warn the entire family.

Olives could not be left unsupervised in open containers at family gatherings. Olives could not be left in an open can on the counter unguarded in the kitchen. French Fry knew when olives were anywhere in the vicinity, and the cat did everything in her power to obtain them.

French Fry did not eat the olives though, as one might expect. If it had only been that simple.

First, French Fry stole the olives. Then she licked them. She rubbed her cheeks on them. She rolled on them. French Fry groomed the olives. She carried them about in her mouth. She rolled them around on the floor. She slept with them. She cuddled them and she nuzzled the olives lovingly to her belly.

French Fry sat on the olives, she pawed them and she talked to them. She played with them. She did everything conceivable to and with the olives except scold them. French Fry never scolded her treasured olives.

What were these items to French Fry? Was it the scent or the shape or the color or the fat content that attracted her to them? Were they surrogate children? Were they toys? Were they curios or keepsakes or collectibles?

It's a mystery which cannot be explained, and French Fry kept an entire family on guard.

Diane Arrington

Chapter 41
Sissie

Evidence of associative learning exists in all living things possessing a brain. Dogs are no exception, and Sissie's story is a shining example. With heartrending thoughtfulness and mysterious ingenuity, Sissie indeed exhibits a covetous degree of dog patience.

She was a stunning tri-color Border Collie possessing the noble "living" eyes for which the breed is so noted. Sissie lived with a middle-aged couple in suburban Oklahoma. Named for her cowardice, when she was three Sissie displayed a behavior that dumfounded her owners, Ruth and Edward. If she was not smart enough to learn how to relate to other dogs, they thought, how could she do something like this? They could not know that canine intelligence and canine social skills are not necessarily interrelated.

For reasons unknown and to her misfortune, Sissie was an "outside" dog. Difficult though it may be for them, dogs adapt to even the worst of situations. Sissie used fair days to rediscover her yard or snooze dreamily in the yellow Oklahoma sun. On days when the weather would be unkind to outside dogs, Sissie had a big, clean two-car garage inside which to keep as warm as she could and at least dry. Her food and water were kept inside her garage, tucked away from birds, squirrels, ants and roaches.

For her full three years of life an old red tricycle, rusty and faded, had propped open the door leading from Sissie's yard into her garage. She was content with the arrangement. The agile dog, bred for athletics, simply hopped over the rear wheels of the once-red trike to get inside for sleep or sustenance.

One day in the fall of the year a lusty and persistent wind swirled crisply-colored leaves through the air and whipped brown dust up the streets of the neighborhood. Throughout the

Diane Arrington

morning the wind worked at Sissie's door, causing it to bump repeatedly against the tricycle. Eventually the tricycle was knocked loose. The door fell shut. The trike was pushed outside. It sat a foot or two in front of the closed door which was now latched tightly.

Ed happened to be looking out at the window when he saw Sissie awaken from her afternoon nap. A little bit hungry and a big bit thirsty, she stretched lazily, fore and aft. She wandered to her garage door.

Sissie approached the door. She stopped abruptly. The door was closed. She had never seen it closed. Sissie appeared bewildered. She thought for a moment, then sat down to wait for the door to open. Ed watched as Sissie looked at the trike, then gazed up at the door. The trike had always meant an open door. But the door did not open. She sat on the concrete as the wind whipped her white ruff. The smell of dust roiled in the air.

Forty seconds passed. Ed watched. Then Sissie did an amazing thing.

The shy Border Collie raised herself up, put both paws on the tricycle and pushed it closer to the door. Then she stood down and waited. She again looked up at the door, down at the trike, up at the door. Confusion ruled her demeanor when the door did not open. Confusion and forbearance.

Captivated, Ed watched his dog thinking.

With both front paws Sissie moved the three-wheeler a second time, closer to the door, at a slightly different angle. Then she waited. The wind continued to ruffle her shiny black coat as she gazed from the trike up at the door and back again. The door did not open. She appeared perplexed by the situation.

But Sissie persevered. After waiting longer this time, she moved the tricycle a third time to still a different angle and again sat down to wait. She seemed to reason *if* the trike were positioned just so, *then* the door would open.

Sissie yawned a big dog yawn. She looked up at the door with translucent, tolerant, questioning eyes. She scratched a flea with a white back foot. She thought for a moment. Then suddenly she jumped to her feet, wagged her tail at the tricycle and looked expectantly at the door, perhaps inviting it to open, willing it to open. Still nothing. She was thirsty.

Three times Sissie tried, her patience never wavering, to complete the association she knew existed between the tricycle and the door.

It is not known how many times Sissie would have tried moving the tricycle, which may be the true mystery of her story. After her third try, Ed's compassion overcame his fascination and he quickly rescued Sissie from her dilemma.

How Sissie thought to move the tricycle is a mystery that will remain forever locked inside her sweet and thoughtful mind.

Diane Arrington

Seventh Sense

Chapter 42
Clique

As with humans, every dog on Earth comes with a distinct personality, each one unlike the next. Whether Clique's mysterious behavior was a result of personality, an added gene or Divine Intervention, no one can say. The intriguing randomness of her behavior left her owner mystified.

It didn't matter to Clique (pronounced "Kleek") that she closely resembled a Niemann-Marcus cake with legs. She was the Idea Dog and she planned to extract from life the most fun possible.

Her deep golden eyes looked at you steadily, intelligently, as if there were a person inside. Happiness sparkled there, in her eyes. Obedience training Clique was unnecessary — an explanation of the matter at hand was sufficient for this chocolate Standard Poodle to understand.

Marnie Simon adopted Clique as a puppy in Philadelphia, Pennsylvania where she lived as a young adult with her parents and grandparents. Covered in chocolate shavings, the lively, affectionate dog didn't begin her truly strange behavior right away. For two years she warmed up to it with some of her Big Ideas.

Clique had a roommate, a Beagle named Christine. Christine could never quite get enough to eat. Clique could never quite have enough fun. Clique seemed to know Christine was always hungry. Clique also knew where the cereal was kept. One of her first Big Ideas was to feed Christine's addiction, and she acted on this idea more than once.

While owners were away the two dogs, one tall one short, broke into the floor cupboard harboring the cereal. Like two robbers hitting up an ATM machine, Christine waited while Clique used one curly brown paw to slide open the cupboard door. Then together they rooted out the boxes of flakes, loops and squares, one by one. Christine stuffed herself full. Clique spread the cereal artfully across the floor. Christine invariably got sick. Clique got in trouble for opening the cupboard.

Very early in her life Clique taught her family to lock up any and all vitamin pills. In a house with no need for childproof caps, Clique had a passion for the energy-loaded pills. She watched where they got put. When everyone left, she simply opened the cupboard or drawer, dug out the bottles, removed the caps and downed the contents. Perhaps this early practice fed her brain cells in a way that set her up for the strange behavior she would later develop. Clique was so consumed with the idea of ingesting vitamin pills that the only place left to secure them was inside the refrigerator.

Clique regularly opened the cupboards, but she never closed them after herself to cover her tracks. It might appear she wasn't smart enough, but from what we know of Clique, this isn't possible. More likely she simply didn't care if she was found out, at least on the issue of opening the cupboards. It wasn't long before it became necessary to install locks on all cupboards and drawers within her reach.

If Clique misbehaved during the day while Marnie was away, she seemed to know she was in Dutch when Marnie came home. It was too late to hide the evidence even if she had chosen to. There was only one thing to do. Clique had an idea that if Marnie couldn't see her, then she couldn't scold her.

Before Marnie even discovered the mess, the dog wedged her head beneath the couch skirt, thinking this made her invisible. But eighty pounds of headless Hershey's chocolate was spread across the floor behind her hidden head. Interestingly, she did not hide her head if she had not been naughty.

One of Clique's Entertainment Ideas was to do impressions. On the cue, "Where's Jimmy Carter?" she tossed her great head and drew back her lips, exposing rows of gleaming teeth. She opened her huge jaws in imitation of the famous Jimmy Carter smile and bobbed her head up and down.

On Clique's first Christmas she was still warming up to her most bizarre, which would not occur for another year.

On December 18 the family, to which belonged a politician, received an unusually large delivery of mail. The housekeeper hurriedly piled the cards and parcels on the coffee table for later perusal. Mixed in the pile was a small box wrapped in brown paper, but the housekeeper thought nothing of it. Two days later she remembered it, but the box had vanished. A week later she found a business card mysteriously buried in a floor plant. The family put two and two together.

The box contained homemade scrapple, a mixture of sausages reciped by an uncle who had sent a batch for Christmas. It had arrived in the particular large delivery. Alone in the house, Clique's needle nose discovered the scrapple. Her idea was to eat it. She did. The smart poodle then realized an empty, shredded box and brown wrapping left on the floor were evidence to give her away, so this time she covered her tracks—she ate them. However she was apparently just too stuffed to eat the accompanying business card. She buried it in the plant. It was the perfect crime.

Clique loved her family dearly. Her grandparents, the housekeeper, the groundskeeper. But Marnie — Marnie was Clique's mentor. Clique would tolerate any amount of discomfort to be with Marnie. She went with her whenever possible. On car trips in the heat and cold, to work where she was required to shoehorn her huge self into a three-foot cubicle beneath Marnie's desk and remain the entire day. But soon Marnie began to work too many hours for Clique to go along. Her loneliness may have triggered her ultimate mystery.

One Saturday Marnie had to work, an unusual situation on a Saturday. Hefty Christine was asleep as always. There was nothing for Clique to do all those hours alone. The Poodle was bored. She wandered aimlessly through the empty, rambling house. Suddenly the inventive dog hit upon an idea.

Clique trotted into Marnie's room and nudged open the closet door. She found a red sweater on the floor. She carried it to the center of the living room and placed it lovingly on the blue carpet. Then she loped into the kitchen to look around. She pulled a white tea towel from a rack and added it to the sweater on the living room floor. She found a tennis shoe in the laundry room and brought that in, putting it on top of the sweater and the towel. With her long Poodle muzzle she discovered a silk daisy lying outside its vase and carried it in her teeth to the living room. Just when she was getting tired she spotted her tennis ball by a chair in the den. With a flourish, she topped off the pile with her ball. Her signature.

The autumn morning had turned to afternoon by the time Clique finished her project. The day was almost gone. She would first catch a nap, then wrestle Christine awake for a game of Tug, and then her treasured Marnie would be home.

And soon Marnie did come home, to find what Clique had done. To Clique's eye the assemblage was perfect. To the human eye it was imperfect, haphazard items scattered on the floor. The family mistakenly assumed it was an incident as random as the items involved. Since none of the articles had been chewed, all were returned to their proper places without incident, and the family went on with life.

Two weeks later on a Tuesday, Marnie was past due from work. Clique paced and fretted, but this didn't bring Marnie, her beloved, any sooner. Once again she decided to occupy herself with work. Every good dog needs a job.

Clique found Marnie's bedroom slippers in the bathroom. She carried them *both* to the middle of the living room and set them on the floor. She went into the den and found grandfather's pipe on the small table by his chair. She lifted it with care, just as she had always seen him do, and carried it in her mouth to the living room. She arranged it next to the slippers. The housekeeper had cleaned thoroughly on Monday, so Clique was hard-pressed to find things lying around. The Idea Dog had an idea. She simply opened a drawer, pulled out a white wool scarf and assigned it a place on the pile.

Minutes, then hours ticked by as Clique found things to add to her creation. She pulled an empty cereal box from the trash without spilling over the can. She discovered one green sock hidden far under grandfather's bed. She pilfered a magazine from an end table. She brought a banana from the wooden bowl on the kitchen table without eating it on the way. She slid one small book out of a bookshelf. She engaged a blue T-shirt. She opened the utility closet and lifted a feather duster from its hook inside the door.

Clique worked and worked. With each item she was required to reach higher to the top of the neatly-crafted stash. Finally, just before Marnie got home, she added the crowning touch to the stack: a golf club.

Marnie came home just before ten o'clock that night to a mysterious mound in the center of the living room rug. The pile was almost two feet high.

Clique never chewed any of the items. Not a toothmark to be found. Clique did her housekeeping only when Marnie worked late. She did not build her creations every time Marnie was gone, only when Marnie was gone too long. The longer Marnie's arrival was delayed, the higher grew the pile.

Clique's work became so regular and so thorough that the family felt it necessary to warn workmen and other visitors to not be alarmed at what they might discover. The house had not been ransacked, they told them, at least not by human hands. Ultimately the family was forced to put locks on the rest of the cupboards throughout the house and install baby-proof latches on all drawers.

There was one aspect of Clique's housekeeping behavior that was most appealing. Never, upon discovery, did she disappear beneath the couch skirt. She did not act ashamed, nor did she seek praise or accolades for her daytime pleasures. Apparently in a dog's mind, housekeeping is not considered malbehavior.

Diane Arrington

What in Clique's mental processes could account for her housekeeping activities? Though anthropomorphically it seems she was bored and looking for things to do, what of her natural wolf instincts could possibly initiate such bizarre activity? Most dogs when bored sleep or chew, many destructively. Not Clique. How did she decide which item to select from a drawer full of many items? And when she first displayed her behavior, that first Saturday when Marnie had to work, did she know it was a day Marnie should not have gone to work?

A dog's main learning tool is mimicking others but Clique had no one to emulate, no one after whom to pattern this particular behavior. She could certainly not copy the housekeeper; she tidies up and puts things away. Clique's behavior could only have originated from deep within the mysteries of her own canine mind. It is behavior for which there is truly no known cause.

Whatever the origins, motivations and goals of Clique's strange housekeeping activities, she remains, without question, the World's Greatest Idea Dog.

Seventh Sense

Diane Arrington

Chapter 43
Sasha

Sasha's story is subtle, but significant of the canine mind's need for stimulation. Perhaps, if Sasha had been human, her choice of career would have been home decorating. Rearranging things appears to be how Sasha, who had a low sleep requirement, amused herself for eight hours in the bathroom.

Sasha was a solid black miniature Schnauzer. Perhaps it was the alacrity with which she met life head-on that made her one of the most appealing dogs in existence. She was happy and sweet and smart, one of those small but sophisticated dogs who wins your heart the instant she lays mahogany eyes upon you. She was eighteen months of age and about twelve pounds when she displayed a most curious behavior.

Sasha was having a carpet-wetting problem and was confined temporarily to a bathroom. She loved everything and everybody, and every incidence that came her way she made the best of. She was a dog who made lemonade of lemons. So Sasha loved it in her bathroom, too.

In her room with her, Sasha had everything she needed: her bed, food, water and all of her toys — eight of them, to be exact — a menagerie ranging from squeaky animal figures to a five-inch dried leather chew, the kind with knots on the ends.

The room was brightly-lit and fairly large, about ten feet by ten feet. Lemon yellow ceramic tile covered walls, floor and one long, single stair eight inches high and wide and running the length of the raised bathtub.

In the mornings Sasha went willingly, indeed, almost eagerly, into her bathroom to wait for her owner's evening return. As Jane left for work, Sasha was camped happily in her "fort."

Her bed, a huge thing four times Sasha's size, was against the end wall. Her toys were scattered hither and yon, the full length and breadth of the room. It was a disaster area.

Sasha had been in her confinement area eight hours a day for two work-weeks. This may have been some intangible limit for Sasha, because it wasn't until the last day of Sasha's confinement that her owner returned home to a queer thing.

Jane opened the door to the bathroom to free Sasha. Something in the room looked different, but Jane could not immediately put her finger on what it was. As she looked closer, she discovered that everything in the room had been mysteriously repositioned.

The housekeeper had not been in that day. Deductive reasoning reveals that Sasha had had a busy day all by herself.

First, little Sasha had managed to move her gigantic bed away from the wall and drag it across the room. Jane found it at least six feet from its original location. Considering its bulk, this was a sizable task for a dog as small as Sasha. The bed had not been haphazardly moved but was neatly snugged up against the stair by the bathtub. Still, in view of any puppy's legendary affinity for Tug-Of-War with any available item, this could be passed off as idle play. But there was more, and Jane's second discovery cannot as easily be dismissed.

In disarray in the morning, the floor was now clean and uncluttered of Sasha's toys. Just to the side of her new bed location, Sasha had moved each and every toy in the bathroom. But Sasha had not simply moved the toys around. Sasha had neatly lined up her toys *along the stair in front of the tub*. The toys, most of them long and vertical in shape, were placed perpendicular to the tub, systematically, like little tin soldiers. Not one toy remained on the floor.

Sasha had placed each toy exactly three inches from the next. She had arranged them precisely parallel to one another, and just as parallel to the lines in the ceramic tile. With only one exception, all the heads were pointed up to the tub and the feet pointed into the room. Foghorn Leghorn was upside down. Each

Diane Arrington

toy had also been placed face up, again with only one exception: Mr. Snowman was face down. Even her rawhide chew was placed perfectly perpendicular to the tub.

The toys lay left to right in the following order: red rubber ring, Chewman, reindeer squeak, black-and-white snowman squeak, rawhide with knots, yellow Foghorn Leghorn squeak, red rubber spring ring *carefully placed into a figure 8,* and Wile E. Coyote last on the right. All toys were placed with care, perfectly and precisely.

One wonders how long it took Sasha to arrange her toys just so. Did she stop to think and wag her tail, paw-to-whiskers like Martha Stewart? Could Sasha have had a reason for placing Foghorn and Snowman upside down, or was it just a puppy's lack of imagery, an oversight? Did she place the articles there for clear selection, as a human selects from a carefully-arranged smorgasbord or salad bar buffet? Or, was this just a random, amusing behavior designed to fill her time until her owner returned home?

Sasha's reasons for her behavior will forever remain locked away in some secret sector of her canine brain. What else can a good dog do alone in a bathroom all day?

One cannot avoid a mental picture of Sasha in the midst of her work, fretting over whether to place Wile E. here, next to Snowman, or *shall I put Foghorn here and my chewie over there ... No, no ... hmm ... let's see now ...*

Docktale 12
Abbey

Abbey is a name pertinent to the church or clergy. It is a clever and befitting name for a dog who did what she did.

Abbey was a curly-backed Labrador as shiny black as they come. She was 2 ½ years old. Her golden eyes gazed intelligently from her sweet ebony face. Abbey carried her ears low and her tail quietly. She was the ever-respectful dog at your feet. Though small in stature, Abbey was the proud guardian of twin baby girl humans who were six months of age at the time.

One day the twins, Samantha and Jordan, were resting on the sofa. Mom was out of town and Dad had been left alone to care for the girls. Preparing for a photo-op, Dad had just set the girls upright like two adults when Jordan's cry indicated a diaper change. Dad scooped her up and carried her upstairs to take care of business. Abbey was lying across the room, keeping an eye on Samantha but not interfering.

Suddenly Samantha, the more active of the two babies, squirmed and rolled herself into an uncomfortable position on the couch. She was dangerously close to the edge. Whether Samantha sensed her own danger we cannot know. She began to cry while she struggled to rectify the mess she had gotten herself into. The baby teetered on the edge of the couch, just about to roll off.

At Samantha's cry Abbey glanced quickly around the room to see that, despite the presence of two other larger and she thought goofier dogs, she was the only one present with enough sense to prevent a disaster.

With barely a hesitation, Abbey sprinted across the room to Samantha. She did not race over and lick the baby's face, as dogs often do when the kids are crying. No, Abbey placed herself in an unnatural position at the side of the couch. She pressed her body against the edge of the couch directly beneath the baby, sitting but stretching herself upward. This enabled her to keep

Diane Arrington

Samantha from falling to the floor. Despite the baby's desperate cries, Abbey stayed put.

Heroically, Abbey propped the baby up and held her there until Dad, hearing Samantha cry, hurried back and rescued his baby daughter from a potentially catastrophic fall. Abbey had sized up the situation correctly and acted upon it.

How did Abbey know the child was in danger? And how did she know that placing her shoulder at just the right spot would protect the baby from harm? Even more mysterious, how did Abbey know exactly how to place her shoulder, and how did she know to wait there until a rescue could be made?

Only Abbey, Samantha's rescuing angel, knows the answers to these questions. When Dad rubbed her head and spoke gently a dog's favorite words, "Good dog," Abbey, the little shy angel, beamed with the pride of a lion.

Seventh Sense

Diane Arrington

Chapter 44
Meisha

The behavior Meisha displays could change all of human nature as it relates to pets. If all pets undertook to let their owners know how they feel in the way that Meisha does, it would be the scourge of pet-haters and an affirmation for pet lovers the world over.

She was a Siamese cross. Any cat-lover knows this usually means trouble. It means intelligence, inventiveness, noise, mischief. These things owner Ronni could expect. But never could she have expected the rare if not first-in-history behavior that Meisha displayed one night in early winter 1994.

A recent divorcee, Ronni needed a friend. She found Meisha at an Eatontown, New Jersey SPCA shelter in spring 1992. Just a tiny thing to fit in the palm of a hand, she was in a cage crammed full with a litter of five. Four were tiger-striped, one had Siamese markings sans blue eyes. This one Ronni took home. The little girl orphan seemed the oddball of the litter, which would indeed prove true.

During her first year of life Meisha watched Ronni eat every meal. She seemed fascinated that Ronni had a utensil — a fork, spoon or hand — with which to move the food to the mouth. The cat was captivated. An intensity illuminated her gold-green eyes and her wedged head moved up and down with every bite Ronni took. This may have been a learning experience for Meisha.

Somewhere along the line, chubby, twelve-pound Meisha developed an eating disorder. She was a food addict. When upset, she bolted for her dish. Indeed, anything out of the ordinary sent Meisha to food. She was fed in the bathroom and had free access to dry kibble with greasy, scrumptious canned food served up in the evenings. At the age of sixteen months, Meisha spontaneously improvised a radical new method for the intake of her cherished wet food.

Since Ronni loved Meisha and Meisha loved the fatty richness of wet cat food, Ronni acquiesced, albeit against doctor's orders. Meisha was not understimulated by the aroma and flavor of the pasty stuff. She was unable to wait to eat with her mouth like any normal cat. She could not ingest the food fast enough to suit her.

So she scooped it up with her paw.

With a smirk on her lips and civility abandoned, she sat like a dog and used her foot like a shovel. Always the left paw, never the right. In one continuous, rolling motion she dug up great gobs with a curled paw and crammed it into her mouth. This was cute and this was funny. But this was a problem. Ronni could not imagine what it was glazing the walls in the bathroom until she happened one evening to see Meisha eat.

As Ronni watched she realized Meisha could not take the time to lick all the food from in and around each toe before gouging out another slab of meat. She chose the quickest method to rid her paw of the excess globules. She shook it. With a swift, hearty flick she spattered cat food far and wide. So violently did she flip her foot that food did not stick to the walls in a limited area around her feed station. It flew clear across the room. It stuck on towels, walls, mats, shower curtain, cupboards. Despite Ronni's strong desire to please Meisha, she ultimately limited Meisha to dry food only.

Meisha was a bit of a trick to raise. Her intelligence wanted to compete with Ronni's. Meisha overdid biting and scratching as a youngster, the way a kitten plays with another kitten. Ronni was anti-violence and was careful not to strike the kitten. She raised Meisha with utmost care, kindness and patience. Still, humans cannot bend cats entirely to human will, and Meisha had her own temperament and her own ideas about things.

Almost all healthy kittens think feet and ankles are the most magical of moving targets. Veterinarians report many minor injuries to humans occurring as a result of this normal kitten fascination. Most grow out of it or, sadly, are accidentally kicked out of it, by the age of a year or so. Not so with Meisha.

When she was almost three the sturdy cat was still attacking Ronni's ankles. Ronni had not been able to get Meisha to stop her annoying and painful habit. Short of spanking, she had tried everything else recommended by the vet, friends and relatives. It seemed Meisha was getting more, not less, enthusiastic about the practice. She grabbed with eighteen fully extended razor claws and bit to the bone. A wee kitten cannot do much damage, but Meisha was a full-grown cat, and a hefty one at that. It was only play, but still it hurt.

Nightly ritual in the Meisha and Ronni's house included an hour or more of kitty quality time. As Ronni got into bed, settled, and began to read, Meisha leaped obtusely onto the bed, making her presence known. In the way two human friends can share, Meisha knew she did not have to ask permission. She curled up on Ronni's chest, permission silently granted. There Meisha would lie for hours, purring and holding very still as Ronni stroked her. Both participants enjoyed the time together and could not imagine bedtime any other way.

One particular February Tuesday in 1993, as will all humans, Ronni had had an overwhelmingly stressful day. When she came in from work that evening, she was glad to have a nice, stress-lowering cat to pet.

But later, as Ronni prepared for bed, Meisha apparently entered her Evening Crazies. As Ronni walked down the hall in her nightgown, Meisha attacked Ronni's bare ankles. This assault hurt badly and indeed drew blood. Stress and pain put Ronni into overload. With her hand she smacked Meisha once firmly on the rear.

Meisha was stunned. She looked up at Ronni, a startled, hurt expression in her gilded eyes. She bolted, disappeared and stayed hidden for half an hour. When she hesitantly reappeared, Ronni did not speak to her. It was The Silent Treatment.

Seventh Sense

Outside, lamb's-wool clouds were lit by an icy full moon. Inside, Ronni climbed into bed. She pulled up the blankets and opened her book. Meisha did not bound raucously onto the bed. Instead, she simply appeared, as if by magic, near Ronni's head. She did not climb onto Ronni's chest. She sat very still beside Ronni and hung her head. Her demeanor seemed to ask, *Are you still mad at me? Do I have permission to lie on your chest?* Ronni was still frustrated and continued the silent treatment.

What happened next may never have happened before.

Ronni continued to read, ignoring Meisha sitting silently and dejectedly by her head. A few minutes passed. Suddenly Ronni was aware of something dripping onto the blanket. Unbelievably, when Meisha lifted her face, her eyes were filled with tears.

The tears ran down her cheeks through her whiskers and spilled onto the blanket, two or three large tears from each eye. Initially Ronni thought Meisha had an eye irritation of some sort, a particle of dust or a length of hair. But it was not so, as the vet would confirm the following day.

To Ronni's chagrin, Meisha had been crying. Her cat had cried real tears.

Ronni was heartbroken. So was Meisha. Ronni had never struck her before that night. In Meisha's mind she was only having fun and enjoying life the way cats are supposed to do.

There is little question that Meisha was expressing a true emotion. But that she expressed it with human deportment was startling. Ronni had the strong sense not that Meisha had been physically hurt by the slap, but rather that her "feelings" had been hurt.

Physiologically feline emotions do not trigger tear duct activity as do emotions in humans. How this happened with Meisha will forever remain a mystery.

And Ronni made the only vow she could, to herself and to Meisha.

Diane Arrington

Chapter 45
Silkie

Every millennium or so there is sent to this great, blue-green ball we call Earth a dog wizened from birth. This is a dog with such an incredible skill for concept, for communication with and comprehension of humans, the critter seems older than we. Silkie was such a dog, and she undertook a startling act of canine heroism.

Silkie, a fetching, champagne-colored shaggy dog who thought fetching was for fools, circled and wagged and panted in the heat. Her all-American bearded face was alive with anticipation at the new adventure at hand, but her stunning, almond eyes held a tinge of worry.

As the thirty-five-pound dog watched family possessions being loaded into a strange truck, she knew someone was moving. She decided to help; one by one she unearthed old toys from beneath beds, cabinets, corners and the refrigerator. She carried them outside and dropped them on the sandy, pine-lined driveway near the back of the truck.

It was 73 degrees and sunny in Palmetto, Florida as owner Kristen loaded her belongings into the rented 33-foot U-Haul truck. The truck was the largest one available, cavernous enough to carry Kristen's new Toyota tucked inside. The small, compact car had been securely tethered for a safe trip, and Kristen tucked her things in available spaces around it.

Last to be carried to the truck was Silkie's bed. Silkie, in her one year of life, had moved once, camped several times and gone on weekend trips with Kristen many times. Seeing her bed go was the clincher. When her bed went, she went, and she knew it. Worry fled her eyes as reality hit: she was getting to go along.

Diane Arrington

Silkie tried to leap into the open passenger door, missed and tumbled back, undaunted. The seat in the big truck was several feet higher than the Toyota she was accustomed to. She needed a bit more mustard. With Kristen's gentle encouragement, the dog whose courage knew no limits backed up, licked her lips and went for it, landing easily upon the wide bench seat. Kristen returned the key to the landlord, climbed into the truck and fired up the mighty engine.

The massive vehicle was a bit cumbersome at first for 5'2", 103-pound Kristen. The relative size of the steering wheel alone, Toyota to truck, was tea saucer to turkey platter. The Toyota was a four-speed, the truck had six gears. The clutch took some leg muscle, the gear shift was a baseball bat, and there were six wheels, not four. But both the dog and the woman rose to the challenge. With $500 in cash and a cooler full of food and chewsticks, the pair set out north from Palmetto on I-75. Destination: Dallas, Texas.

For the first two hours Silkie stood on the seat, pink tongue bouncing and dropped black ears perked, expecting to be there any minute. This was to be the longest trip she'd had yet. At rest stops the confident dog breathlessly investigated every post and bench. Her nose stayed in high gear as she untangled the scents of other traveling pets. But when it was time to move on, she did not hesitate.

Sometime during her first year of life Silkie had developed an eery knack for telling time. Consequently, it was never necessary for Kristen to set an alarm clock. If Kristen asked Silk to wake her at seven, Silkie did. If she asked to be awakened at 8:15, Silkie woke her at 8:15. Even more amazing, if Silkie was asked to wake Kristen "in one hour," Silkie obliged, without fail.

For perhaps eight of her twelve months the dog had been able to tell time. Kristen has no idea how Silkie learned this. She had obedience trained Silkie, but telling time was certainly not something a dog could be taught. With a hip check against the bed, whiskers up the nose or a tongue in the eye, Silkie never let her owner down. Almost without fail, Silkie was at the side of the bed when requested, bright-eyed, grinning ear-to-ear, gray shaggy tail high.

There was one thing most uncanny about Silkie's time-telling. Two times a year, once in spring and once in fall, the two exact days of the year when humans change their clocks, Silkie was an hour off in waking Kristen.

Can dogs tell time? How could a wolf descendant possibly adapt so thoroughly to the time clock, to the digital, electrical, mechanical world of man? A wolf with all her instincts "tells time" by the angle of the sun. But how can a canine mind equate, say, a ten degree angle of the sun with 7:15 a.m. by human standards? And how was Silkie able to wake herself in order to be able to wake her owner? It's an unsolved mystery, and so is the action Silkie took the night the travelers reached Dallas.

The first overnight stop to sleep on the trip was in Tallahassee, Florida. It was 1980. The world was still a relatively safe place then, and Kristen felt safe in pulling the huge truck into an expansive grocery store parking lot to sleep. She locked the doors and stretched out on the bench seat which was just long enough to accommodate her full height. Silkie curled up on a blanket on the passenger floor next to her water pail.

"*Silkie, wake me up at six tomorrow, okay?*" Silkie must have been happy to be useful, because she woke Kristen at five minutes to six the next morning. At home or away, Silk retained her uncanny sense of time.

Through the long, boring flats of Louisiana, after twenty-eight hours of traveling, Silkie developed an odd, stereotypic behavior. She rocked. She stood on the seat and, with her chin over the wide dashboard and her nose just inches from the front glass, she swung back and forth, back and forth, back and forth. Her wheaty hair flowed as she shifted her weight from one front foot to the other and back again. Her black-lined eyes were bright, her black nose shiny and wet. She looked healthy and happy, she simply rocked without stopping for about two hours straight. Was she dancing to some silent music in her mind? The

Diane Arrington

truck radio had quit on the first leg of the trip. Or was she getting her exercise the only way she could in such a confined space?

For a total of thirty-six hours the pair drove through sunlight, darkness, midday heat and morning mist. They talked and sang, stopping only to eat, rest and sleep.

The woman and the dog could not know the cold danger that lay just ahead.

***

The pair pulled into Dallas, tired and ready for a real bed, just after midnight on an icy night in January. Unknowingly they had driven from tropics to cold. 73 in Florida, 37 and dropping in Dallas. In the morning there would be five inches of snow on the ground.

After almost three days in the mammoth truck Kristen had become skilled at handling it. Nevertheless, Dallas traffic stunned her. Drivers tailgated. They honked impatiently. They sped by, pulled in and cut her off, forcing her to slam on the brakes and throw Silkie off the seat to the floor. She had seen the signs, "Drive Friendly," and thought it quaint until she realized nobody did.

The city seemed huge and cold-blooded. The traffic made her feel unwelcome, a stranger. She was glad to have Silkie with her, someone familiar to talk to and sing to. Silkie loved being sung to, and dreamily hung her eyelids at half-mast until the song was over. Her favorite song seemed to be "My Girl."

Kristen struggled to find her way on the streets of a city not designed for tourists. Avenues were poorly marked, drivers unruly. Both girl and dog were tired and cold. It was one a.m., and the gas gauge was on empty.

For Kristen it was a scary night in Dallas, and it was long before the advent of cell phones. Searching for a friend's apartment hotel near Old City Park, Kristen at last realized she was lost on a street called Forest, just south of downtown Dallas.

Seventh Sense

A Florida innocent, she could not know the area's notorious reputation as one of the most dangerous and crime-ridden in Dallas.

Through the darkness Kristen peered out through the massive windshield, searching for a gas station. Everything seemed to be closed and dark. She talked constantly to Silkie who stood eagerly on the seat and watched out the window. The wise dog sensed they were almost there.

The rented truck's heater was poor. Kristen had not expected cold this severe. It was slowly freezing her feet, which were clad only in light tennis shoes. Her eyes felt dry and scratchy. She was tired. She wanted to pull over and sleep, but she could not afford that luxury. She had to find a gas station or risk running out of gas — and heat — in the middle of the night in an unfamiliar neighborhood.

At last, off to the right, two gas pumps stood outside a minuscule, dimly-lit corner store. Above the store an ancient, faded, red-on-white sign read "COLD BEER — CIGARETTES — GAS." There were only two pumps, side-by-side, but one was all she needed. Innocently, Kristen maneuvered the oversized truck into the small parking lot.

An old, beat-up, once-red Pinto stood at the pumps, blocking both. Kristen moved the huge, rumbling truck in behind it, put it in neutral and waited with her foot on the brake. She kept the engine running for heat. Minutes passed; gas burned. She wished the Pinto would finish. Silkie stood on her side of the bench seat watching eagerly, carefully taking in all that she saw.

Kristen waited. And waited. And waited some more. As gas burned, so did her patience. Then something strange happened.

Slowly, like a wayward drop of syrup creeping down the side of the bottle, an uneasy feeling slid down Kristen's spine. She looked around. So did Silkie. Despite the lights, the night seemed very black. Dark men in jeans and shabby jackets loitered in clusters of three and four, smoking, talking, drinking beer — watching the stranger. None of them moved. There was not another woman in sight. Kristen felt suddenly aware of her appearance; flowing dark hair, blue eyes, tanned, white skin. She wished the radio worked. Anything to break the silence. The emergency brake and the radio had each gone out at the beginning of the trip.

By now Kristen had been waiting at the pump for perhaps twenty minutes. Several more minutes passed before she realized the Pinto was not using the gas pump at all. No one was in or around the car. Suddenly she saw that the Pinto was simply parked there, sitting silent. Perhaps fatigue had kept her from noticing this fact earlier. Hoping the owner would realize she was waiting and come out from the store, Kristen tooted the truck's horn.

Nothing happened. Though there were perhaps twenty people hanging around, no one moved. Kristen and her dog waited a little longer, then honked again. The big engine was rapidly gobbling up the last of the gas in the tank. If it idled long enough, she would not have enough gas to drive to another station.

After a minute more, Kristen pressed the horn a third time, considering the circumstances, a bit more insistently this time. From somewhere behind her, a male voice shouted ominously, *"Go back to Florida, honky!"* What happened next was any woman's nightmare.

Three men who had been lounging against the ice machine stirred. They took their time as they ambled across the pavement to the Pinto. They did not get in it. Instead, they moved into the space between the two vehicles. Very deliberately, they turned their backs and leaned directly against the front grill of Kristen's truck. One of the men slowly lit a cigarette. Impudently the men lounged against the truck that was not theirs, smoking and talking in low tones. They were not laughing.

Now Kristen could not pull forward. Nor could she back up; in her side mirrors she could see a dented brown Buick blocking her from behind. She was trapped. Petite and attractive, she was ensnared in a different world. She had traveled more than eleven hundred miles from a tiny town where neighbors baked cakes for one another, smiled and waved good morning, where no one even locked their doors at night. To Kristen, this hostility was unfamiliar, unexpected.

Kristen would not realize until later that Silkie stood quietly alert on the seat, her full, elegant tail hanging still. Her bearded face was serious. She watched. She listened. She saw, with her hunter's instinct, every movement in that parking lot.

Cold, tired, threatened, ticked, and unwilling to sit idly and do nothing, Kristen laid on the horn. She thought the men leaning against the truck might stand forward, giving her a chance to get the truck in motion.

Then she saw them. Two groups of men. Five on her left, twenty feet away, four on her right, fifteen feet away. They had come forward from their corners and were standing in the open, looking directly at her through the truck's windows. The three men in front of the truck stood and turned around. They placed their dark hands on the white hood of the truck. Ominously, they leaned forward and stared right at Kristen through the windshield. Kristen found herself face-to-face with three menacing faces, the whites of their eyes spitting belligerence.

The two groups began to move slowly towards the truck. They were focused, moving in tandem. Her blood chilled and her mouth went dry as she realized what was happening. She quickly locked her door. In a split second, she saw that Silkie's window was open just enough to put an arm through and unlock the plunger-type lock visible through the glass. She could not reach the handle to wind the window up without taking her foot off the brake. With no emergency brake, the truck might roll forward and crush six legs against a Pinto.

She glanced to her left, past the men to the street. The neighborhood was vacant, deserted. Storefronts up and down both sides of the street had long since locked up tight for the night. There was no traffic, no help in sight. She could not move the truck. There was no way out. She was a fish in a barrel.

Diane Arrington

A few of the men threw whole cigarettes to the pavement as they advanced on the truck. They bore no weapons that Kristen could see, but their hands were stuffed deep into jacket pockets. Their breath jetted blades of gray mist in the cold night.

Suddenly things seemed to be moving in slow motion. Kristen watched the men approach her, one sinister step at a time. They were closing in on the truck from out-of state with the lone girl and her fluffy dog inside. Who would miss her? The hair on her neck stood up. She had forgotten about the cold, and was not even thinking of Silkie.

But Silkie watched with keen eyes. She held perfectly still. She did not bark, growl, or raise a hair. She did not display the freeze-warning dogs posture before an attack. She was sitting, not standing, on the seat. She looked utterly passive, harmless. In retrospect, this may have been intentional.

The men on the left were now five feet from her door. The men on the right reached the truck. Suddenly, as if to take advantage of the element of surprise, one of the men leaped onto the narrow running board on the passenger side, Silkie's side, of the truck. He reached to shove his arm through the open window and unlock the truck door. That was enough for Silkie.

Suddenly the quiet dog exploded. With the quickness of a cat, all teeth exposed, hair and spit flying, she let out a roar that came from her belly. She lunged violently, not at the man's arm, but at his face. *How dare you touch this truck!* She hit the glass and tried to throw herself through the four-inch opening at the top of the window. She snapped and bit viciously at the intruder, at the window, at the air.

The dog's savage snarls were audible even outside the closed truck, and echoed across the parking lot. A guttural sound escaped the man's throat. He panicked and leaped backwards off the truck, almost falling foolishly over his comrades. In a nanosecond his fear spread among them and the men on both sides of the truck jumped back in fear. When they did, Silkie stopped instantly and fell strangely silent.

Seventh Sense

Her mind at full speed, Kristen seized the moment. She threw the huge gearshift into reverse, manipulated the clutch, and floored the gas pedal. At this point she cared not if anyone was standing behind the truck. All she wanted was to get the truck in motion. In a series of quick movements she backed up, smashed broadside into the Buick, slammed the lever into first gear, turned the wheels left as far as she could, finessed the clutch and prayed. With all the weight of an automobile inside, the truck moved forward surprisingly fast. With the truck now in motion she could turn the wheels further, heading desperately for the exit to the street.

The men ran in angry pursuit as she worked the clutch and speed-shifted into second. The truck careened out of the small lot and onto the street. She jammed it in third, pressed the gas to the floor — and she was free. She looked in her mirrors as she sped away. She could see the men standing on the street, gesturing and cursing after her. Thanks to one brave dog and their surprised fear of her, the men had lost a fish.

All the while thanking God for enough gas left to do so, Kristen drove the truck almost a full mile before she felt assured no one was following, and before her nerves would let her stop and breathe. She pulled to the curb and wrapped her arms around her beloved Silkie. She buried a tearful face in her dog's coarse, shaggy fur. Silkie wiggled happily inside the grateful, loving arms of her owner, pride all over her beautiful stuffed-toy face.

Kristen had never seen an aggressive side of Silk. She was a happy, smart, affectionate dog who slept flat on her back, loved to be sung to and was a nut for foot massages. She was a dog at once sociable and independent. Kristen had always wondered, in the back of her mind, if Silkie would be there for her in a situation of real danger; she discovered the best truth. Silkie had done only what was necessary and nothing more. Kristen thanked Silkie, and thanked God for giving her the perfect dog, one sentient enough to read a situation and save Kristen's life.

It cannot be known what the men would have done to Kristen had they succeeded in pulling her from the truck. Killed

Diane Arrington

her? Or worse, raped her? Too often, in south Dallas, the story has a tragic end. That their intent was evil, there is no doubt. Silkie's intuition saved Kristen from an unknown fate, and made Silkie a hero.

As for Silkie, about one minute of the gushy stuff was enough for her. Ho-hum, all in a dog day's work. All she wanted to know was, *are we there yet?*

Seventh Sense

Diane Arrington

Chapter 46
Sandy & Waldo

This tale of remarkable cross-species communication took place long before dogs were as advanced as they are today. It is a story about improbable compatibility between two unlikely subjects. Ultimately, it is about imposing one specie's idea of domestication upon another whose ancestors carry with them no knowledge of such domestic habit.

In 1955 in rural Mississippi, when Marvin Whitehall was a boy, he lived with his mother and father at the outskirts of town on four acres of pristine pastureland. Young Marvin had two pets: a quarter horse mare named Tootsie, and a very special dog named Sandy.

Sandy was a rather serious fellow. An English Shepherd whose body size and fur density approximated a Sheltie, he had a coat of fine dark chocolate with mocha mixed in. He carried high a long, lean, clean muzzle and a smooth head capped with upright, tipped-over black ears. His fluffy white chest was proud, and he had white socks to match. The white tip on Sandy's thickset tail was like the flag on a dirt bike, signaling not only where he was in the high green grass of the pastures, but how he was feeling that day.

Sandy had been the only housepet for five years when Waldo came to live with them. Waldo's arrival was not to Sandy's particular delight.

***

Mr. Whitehall's boots echoed on the wood floor of the country store. Outside, the Mississippi springtime was replete

Seventh Sense

with snowy, blossoming Dogwoods and extravagant purple iris. Inside, there were baby ducklings for sale. A dozen of them peeped pitifully from a box in one corner of the store. Dad could not resist them. He returned home with a bag of feed for Tootsie and, in his jacket pocket, a fuzzy golden duckling for Marv.

The duck was palm-sized. He had the tiniest orange beak Marvin had ever seen. The little duckling was also outfitted with bright yellow fledgling fluff the color of a canary. It was stuck all over his tiny body as if it had been haphazardly glued on. Marv was thrilled with his new Easter pet. He made a house for him out of a cardboard box, and named the baby Waldo.

When he was very small, Waldo lived inside his box in the kitchen. Had he been able to speak English, Sandy might have had a few things to say about Waldo moving in. But being the nice, well-mannered, domesticated, cultured dog he really was, he kept his mouth shut.

Just a few hours after little Waldo took up residence at the Whitehall home, Sandy began to notice an offensive odor wafting through the house. His alert Shepherd nose traced the smell to a strange cardboard box in the kitchen. The box had four sides and a bottom, but no top. Investigating, his ears tipped in puzzlement, the dog wandered over and peered down inside. There was Waldo.

When Waldo spotted Sandy he all but screamed, *"Dad-deee!"* and scrambled madly for the dog. Sandy leaped back in fright, then slid his eyes around like Wile E. Coyote, hoping no one saw.

Not to be put off by this weird, helpless thing the size of his snout, Sandy ventured another peek over the side of the box. He was anxious to determine the source of that lingering, vociferous odor. When he got a good look inside the box, he found what he was looking for. In one corner of the box was a small pile of something unpleasant, even to a dog. Sandy growled. Undaunted, little Waldo continued to pursue the great hair face appearing in the sky above his house.

As the days passed Sandy grew increasingly annoyed at the odor emanating from Waldo's box. Although the box was cleaned regularly with fresh newspapers laid in, Waldo was prolific. As far as Sandy was concerned, it was much too near his food dish.

He began to growl and complain more often at Waldo's unsophisticated hygiene. Waldo, it seemed, was bent on filling up his box with the obnoxious substance. Soon Sandy was running to Waldo's box and growling whenever he smelled Waldo passing a meal. This happened so often that Sandy was running ragged. He decided it would be simpler just to stand and hang his head over the side of Waldo's box and wait for the next occurrence. When Waldo messed, Sandy showed his teeth and growled threateningly, glaring at Waldo. Little Waldo was clueless.

Soon Waldo grew large enough to hop out of his foot-high nest. On little duck feet he paddled the linoleum back and forth around his box, but was as yet too timid to venture far. He went as far as he dared, though, looking for Sandy. When Sandy escaped to other parts of the house Waldo looked bored, pecking at small crumbs that had dropped to the floor or settling on his belly for a snooze. When Waldo needed some real sleep, he wedged himself beneath the small ceramic heater which stood in the kitchen near his box.

When Sandy entered the room, Waldo raced to him on webbed feet as though the dog were his lost mother. It was clear Waldo had imprinted on the dog whose chest resembled the puffed white of Mom's. The family had great fun watching the endearing scenario. For his part, Sandy was not amused.

Sandy was particularly disenchanted that Waldo, now hopping easily in and out of his box, chose to leave ugly things on the kitchen floor. When Sandy discovered Waldo's fresh messes he stood over the offending area and complained, growling his most meaningful growl. Waldo was unaffected. He was driven by his obsession to be near his beloved daddy.

Sandy's frustration with the situation mounted to the point of desperation. Finally one day he wrapped his lips around his teeth, reached down, and wrapped his jaws around Waldo. Sandy did not mean to eat Waldo, but to lift him and place him gently back inside his box. This became ritual. When Waldo messed, Sandy put him in his box.

But soon Waldo grew to the size of a large white pigeon, too large for Sandy to lift safely. Now when Sandy caught Waldo in the act, he growled and scolded Waldo, then herded him, in the way of a Shepherd, to the back door. After all, out the back door is where any self-respecting creature goes when that special need arises.

Soon Sandy was spending most of his time babysitting Waldo in the kitchen. He tolerated the duck's affections in favor of keeping the house free of Waldo's emissions. Through some mysterious cross-species communication undetectable to man, Sandy developed a sense for recognizing when Waldo had the urge. He would rush to Waldo, growl, and with his mouse-whiskered muzzle shove the duck across the kitchen floor to the back door. There Sandy would keep Waldo pinned against the door, growling and scolding. If Waldo dared to try waddling away, Sandy would slide him back against the door.

Waldo, annoyed at being held captive, honked in loud protest. The family could hear the honking and commotion from all parts of the house, which of course resulted in someone coming to let Waldo out. It wasn't long before Waldo was deathly intimidated when it came to his bathroom habits.

One day the family got a shock. They could hear Waldo honking in the kitchen and assumed Sandy had Waldo cornered at the door again. But when they got to the kitchen to let him out, Waldo stood at the door alone. Sandy was nowhere in sight. When they opened the door, Waldo hopped outside and performed on the step just beyond the threshold. This began to occur with regularity. Waldo would ask to go out, waddle across the threshold, do his thing, and waddle back in.

Diane Arrington

As Waldo matured and his feathers turned from yellow to white, he began to understand Sandy's signals. Sandy was still displeased and Waldo could tell it. Now when Sandy saw Waldo on the porch, he nudged him dangerously close to the stairs. To save his own life, Waldo began to hop down the dozen stairs to the ground for his needs.

When he went out with Sandy, always his preference, Waldo followed Sandy everywhere. Where Sandy went, he went, and when Sandy went, Waldo went. When finished they climbed the stairs together, Waldo hopping two-footed up one stair at a time behind Sandy. The unlikely pair would come through the door, disgruntled dog leading the way, pudgy white Waldo waddling earnestly behind.

Spring turned to summer. To Sandy's dismay, he and Waldo were constant companions. When anything startled Waldo he fled in terror for Sandy's comforting fur. Sandy looked embarrassed.

But in secret, when he thought no one was looking, Sandy permitted play between the two of them. How do a duck and a dog play? Sandy's method was to pin Waldo to the ground with his paw. He held the duck fast, licking him and pushing at him with his nose, perhaps considering a meal. Waldo seemed to enjoy this. He must have taken it as a sign that his idol loved him as much as he loved the big dog.

Winter arrived. The sky turned bleak grey and the weather icy cold. Waldo tried to sleep with Sandy at every opportunity, seeking his warmth. He paddled over to where Sandy napped on a throw rug. Sandy got up and moved to another part of the house. Waldo followed behind. Sandy moved again. Waldo followed. In Dogdom, when it's nap time and mother moves away from puppies, the puppies don't always follow. In Duckdom, baby ducklings routinely follow mother and stay glued to her like moss on a tree.

To Sandy, Waldo's custom was tiresome. To Waldo, it was perfectly natural. Finally Sandy, desperate for slumber, gave in

Seventh Sense

and permitted Waldo to sleep on him. Other than sleep deprivation, it appeared to him he had no other choice.

Waldo's persistence had paid off. He snuggled ecstatically against Sandy's ribs or under his thick, bushy-warm tail, a heavenly look upon his duck face. Sandy put his dog lips in a line, rolled his eyes, turned his head away and begrudgingly tolerated naps with a duck. At least the brainless, quacking barbarian was finally housetrained.

Waldo may be the world's first housetrained duck, certainly the first to be housetrained by a dog.

The common bond Sandy and Waldo shared was rare. Both mysterious and reassuring were Sandy's ability to teach and Waldo's ability to learn, even if they did speak separate languages.

***

Marv kept Waldo as a pet for three years. Waldo grew into a stunning creamy white, orange-beaked, flat-footed fourteen pounds. Marv had spent time petting and entertaining Waldo. It was clear that Waldo recognized Marv as some sort of flockmate.

When Marv came home from school, Waldo heard the bus in the distance, the sound of its engine floating across open pastures. Waldo excitedly interrupted his duck day and perpetual pursuit of the peevish Sandy to waddle as fast as his short legs and webbed feet could carry him down the driveway to greet his boy. He spread his magnificent white wings in welcome, his beak wide open, honking madly with joy.

There came a time when the family sold the farm and moved to a suburban subdivision where "livestock" was not permitted. Waldo was transplanted to the grandparents' small farm to be with other ducks. But Waldo had imprinted so strongly on Sandy and Marv that when he was put with other ducks he did not recognize them.

Diane Arrington

At first Waldo wasn't sure what the weird things were. Their appearance and behavior startled him. He screeched and ran for cover beneath Sandy. It took some time for Waldo to recognize and understand the language these two-footed creatures spoke to one another, but eventually he merged with the flock.

After Waldo left their new home, Sandy searched for him, secretly of course, for about three weeks. For all his disgruntlement, Sandy seemed to miss the big duck. One day Sandy was taken for a visit to the farm where Waldo then lived. As he hopped down from the truck, Sandy recognized Waldo before Waldo recognized him.

The other ducks, unaccustomed to dogs, fled the area squawking when Sandy approached. Waldo watched their panic with a bewildered look on his beak. The duck and the dog approached each other joyously, like old friends greeting after a long absence. Waldo made throaty, loving noises similar to the guttural sounds ducks make when feeding. Sandy swung his tail wildly, unabashedly. He sniffed and lapped at Waldo eagerly, all the while whining softly, as if worrying over Waldo's welfare.

Then, just like the old days, Sandy lifted one big white paw and pinned Waldo to the ground. As Waldo lay there, helpless and smiling, Sandy licked and nuzzled him, the ultimate sign of affection within the warm understanding shared between the dog and the duck.

About the Author

Diane Arrington has been a professional practitioner of punishment-free pet training and behavior modification for more than twenty successful years. She regularly appears in the media and in person to help audiences with educated, experienced advice on gentle companion animal management. A previous talk radio host, Ms. Arrington's gift for understanding animals gives her the ability to write with sensitivity and caring about the animals with whom she has worked for more than two decades. During her career she was the first to develop a method for obedience training dogs using a body harness to prevent pain, fear or force during the education process. The animals she has trained for advertising have appeared in ads for Chrysler, Pepsi, Frito-Lay, Pet Milk and an ABC Movie of the Week, among others. She also developed a behavioral rehabilitation program for retraining cats to the litterbox which is 99% successful. She writes, edits and publishes The Pet Gazette, a national pet behavior newsletter, and she has been published in the Journal of the American Veterinary Medical Association. Ms. Arrington can be reached through her website at www.petperfect.com.